Attorney to the Stars

ATTORNEY
TO THE STARS

A Memoir

CLAIR BURRILL

CLAIRIFIED LIBROS PUBLISHING

ATTORNEY TO THE STARS: A Memoir

Published by Clairified Libros Publishing
First Edition March 2025

Photos licensed by Getty Images

For a complete list of photo credits, please see Photo Credits at the end of the book.

For a complete list of song lyric credits, please see Song Lyric Credits at the end of the book.

Jacket design: Eric Labacz

Library of Congress Control Number: 2024916349

ISBN 979-8-9912942-1-8 Paperback Edition
ISBN 979-8-9912942-2-5 Hardcover Edition
ISBN 979-8-9912942-0-1 Digital Edition

Printed in the United States of America

v24

To Denise, Leigh, Kate, and Tracey

CONTENTS

PREFACE

Attorney To The Stars is a collage of vignettes portraying the personal relationships I developed and adventures I encountered along the way with various famous folks, family members, friends, and others, during my forty plus years as an attorney in the entertainment industry.

MR. MAMBO

It is 1979. I am sitting at my desk in my law office in West Hollywood, California, a supposed attorney to the stars, when Debbie, our 20-something receptionist pokes her head in my door and tells me there is someone in the reception lobby who didn't have an appointment but who would like to talk to an attorney.

Curious, I went out to the reception area. Seated on the couch behind a table strewn with newspapers and magazines was a quite jovial-looking young man with a round baby face and a big frame.

He stood up and respectfully extended his right hand toward me. His blousy shirt covered with bright flowers hung out over bright blue shorts. His legs were noticeably white—he obviously was not a native Californian—and he was wearing athletic socks and giant Nike sneakers. He had to be six foot four and 250 pounds.

He looked a bit apprehensive.

"My name is John Candy. Yeah, that's my real name," he said with a bashful chuckle.

I introduced myself and asked him about his last name. He said it was Irish as he followed me into my office. On the way, he mentioned that he was born on Halloween.

"So, I am Halloween Candy," he said with the same chuckle.

He looked around the office and out the window.

He said, "You sure have a very nice office here. I really appreciate you agreeing to see me."

I told him it was my pleasure and asked him what brought him to us. He explained that he was from Toronto, Canada, and was in California working on a movie entitled *1941* being directed by Steven Spielberg. He went on to say the movie was a World War II spoof starring his friends John Belushi and Dan Aykroyd. He knew Aykroyd from the Second City troupe in Toronto and Dan had suggested to Spielberg that he would be great for the part of Private Foley in the movie.

I said, "So Dan Aykroyd did you a real solid."

He said, "He sure did, but then my manager, Marty Epstein, got involved and that's why I came to see you."

I asked him to explain. He said he was worried that Marty didn't know much about what goes on in Hollywood and that he couldn't do much for his career. He talked to a production assistant on the film, Maddy Smith, and she said maybe he should consider getting rid of Marty and that he should talk to a lawyer. She recommended us.

Maddy Smith was a close friend of Mary Kay Place, whom our firm represented in connection with her appearances on *Mary Hartman, Mary Hartman.*

Candy's voice, his facial expressions when he spoke, and his body language all made him appear like a lovable little boy, although I guessed he was probably in his mid-twenties. He had a way with physical humor, with his bulk, the boyish smile and twinkling eyes, and the way he gestured with his eyes. There was innocence in those eyes, but something devilish was hiding underneath. There was a comedian in there.

"Do you have a contract with this manager?" I asked.

"I sure do. Maddy said I should bring it along. Here it is."

I took the one-page document from him. There was the name, address, and phone number of a management company in Toronto at the top. It was signed at the bottom on behalf of the management company by Marty Epstein. John's signature was next to Marty's.

"Did this management company, did Marty Epstein, procure this job for you, this Private Foley part you play in *1941*?"

"Yes, sir. He did. Why?"

I explained that if Marty did that and he really wanted to get rid of Marty, to fire Marty, there was a way I could help him do that. He asked what I meant by that. I went on to explain that since the movie was being shot in California, under California law, to do what Marty did, procuring work for him on the movie, Marty would be required to be licensed by the California Labor Commissioner.

I said, "So, first, I am going to call the California Labor Commissioner's office."

He was all ears.

Thumbing through my Rolodex, I found the number and dialed the Office of the California Labor Commissioner in San Francisco. A woman answered.

"Good morning, ma'am. My name is Clair Burrill. I'm an attorney in Los Angeles. I am calling to ask if a certain management company is licensed by your office."

She said she could help. She put me on hold. As we waited, we could hear the traffic on the street below and the sound of an approaching siren. John got up, walked over to the window, and looking down said, "Here comes my ride."

I smiled. The woman came back on the line and said no such company was licensed. I asked her to check under the name Marty Epstein. John gave me a thumbs-up. The woman again said there was no license issued under that name. I thanked her and said goodbye. Hanging up the phone, I looked at John. He held my gaze.

"Marty's not licensed. You can fire him."

John got up again and walked over to the wall, saying nothing. Unconsciously, he adjusted one of the pictures. He was deep in thought. Returning to his chair, he sat down and straightened himself. His face showed me that the comedian in him was on hold for the moment. He was very serious now. It was decision time.

"Well, I guess I'll do it." He looked conflicted. "But I want to call my wife."

"Of course," I said. "Here, you can use my phone. I'll let you have some privacy."

I walked out of the office and closed the door.

In a few minutes, my office door opened and John stood in the doorway, looking as if he didn't know what to say.

"Did you talk to your wife?" I asked.

"Yes." He looked concerned. He was still grappling with the situation.

We walked back into my office and sat down. There was a moment of silence. Then he broke it.

"Rosie says I should do it, so I'm gonna do it."

"OK, that's it then. You want to fire Marty."

He nodded yes and asked. "What is this going to cost?"

Some clouds were rolling across the sky outside my window.

"For now," I said. "I will accept a retainer of $125. Is that OK? Do you have $125?"

He pulled out his wallet and opened it. I stopped him with a wave.

"We can deal with that later."

Then picking up the phone again, I said "Here goes" and dialed the number of the management company on the contract. The phone started ringing.

John looked at his watch and then rubbed the side of his face with his hand. A clock on the wall struck three o'clock.

The phone rang six or seven times before a man answered.

I asked if he was Marty Epstein; he said yes and asked who I was. I told him and asked if he had a management contract with John Candy. He said yes, so I asked him if he booked the job for

John on the film *1941*, presently in production in Los Angeles, California.

He said, "Wait a minute. What is this all about? Do you represent John Candy?"

I said yes and that John Candy was sitting in my office with me and had told me that he, Marty, procured the job for him in *1941*.

John dropped his hand from his face and stared at the phone as if he could see Marty on the other end of the line.

Marty said, "Of course, I booked that job. I'm John's manager. We have a contract."

"Marty," I said. "I have some bad news for you. You are fired."

"What the hell? You can't do that."

"Yes, sir, I am afraid I can. Your contract is no good."

"He signed it."

"Yes, but it is void. The California Labor Commissioner's office tells me you are not licensed as a Talent Agent as required under California law. So your contract is no good, and you are fired."

"What the fuck? Tell that prick I'll sue his ass, and I'll sue your ass too."

I said, "You might want to check with your lawyer before doing that."

I looked over at John and continued.

"Because, I have to warn you, if you have collected any commissions, John will countersue you, and you will have to pay the commissions back."

Marty said nothing. John froze in his chair, looking scared at the mention of a lawsuit. He got up and started to pace.

I told Marty I would be sending him a letter formally restating everything I had said and fully explaining Mr. Candy's legal position. I bid him goodbye and hung up.

John stood in disbelief. "Is he really fired?" he asked.

"Yes, he is," I said. "Now about the $125 retainer."

John came to my desk and opened his wallet again. Still a

bit bewildered, he counted out the money and said, "You know, I really can't believe this. Marty is fired. Wow."

I stood up, John reached out, and we shook hands.

Then, coming around my desk and putting one arm over his broad shoulders, I flashed on that great scene from *Casablanca* with Humphrey Bogart and Claude Raines. Walking together toward the door, John also put his arm around my shoulders. I said, "John, I think this is the beginning of a beautiful friendship." And it was.

After John left, I went back to my desk and gazed around the room. The firm's office was located on the fourth floor of an eight-story building, and my office had a floor-to-ceiling window overlooking Sunset Boulevard. My office décor was provided by others, drab, grassy pale green wallpaper and pictures of flowers and outdoor scenery. Staring at it, I mused that one day I would have my own firm and then I could do what I wanted with my office furnishings and put whatever I wanted on my walls.

Our law firm specialized in entertainment law. I joined the firm on a whim. I was practicing at a law firm in Cleveland (after a stint in the Navy and law school at the University of Wisconsin), when I got back in touch with a close friend and fellow Harvard graduate, Gerry Margolis, now a lawyer in Los Angeles. Our common interests not only included the law but also our years of playing together in a rock band at Harvard.

My wife, Denise, and I and our two daughters, Leigh and Kate, moved from Ohio to California in 1975, and by that time, Gerry had become a partner in the firm and had transferred to the California office. He lured me back into the entertainment world that he and I had shared in college. I welcomed it. I loved being around performers because I loved to perform myself. I was dying to tell Gerry about our new client, John Candy.

A week or so after our introductory meeting, John called me from his home in New Market, Ontario, and said he wanted me to get involved in his work on SCTV, short for Second City

Television, a send-up spoof sketch comedy show originally on the Global Network and then the CBC Network, both in Canada. He said he loved doing the show and working with the friends he had met over the years, ever since Dan Aykroyd and Gilda Radner had convinced him to try out with the Toronto-based Second City comedy troupe at the Old Fire Hall Theater in downtown Toronto.

John told me that as part of his performing on SCTV, he had developed several characters, including Mr. Mambo, Johnny LaRue, Doctor Tongue, and Harry the Guy with the Snake on His Face. I will tell you more about John and SCTV a little later on, but first I would like to introduce you to Little Andrew.

Do the mambo, Jim
John Candy and Jim Belushi - Saturday Night Live

LITTLE ANDREW

It was about that same time, in the late 1970s, that one of the biggest hits on television was *Happy Days*, on ABC. Anybody who watched television back then knew the Cunninghams: Howard, Marion, Richie, and Joanie. They also knew Richie's pals Potsie and Ralph and, of course, bad boy Arthur "Fonzie" Fonzarelli. The Fonz. Legend has it that producer Gary Marshall's young son insisted that the show needed a spaceman. Enter Mork from Ork in a red and silver space suit, with a fast-talking, crazier-than-crazy comedian playing the part.

Mork was such a huge success that the executives at ABC decided he should have his own show. But there was one problem. The comedian playing Mork was under contract to George Schlatter Productions, which had produced the very successful *Rowan & Martin's Laugh-In* and was anticipating a *Laugh-In 2*. A veritable war broke out between Schlatter and ABC, with the comedian caught in the middle.

A large, prominent law firm in Beverly Hills represented ABC in the melee and two of the attorneys at that firm were principally involved in the representation. My partner Gerry Margolis and I knew both of them. Gerry told me he received a call from them to discuss the whole situation concerning the dispute between their client, ABC, and Schlatter and said the comedian who played Mork, Robin Williams, needed legal representation.

Gerry and I met with the attorneys. By this time, the ABC/Schlatter situation had boiled over into a threatened lawsuit. The meeting was memorable. One attorney was pompous and arrogant; the other quiet and withdrawn. Years later, the quiet one made headlines in the *L.A. Times*. He went off the deep end, murdered his triplet daughters and took his own life. The good news is that we wound up with Robin Williams as a client.

We stepped into the fray on Robin's behalf and eventually the Schlatter versus ABC matter was settled. As part of the settlement, Robin was released from his Schlatter contract and the result was *Mork and Mindy*.

Mork became so popular that his image popped up almost everywhere, with one memorable image of Mork in his red and black horizontal striped shirt and rainbow striped suspenders peppered with badges and buttons on the cover of *People* magazine. It was that image that would come into play in the future.

In the interim, one of my jobs was to put together a so-called "loan-out" corporation for Robin, through which he would provide his personal services to the ABCs of the world. Robin and I met for the first time at our offices in Century City.

He was wearing an open-at-the-collar cotton shirt and baggy khaki pants held up by his signature rainbow-striped suspenders but without any buttons or badges. He had a full head of well-coiffed dark hair that surrounded his face and obscured his ears. His piercing bright eyes engaged mine immediately, and his mouth was set in a gentle smile. He had a lot of chest hair visible at the opening of his shirt. He spoke in short quick phrases and sentences; you had to pay strict attention to what he was saying or you surely would miss something.

Seated in my office, he was relaxed, and no matter what I said, he always had an instant quip, a jerky almost nervous response, usually followed by a chuckle.

I eventually got around to explaining what a "loan out" corporation was.

"Maybe I should be a bank," he mused.

When he returned to seriousness, he said he wanted to call his corporation "Little Andrew Productions." He said he grew up as an only child and played by himself, including soldiers and animals and Little Andrew, whom I took to be one of his imaginary friends.

"No, that would be my penis," he explained, straight-faced.

He was always "on," always performing—the quickest mind and wit I had ever encountered. Anyone could tell he was going places.

Now there are those in the world who cannot help themselves from feeding off of those more popular and more successful than themselves. So back into the world of Robin Williams came a man, I will call him Peter, who ran a second-rate comedy club where Robin had appeared before anyone knew who he was or who Mork was. He did improvisational stand-up routines for peanuts and the right to have a stage upon which to hone his "I want to be a comedian" craft. Peter video-recorded the performances of Robin and others who appeared at his club and archived the videos for a rainy day.

When Peter saw what had become of Robin Williams, he went into his archive to search for footage he might have saved of Robin doing stand-up or skits.

Peter and some of his friends had previously spliced together a bunch of his videos of various performers at his club, not including Robin, and released a movie entitled *If You Don't Stop It...You'll Go Blind!!!* It was not successful.

But now, rummaging around in his collection of videos, Peter found what he was looking for. It was Robin acting out two short separate bits totaling about 30 seconds. Peter spliced the two bits into the movie that had flopped, and he re-titled it *Can I Do It... Till I Need Glasses?* Peter then took out full-page ads in various publications, including the *L.A. Times*, with a very large picture of Robin in his striped shirt and rainbow striped suspenders. Splashed across the top of the ad, above the title of this new movie, were the words "Robin Williams' Film Debut."

We saw this clearly as deliberately misleading advertising in that Robin's appearance was a mere 30 seconds, in a one hour thirteen minute film, consisting of the following sketches:

First bit: The scene opens and Robin appears in his rainbow suspenders and a large towel-like bandage encircling his face and tied at the top of his head. He is standing in front of an office with a large molar tooth hanging from a bracket above the door. He is moaning and holding the side of his face with an obvious toothache. A man in a suit approaches and starts to unlock the door. Robin says:

"Thank goodness you're here, Doc. I'm new in town and this tooth is killing me."

"I'm afraid you made a mistake, young man," the doctor replies, "I'm not a dentist. I'm a gynecologist."

Pointing up at the molar hanging above the door, Robin says, "But..."

And the doctor says, "Schmuck, what did you expect me to hang up there?"

We hear the sound of a slide whistle and a ringing bell and the screen cuts to black.

Second bit: Robin is an attorney in a suit and bow tie, wearing John Lennon glasses, and questioning a large-breasted woman in a low-cut top.

He asks her, "Is it true, Mrs. Frisbee, that last summer, you had sexual intercourse with a red-headed midget during a thunderstorm, while riding in the sidecar of a Kawasaki motorcycle, performing an unnatural act on a Polish plumbing contractor, going 60 miles an hour, up and down the steps of the Washington Monument, on the night of July 14th? Is it true, Mrs. Frisbee? Is it true?"

The witness looks up at Robin and asks, "Could you repeat that date again, please?"

Robin stares into the camera and we hear a sad wah-wah trumpet refrain.

That's it. Robin Williams' film debut.

I received a call from Buddy Morra, Robin's manager, who had seen the ad in the *L.A. Times* and brought it to my attention. Buddy was not happy with the ad. He said we have to stop this. He sent me a copy of the Times ad, and I went to work.

Buddy also sent me a copy of a release that Robin had signed. This presented a problem. The release, along with California law, made it impossible to stop the film itself. But there was a chance that the advertising could be stopped and stopping the advertising would certainly have an adverse effect on the proliferation and success of the film. My job would be to show that the advertising was false and misleading. I explained all of this to Buddy.

Time was of the essence. The advertising had to be stopped as quickly as possible. The filing of a complaint demanding that the court stop the advertising would have to be accompanied by a declaration, under oath, reciting the facts from firsthand knowledge that would establish the advertising as being false and misleading. Such a declaration would be required of Robin himself, the guy with the necessary firsthand knowledge.

Robin and I had a lengthy, serious conversation about the facts and I drafted a declaration for him to review.

I met with Buddy in his office and we went over the plan of attack on the advertising. I showed him a copy of the declaration I had prepared for Robin to sign. Reading through it, Buddy suggested we call Peter and see what he had to say. We called him and recorded the conversation, which was legally permissible under the circumstances. He made some very useful admissions that coupled with Robin's declaration would make for a strong argument before a judge in our effort to stop the advertising.

Robin was shooting *Mork and Mindy* on the Paramount lot. Buddy arranged for me to meet with Robin during a lunch break. I found my way through security to the set where the program was being recorded. I watched the last several minutes of Robin and Pam Dawber acting out a scene. Robin was, of course, hilarious.

During the break, Robin and I went to his trailer. I explained in detail everything that we had put together to try to get a judge to stop the advertising. I recited to Robin what Peter had said during the recorded conversation. I began.

"First, Peter said this….."

Robin responded, "What an asshole."

"Then he said this….."

"What an asshole."

"Then he said this….."

Robin paused for a second and then said, "That man is the Grand Canyon in the Land of Sphincters."

I cracked up and once again marveled at his quick wit. No matter how serious or important the circumstances, he was always there with a quip.

He read through the declaration and confirmed that it was completely accurate. He signed it and thanked me, and I was on my way to Department 85 of the Los Angeles County Superior Court to seek an injunction to stop the advertising of the film, but before I get to that, I digress to tell you a bit about an adventure I had with an English rock band that called itself The Rolling Stones.

No, that would be my penis
Robin Williams

THE STONES

I n the late 1960s, before I joined the firm, the litigation department in our New York office had launched what became famous lawsuits on behalf of The Rolling Stones, against their manager, Allen Klein. The cases settled with Klein keeping rights to some pre-1968 Stones songs and the Stones free from Klein's management.

Rid of Klein, the Stones toured the U.S. in 1972, 1975, 1978, and 1981, and our firm was involved with each of those tours. I joined the firm in May of 1975 and was almost immediately thrust into the middle of the Rolling Stones 1975 Tour of the Americas.

My first job for the Stones was to hire law firms in each of the tour cities in case they needed legal advice. This was smart, since memories lingered of the mayhem and disastrous events that occurred at the infamous Altamont Free Concert held at the Altamont Speedway near Livermore, California, in December 1969.

To address my assigned task, I consulted the most recent volume of the encyclopedia of U.S. attorneys published by Martindale-Hubbell for the top litigation firms in each of the tour cities. When I found the best two or three, I called my first choice firm and asked to speak to the head of the litigation department. When I mentioned the Rolling Stones, my call was most often taken, and I was transferred to an attorney who was all ears.

I explained that my client was Sunday Promotions, the entity that presented the Rolling Stones' performances on the tour. I needed contact information in the form of the direct office and personal home phone numbers of the two top litigators in the firm. Further, I needed an agreement that each litigator would be available by phone at any time, day or night, 24 hours a day, for each day of the Stones' tour performance or performances in their city, as well as the day before the first performance and the day after the last performance.

In exchange, Sunday Promotions would pay their firm a $100 retainer *and* provide four best section tickets to each of the Stones' performances in their city. Sunday Promotions also agreed that, if necessary, their firm would be retained to handle any legal matters that might arise out of or relate to the tour in their city at their regular hourly rates.

No one turned me down, and in the unusual situation when no one was available to take my call, I would call my second choice firm. I never had to call my third choice.

After I had all of the contact information and phone numbers for the top litigators in every venue city on the tour, I sat back and waited for the tour to begin.

Officially, the Stones' Tour of the Americas was to begin with two shows on June 3rd and 4th at the Convention Center in San Antonio, Texas, but the Stones decided to play two warm up shows on Sunday, June 1, at the LSU Assembly Center in Baton Rouge, Louisiana. It was in the early evening, Louisiana time, that Sunday that I got a call at my home from Peter Rudge, the Stones' tour manager.

Peter, speaking in his marked English accent, told me there was a problem in Baton Rouge. There was a veritable army of counterfeiters purveying all sorts of knock-off goods, including programs, T-shirts, and ball caps, all with the Stones' logo. They were smart enough, he said, to set up further outside the venue than his vendors with legitimate stuff, so the patrons would come upon them first. I told him I would get on it immediately.

It was getting dark by the time I reached the office. Seated at my desk, I pulled out my tour file and checked the tour schedule. The San Antonio dates were too soon to get done what I needed to do. I chose Kansas City, Missouri, and the Arrowhead Stadium show scheduled for Friday, June 6. That should give my Kansas City litigators enough time to get their stuff together, get into court, and get what we needed to deal with these knock-off bastards.

I was excited. I wanted to take my file, drive to LAX, and get on the next plane to Kansas City. Then, back to reality, I thought better of it. I flipped through my file and called the home phone number for my top litigator in Kansas City. It was 10:30 pm Kansas City time.

"Good evening, ma'am," I said to the woman who answered the phone. "I hate to disturb you on a Sunday night, but is John at home? My name is Clair Burrill and I am calling from Los Angeles. I am sure John will know what this is about."

There was a full moon rising in the eastern sky and shining down on the tops of the buildings across Sunset Boulevard.

John came on the line.

"Hello, Clair. I never really thought I would hear from you. What's up? And by the way, I got the tickets, thank you very much, and my daughter and son thank you also."

I told him he was welcome and that I was sure his family would enjoy the show. Then I gave him a rundown of the whole affair. He gave me a list of what he needed from me and said he and his people would be on the case first thing in the morning. He said with any luck, he would be in federal court by Wednesday.

I gathered together what he needed from me before leaving the office.

The first thing Monday morning, I FedExed the documents

to John. Later that afternoon, John faxed me proposed declarations that he needed signed and returned; I coordinated everything with Peter Rudge, and we were on our way.

Late Tuesday evening, John said he would be in federal court Wednesday morning. Late Wednesday afternoon, he called again and said he got everything he had hoped for from the judge and that he and several federal marshals would be at Arrowhead Stadium early Friday afternoon, waiting for our friends to show up, with a court order to seize all of their counterfeit materials.

I called Peter Rudge at his hotel in San Antonio. He was ecstatic to hear the news. He said he would call me from Arrowhead on Friday.

All day Thursday and Friday morning, I found myself watching the clock. Finally, the first call came in. It was Peter Rudge. He had met John and everything was in place. Shortly thereafter, John called.

"We hit a home run, Clair," he said. "You should have seen the looks on their faces when we showed up with our court order and four uniformed U.S. Marshals."

"That's fantastic, John. Congratulations."

"We got all their stuff. The marshals put it in their van and these guys are still trying to figure out what happened. I think they are out of business."

"So there is some justice in the world."

"Right you are."

"Great job, I know the client will be thrilled."

THE TOUR WAS SUPPOSED to include dates in Mexico, Brazil, and Venezuela, hence the Tour of the Americas, but due to currency fluctuations and security concerns, those dates were canceled. Instead, four additional U.S. tour cities were added. So once again, I pulled out Martindale-Hubbell and was back on the phone lining up litigators in Jacksonville, Florida; Louisville, Kentucky; Hampton, Virginia; and Buffalo, New York.

It turned out that no legal services would be required in those venues, but prior to those dates, when the tour was about half over and the Stones had just performed at the Memorial Stadium in Memphis, Tennessee, I received another urgent call from Peter Rudge, but that's a story I will get to in another chapter.

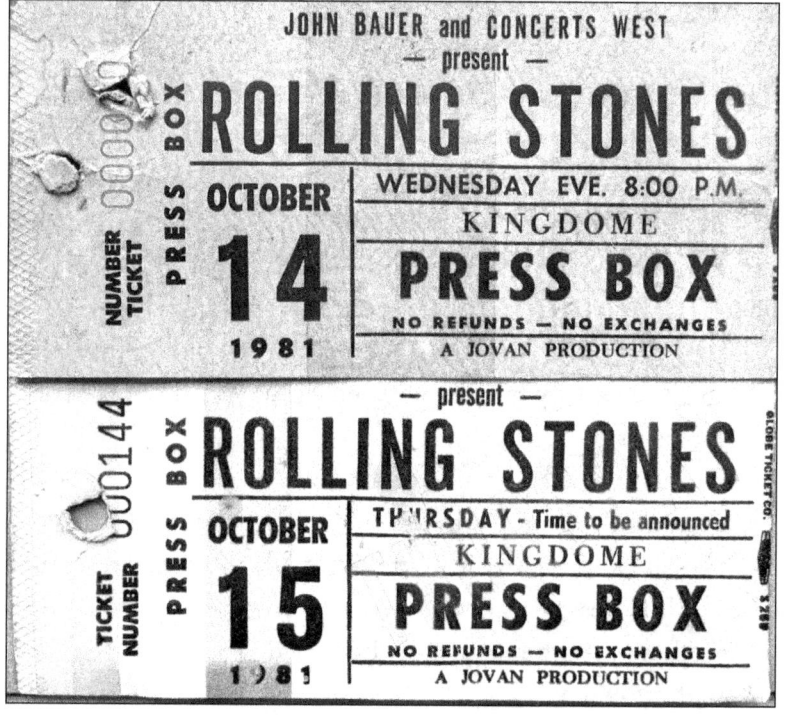

Another sell out

Tongue and Lips
The Rolling Stones

FROM PLYMOUTH TO CAMBRIDGE

So how did I wind up going from a small town in the Midwest to Harvard, joining a law firm and representing the likes of John Candy, Robin Williams, The Rolling Stones, and others?

I was born and raised in Plymouth, Wisconsin, population of around 5,800 during my youth. Plymouth was and is known as the "Cheese Capital of the World," with multiple cheese companies, including Kraft, Bordens, S&R, and most recently Sargento. But it also had a different reputation, one I learned about at a very young age.

Plymouth is located in Sheboygan County, midway between Milwaukee and Green Bay. With the advent of Prohibition in 1920, and continuing throughout the 1920s, 30s, and 40s, lawlessness in the form of bootlegging, gambling, and prostitution ran rampant throughout Sheboygan County.

Indeed, this was so well known that people would travel hundreds of miles from as far away as Chicago and Minneapolis to buy moonshine, place a bet, or spend a little time in a tavern that had been turned into what my mother called a "house of ill repute." At one time, the County was home to more than forty such houses, of which there were three just outside the Plymouth city limits; two to the south, the Tin Roof and Green Bungalow, and one to the east, the Club Royal.

My mother chose not to explain to me what a house of ill repute was, but that's what big brothers are for. So thanks to my older brother, Jack, who was 14, I got a vivid description of the oldest profession in the world when I was a mere seven years old.

Around this time, I recall returning home from my grandmother's house in Sheboygan Falls one evening in the family car with my parents, brothers, and sister. We were driving down County Trunk Highway PP and turning right onto South Street. Right there on the corner to the left was the Tin Roof with several cars in the parking area.

Being the youngest and smallest child, I was seated in the middle of the front seat between my parents. As we drove past the Tin Roof, my mother, looking at the parking area, turned to my father and said, "Is that Ralph Gibbons' car?" My father looked out the window and answered "Yes," and my mother said, "Well I never."

I heard my brother Jack let out a giggle in the back seat before my sister, the oldest of the four of us, made him stop with a jab of her elbow.

I also remember one day when my friend Pat and I were riding our bikes down the gravel road that ran past the Club Royal, with its unique blue glass windows, and Pat asking me what kind of people lived in a house with blue windows.

Now Pat did not have an older brother, so it became my job to fill him in on some of the wonders of life. I felt quite smug in carrying out my duty to enlighten my uninformed friend.

It wasn't until mid-1951 that after serious community action had been taken and pressure applied, the County was cleaned up and the houses were shut down for good.

Some time prior, however, in the late 1940s, according to what I was told years later, a gentleman by the name of Charles B. Windford, known as CB, paid an unplanned visit to Plymouth.

A Harvard College graduate and a successful businessman, he and his good friend, William J. Hallsworthy from Milwaukee, also a Harvard grad, served as a two-man interviewing committee for their alma mater. Their job was to visit certain high schools in Wisconsin to interview potential candidates for possible matriculation at the venerable Harvard College.

As the story goes, on a blustery winter day, CB and Bill set out from Milwaukee en route to conduct an interviewing session at Preble High School in Green Bay.

Traveling north on Highway 57 through Ozaukee County, it began to snow. The flurries increased and before too long, as they were entering Sheboygan County, they were stuck in a good old Wisconsin, take no prisoners, blizzard.

CB was driving and turning to Bill said, "I don't think we are going to make it to Green Bay. I can barely see to drive and it will be dark soon."

Pulling a Rand McNally road map out of the glove compartment, Bill responded,

"Let me see if I can find a place to eat dinner and spend the night. Hey, we're not far from Plymouth. Now how's that for a coincidence? You know about Plymouth, right?"

CB glanced over at his friend and said, "You mean Plymouth like in the Tin Roof and Club Royal Plymouth?"

The men laughed.

They crawled into town, spotted the Hotel Mitchell, and parked.

They walked up to the front door, stomped the snow from their boots, and stepped into a warm, cozy, welcoming lobby. The lighting was dim, the furniture was well-stuffed and comfortable, and wood was burning in the fireplace. To their left was a bar behind which stood a man in his fifties with dark, slicked-back hair, wearing a Green Bay Packers sweatshirt.

CB and Bill sat down at the bar, introduced themselves to the bartender, who turned out to also be the proprietor of the establishment, one Lowell Colbert, and ordered a drink.

There were no other customers in the place. Not surprising, since only a fool would venture out on such a night.

A grandfather clock in the lobby behind them chimed six o'clock.

After several drinks and a lot of robust conversation, CB inquired about dinner and room availability, and eventually said, "So Lowell, is it true what I've heard about something around here called the Tin Roof?"

It is not clear what happened after that, but it is clear that at some point, the next morning, Bill said to CB, "So how do you suggest we are going to explain all of this? How we spent our time in Plymouth?"

"Well," CB said. "I'll bet Plymouth has a high school."

They smiled at each other.

The snow had stopped, a bright sun was shining through some broken clouds, and the men found their way to Plymouth High School on the snow-covered banks of the Mullet River.

Inside, they went to the school's administration office, explained their visit, and were directed to the office of Vera Carlyle, the student Guidance Counselor.

As a result of the events of that day and CB and Bill's having interviewed several prospective Harvard students, Peter Ullrich, one of my brother Jack's friends, applied to, was accepted at, attended, and graduated from Harvard, Class of 1958.

I met CB and Bill when they returned to Plymouth High School in the winter of 1958. I was in my freshman year and was interviewed by them. I applied to Harvard in the spring of 1962. I was accepted and spent four memorable years there.

Veritas
John Harvard

MITZI SHORE AND
THE COMEDY STORE

Once again, it was the late 1970s, and I was seated at my desk going over some paperwork. Judy, Gerry Margolis' secretary and the office manager, and I were alone in the office when she buzzed me on the intercom.

"Clair," she said, "I just got a call from a woman at the Comedy Store. Her name is Justine. She is Mitzi Shore's assistant. She says Mitzi is looking for a lawyer. Can you believe that?"

"Whoa," I said, trying to hide my ignorance.

Judy had lived in Southern California much longer than anyone else in the office. She loved working for an entertainment law firm and was devoted to her work. She was very "hip" as we said then and very knowledgeable concerning the goings on in the entertainment world.

"Go a little slower for me, Judy, would you please," I said.

By this time, she was in my office, beaming with her Judy smile. She said she told Justine I would be coming right over. This is terrific, she said. We can represent the Comedy Store.

I asked her where I was going and for what.

"It doesn't matter for what," she responded. "This could be a killer client for us. You've got to go over there."

She gave me a complete run down on just exactly what the

Comedy Store was, who Mitzi Shore was, and most of the names of the comedians who had performed there in the last decade. She told me the Comedy Store was just up the street on Sunset, on the left-hand side going east, you can't miss it.

I proceeded slowly down Sunset to the Comedy Store. I turned into a parking lot behind the Store and parked in an unmarked spot next to one marked "Reserved for Mitzi Shore." I climbed up the stairs to a landing and a back door. Inside, behind a functional desk, sat a young woman I surmised was Justine.

"You must Justine," I said.

"Yes, and you must be Mr. Burrill."

"I am indeed."

"Please have a seat. Mitzi is on the phone and when she is finished with her call, I will let her know that you are here."

I sat down on a couch across from Justine's desk. Minutes passed. Justine said Mitzi was still on the phone. She asked me where I was from originally and guessed Canada. It was not the first time someone recognized my midwestern accent. I told her she was close but it was Wisconsin.

"Oh my God," she said. "Mitzi is from Green Bay. You will have to mention to her that you are from Wisconsin. Wait. She just hung up the phone. I will let her know you are here." Then she turned to me and said I could go through the door to my right and warned me that it was dark in there.

I smiled a thank you and opened the door. Just inside, I was confronted with a curtain of black beads, nearly opaque. I spread the beads with my hand and walked through them into a large and very dark room. My mind flashed back to when I was a young boy, sitting on the floor in front of the family radio listening to an eerie, scary program called *The Inner Sanctum*. As I looked around, I felt that I had just entered the inner sanctum of the Comedy Store.

The huge room was sparsely furnished, with lots of pictures

lining three of the four walls. They were pictures or portraits of people, but in the darkness, I could not make out who they might be.

To my left, behind an enormous, ornate desk, in a huge chair, sat this tiny, wiry lady. My eyes strained to make her out. She was dressed all in black with unruly black hair that appeared to have been hastily tied up on top, not fashionably, but to keep it out of her face. Nevertheless, I could barely make out her face. I could not tell if she was smiling or scowling.

"Please take a seat," she said in a high-pitched, authoritative voice.

I looked around. There was but one chair, way off to the left of her desk and not facing her, like the witness chair next to the judge's bench. The only other place to sit was a couch, directly across from her desk and a good 15 feet away. I went to it, sat down, and figured we would probably have to shout at each other in order to be heard in the darkness.

"Thank you," I said in a loud voice.

She moved ever so slightly in her chair.

"So why do you want to be my lawyer?" she asked.

"So why do you think you need a lawyer?" I replied. A lawyerly habit of mine, answering a question with a question.

"You may have read about it," she said. "A comedian jumped off the top of the hotel across the street and basically blamed it on me."

I had not read about it.

"What a horrible thing to do," I said. "Why would he blame you?"

"It's a long story. It involves the way I run the Store, comedians wanting to get paid, comedians trying to form a union, and lots of other nonsense. I just think it is time that I should have someone to talk to and protect me."

"Well I bet nothing like this ever happened to you in Green Bay," I said.

"What?" she said. "What did you say? Did you say Green Bay?"

"Yes," I said. "Justine mentioned that you are originally from Green Bay."

She stood up, walked over to the only chair, pulled it over next to her desk facing her, and said, "Please come and sit over here."

Sitting down on the chair, I told her I was also from Wisconsin, from the small town of Plymouth.

She said she knew of Plymouth, that her husband, Sammy, used to do shows in a village near Plymouth called Elkhart Lake. Sammy was a stand-up comedian. They had divorced several years earlier, and that's how she wound up with the Comedy Store. It was originally a nightclub called Ciro's that she changed into the Comedy Store after Sammy agreed she could keep it as part of their divorce settlement.

She switched on a Tiffany lamp on her desk that cast a dim light, and her face became more visible. Her eyes and her smile belied her brusque manner and sharp tone.

I asked if Sammy ever performed at the Schwartz Hotel or the Pine Point Resort in Elkhart Lake. She said he did, that they stayed together in both places, and wondered how I knew of them.

I told her I had a rock band in high school, growing up in Plymouth, called The Ravens, and we played in those same venues.

"This is a wonderful coincidence," she said. "We share some roots. Please tell me more."

In the ensuing conversation, which lasted for several hours, we became close. As it turned out, we had many things in common. Mitzi opened up her life to me as if she had been wanting to do so to someone for a long time. I learned a great deal about Mitzi, her personal family and her professional family, a seemingly never-ending list of who's who comedians, as well as her times and her beloved Store. She gave me a tour of the place, and I can still see and smell the Belly Room, the Main Room, and especially the notorious basement where, it was rumored, she told me, Bugsy Siegel and his boys carried out unthinkable things during Prohibition.

She was the mistress of this domain, no question, and she loved her Store. And she spoke of the comedians who had performed and who were performing there as if they were her children. She said she wanted me to work with her not only to protect her and her reputation but also to become a part of the Store.

It was an absolutely inflating experience and, beginning with that first encounter, in the inner sanctum, Mitzi and I would go on to share many adventures together.

Mitzi Shore's beloved Store
The Comedy Store

SPYDER GIRALDO

Down at the end of the hallway outside our office was the office of another entertainment law firm – Dewey and Howe.

Across the street from our office building was another office building at 9255 Sunset Boulevard, and in it was the accounting office of Gary Haber, a well-known CPA. He was an entertainment business manager who served many individuals in the entertainment business and particularly the music industry. He was street-wise as well as college educated, with a very gentle nature. His calm demeanor disguised his dry wit, deep thoughts, and professional wisdom. He was a problem solver and an effective career guide and advisor in the crazy business of entertainment.

Gary told me that one day a young man named Neil Giraldo came into his office. Neil was the lead guitar player in a burgeoning band featuring the female vocalist, Pat Benatar. Gary was the business manager for the band and Neil had come to Gary for advice. The band had been performing at clubs like Catch a Rising Star in New York and The Roxy on Sunset Strip and had recently been signed to a recording contract with a major record company.

Neil, in addition to being an accomplished guitarist and musician, had written a song that the band was performing regularly and that was going to be recorded on their first album for the record company. Gary informed Neil that he should seek the advice of an entertainment attorney with knowledge in the areas of music publishing and recording agreements. Gary suggested that Neil go to the office building across the street, to the fourth floor, to the offices of Dewey and Howe, ask for Mr. Howe, and tell him that Gary had sent him.

Neil crossed the street, entered 9200 Sunset, and went up to the fourth floor to the office of Dewey and Howe. He told the receptionist who he was, what he needed, and that Gary had suggested that he meet with Mr. Howe.

The receptionist asked Neil to take a seat. She picked up her phone and called Mr. Howe on the intercom, hung up, and said Mr. Howe would see him in a few minutes.

Time passed. The receptionist's phone buzzed, and she escorted Neil into Mr. Howe's office.

The furnishings in Howe's office were dark wood and red leather, the walls adorned with gold and platinum framed record albums.

Mr. Howe was a very serious-looking, older man. He looked as though he did not want to be bothered and said in a raspy voice, "So you are a songwriter, eh?"

"Yes, sir," Neil replied. He was standing in front of Howe's desk. He said Gary sent him over because he needed some songwriting advice. Howe said he required a $2500 retainer before providing any advice. Neil told him he did not have $2500.

An antique cuckoo clock mounted on the wall behind Howe's desk cuckooed two o'clock.

"That's too bad," Howe said. "I am afraid I cannot be of any assistance to you. Good day to you and close the door behind you as you leave."

Howe did not even look up but rather shushed Neil away with a wave of his right hand.

Stunned, Neil turned on his heels and marched out the door, closing it with a loud bang.

Outside the Dewey and Howe office, Neil paused in the hallway. He was pissed and intended to return to Gary's office to tell him what had happened. Halfway down the hallway, he stepped into the men's room. When he exited, he was looking directly across the hallway at our office door. On it, he read the name of our firm and the words "Attorneys at Law." He thought for a moment and then opened the door and walked inside.

He asked the receptionist if any attorneys in the office knew anything about music publishing. Debbie said yes and asked if he had an appointment. He said no, but that Gary Haber, his business manager, told him he needed to talk to a music publishing attorney.

Debbie asked him to take a seat and buzzed my office.

Once again, I made a trip out to the reception area to meet a stranger. This time, however, I came upon a totally different-looking young man. Neil was tall and lean with long fingers. He looked a bit tense and stern as though he had something on his mind. He was wearing a white sweatshirt with Catch a Rising Star printed on the front, black jeans, and black boots.

I introduced myself, we shook hands, he said his name was Neil, and that he was the lead guitar player in a band that just got signed to a recording deal. He went on to say that he wrote a song that was going to be on their first album and he didn't know anything about music publishing.

I said, "You came to the right place. I can help you with that."

"Is it going to cost me $2500?" he asked. "The guy down the hall wanted $2500 just to talk to me."

I told him my hourly rate was $125 per hour. He shook my hand again and said we had a deal.

Seated in my office, he was attentive as I recited everything I thought he needed to know about music publishing that fit his circumstances. We got into discussions about performance and mechanical royalties, and he was genuinely interested. He asked pertinent questions and soaked up the details.

The conversation switched to more personal things. He told me he grew up in Parma, Ohio, on the west side of Cleveland, and I told him that my wife and I had lived in Cleveland Heights for several years. We shared stories of playing in various rock bands over the years and other things that we had in common.

I learned his nickname was Spyder, spelled with a Y, given to him by Pat Benatar, the lead singer in the band comprised of four members that coalesced in performances at Catch a Rising Star. When I said I would like to hear the band perform and meet the other members someday, he invited me to the band's performance at The Roxy scheduled for the following week.

I presented him with our standard engagement letter agreement, which he read and signed on the spot. We went on to discuss the setting up of a music publishing company and a "loan out" corporation, which he dubbed Arachnid T., Inc.

The Roxy was packed and the band's performance featured piercing vocals and powerful guitar licks that had the audience jumping out of their seats and screaming. They rocked out "Heartbreaker" and then Pat sang Neil's song, "We Live For Love," like an angelic bird.

Backstage I met Roger Capps, the bass player, who also wrote several songs on the band's first album, *In the Heat of the Night*, released on Chrysalis Records. And then there was Myron Grombacher, the drummer. All I can say is, Myron was one of a kind. You had to watch him play the drums to fully understand what I mean. He was a show within a show.

Thanks to Gary Haber, I met and worked with Neil.

And through Neil, I was fortunate to come to know all of the talented people in the band and to work with them over the years.

The Spyder
Neil Giraldo

SCTV

S CTV was the brainchild of Andrew Alexander. Andrew was the mastermind behind Toronto's Second City Comedy Troupe. In 1976, Andrew approached John Candy and several other troupe members with his idea of going into television production, and that idea gave birth to SCTV.

The show was built around the premise of a typical broadcast day of a fictitious television station in the fictitious town of Melonville. John explained that everything was meant to be a spoof on what was on real television stations. The Melonville station was run by a cheap, tyrannical owner named Guy Caballero, who, though totally ambulatory, used a wheelchair to get around the station to earn respect. The station had game shows, like "Shoot at the Stars," where celebrities were actually shot at, and commercials for non-existent products, like "Shower in a Briefcase," and news anchors, sitcoms, and soap operas, like "The Days of the Week." It all sounded hilarious to me, especially the way John described it.

After SCTV had been running on Canadian television for several years, Andrew called the cast members and writers together and told them that NBC in New York was going to cancel Burt Sugarman's *The Midnight Special* and would be looking for a 90-minute replacement, the time slot being midnight Friday to 1:30 am Saturday. Did the troupe think they could expand SCTV to a 90-minute show? The answer was a resounding YES, and SCTV would soon move to NBC. This would require new contracts.

At John's request, I went to work on his new SCTV contract, and as things started to come together for the move to NBC, a fortuitous event occurred.

John asked me to fly up to Toronto to finalize the negotiations for his new contract, to meet the people involved in SCTV, to meet Rose, his wife, and to visit his home in New Market. While I was making arrangements, the Writers Guild of America (WGA) announced a breakdown in its negotiations with television producers and threatened to strike.

By the time I got to Toronto, the WGA had gone on strike; this created a shutdown of production of television programs for NBC and all other U.S. television networks and services. When I got to the SCTV studio, I was greeted by Andrew Alexander, who led me into a conference room where a bunch of people, including John, were seated around a table with grim looks on their faces. They were on the verge of something big in their lives, doing a show on a major U.S. television network, and then along came this strike.

Going around the table, Andrew introduced me to each of the members of the SCTV team. In addition to John, there were Joe Flaherty, Eugene Levy, Catherine O'Hara, Andrea Martin, Dave Thomas, and Rick Moranis, performer/writers; Michael Short, Dick Blasucci, and Doug Steckler, writers; and Paul Flaherty writer/director.

I had a thought. I asked if everyone was a Canadian. Most were; some were Americans. I then asked who were WGA members and who were ACTRA members. ACTRA being the Canadian Guild for Canadian television and screen writers, as opposed to the WGA, the US Guild. There were some mumbles and nods; everyone was still in a funk.

"Andrew," I said, "I have an idea. Any of your writers who

are ACTRA members, regardless of whether they are also WGA members, can apply for a strike waiver."

"What do you mean?" Andrew asked.

I explained that I could go back to L.A. and apply to the WGA for an ACTRA waiver of the WGA strike for each of the writers who are ACTRA members.

The fog started to lift; eyes started to light up; smiles replaced frowns.

"There is one hitch," I went on. "Each of the ACTRA writers will have to engage my services to represent them in order for me to be able to seek a waiver on their behalf."

Everyone was pumped up and asked if it meant they could continue writing their show. I said if I get the waiver, yes.

I was hired.

John smiled and Andrew ushered me away into his office for a formal thank you. When I left, echoing in my head I heard—I think this is the beginning of a beautiful friendship.

What WGA strike?
The SCTV cast

LITTLE ANDREW GOES TO COURT

Having left Robin in his trailer on the Paramount lot, I arrived at Department 85 of the Los Angeles County Superior Court just as the court was convening for the afternoon session. Department 85, known as "Writs and Receivers," was presided over by a veteran judge, the Honorable Howard T. Harris. Judge Harris was no nonsense, sort of a "take no prisoners" type. In the wild west, they would have referred to him as "Hang 'em High Harris."

He had a nearly bald head with white bristles of hair on each side, like Bernie Sanders. He wore his black judge's robe with the sleeves pushed up to his elbows, ready to go to work.

I had served the other side with notice, as required, and, before the judge took the bench, I turned to the other people in the courtroom and asked if anyone was appearing on *Williams v. Garner*.

A man in a blue suit approached me, extended his hand, said his name was Henry, that he represented Peter Garner, the guy who produced *Can I Do It ... Till I Need Glasses?*, and took out the objectionable ad in the *L.A. Times*. I handed Henry copies of my papers and we both took a seat in the gallery.

The door to the judge's chambers opened, and the bailiff called everyone to order.

"All rise. Department 85 of the Los Angeles Superior Court is now in session, the Honorable Howard T. Harris, Judge, presiding."

Judge Harris approached his seat behind the bench, looked out at the gallery with squinty eyes, and said through pit bull-like jowls.

"Please be seated."

He picked up the first case file from a stack of about twelve and called case number one on the docket.

Fifteen or twenty minutes later, when case number three was called, Henry and I rose, crossed through the bar, took our requisite places for the petitioner and the respondent, and stated our appearances to the judge.

"Clair Burrill for the petitioner Robin Williams, your honor."

I heard a murmur coming from the crowd seated behind us when I mentioned Robin's name. As I said earlier, his name and image were all over the media at that time. I felt a twinge of excitement and importance.

Henry made his appearance and then, representing the petitioner, I went first and presented my argument to explain and bolster the pleadings I had filed with the court, copies of which I had given to Henry.

The pleadings included copies of the ads for *Can I Do It ... Till I Need Glasses?* with Robin's picture dressed as Mork, a video tape copy with the clip of the twenty-five seconds of Robin's entire performance in the film, as well as Robin's declaration, and my points and authorities on the law. The judge had reviewed all of these before taking the bench, and they were in front of him.

The judge asked me a few questions, which I answered and sat down. He looked at Henry.

Henry rose and presented his client's position. When he had finished, the judge said, "I would like to see counsel in chambers."

Judge Harris took his seat behind his desk and motioned for us to sit. He looked very serious and, staring directly at Henry, said, "Well, sir, I think you have a real problem on your hands here."

Henry fumbled for something to say in defense of his client's alleged wrongdoing, but it was clear to me that the judge wasn't having any of it. The judge, of course, was polite and listened to Henry without interruption, but his facial expressions left no doubt about what he was thinking and how he was going to rule. I would not have to say anything further than what I had argued in open court. I was going to get what I had come for, a temporary restraining order (TRO) to stop the advertising, with a further hearing on the matter being set, most likely, about two weeks down the road.

My brain was pounding. I had to be sure to get as much as possible. In addition to the ads in newspapers, Peter's company had also circulated a brochure of about forty pages promoting his company's various films and other video products and, on the bottom half of page 28, was the same ad for their *Glasses* film, ablaze with Robin's picture and the statement, "Robin Williams' Film Debut." A copy of the brochure was included in my pleadings.

When Henry had finished his attempt to come up with some sort of explanation, the judge paused and moved our court case file to the right and leaned forward. He said he was going to grant the petitioner's request for a TRO and instructed the two of us to remain in his chambers and draft a proposed order for his review. In the meantime, he was going back into the courtroom to finish other business.

There were things I wanted in the TRO that Henry was not willing to agree to and vice versa. After nearly an hour had passed, the judge returned to his chambers and worked with us to finalize the TRO.

The judge was clear that he was going to order that all advertising of the film had to stop immediately, pending a further hearing on the matter in two weeks. I had also asked that all the offensive ads already in circulation be recalled, but the judge said he was not going to go that far. Then I turned to the brochure and asked that its circulation be stopped immediately.

Henry was outraged. The brochure, he said, contained many

very important ads and promotions for items that were not the subject matter of this hearing.

After some wrangling, Judge Harris ordered that all circulation of the brochure also cease immediately.

Henry then demanded that a huge bond be set.

It is normal for a bond to be set when a TRO is granted to protect against any undue harm that might be caused to the respondent if, for example, it were to turn out that the petitioner could not prevail at the next hearing. But the amount of the bond is discretionary with the judge.

Judge Harris listened to Henry and ordered my client to post a bond in an amount less than half of what Henry insisted upon. He next ordered us to return in two weeks for the follow up hearing. I was happy. Henry was not.

On my way back to the office, something suddenly dawned on me. How am I going to know whether or not they stop circulating that brochure?

That evening I basked in my victory but could not shake the thought that it was only a pyrrhic victory. I fell asleep thinking about the brochure.

I awoke in the morning with a plan. I raced to the office and called the private investigation firm we had used in the past and asked for Lori. I explained the situation to her and my plan. She was Johnny-on-the-spot and rip roarin' to go into action.

Lori waited a few days and then called Peter's office and told the receptionist that she was attending UCLA film school and someone at the school had mentioned Peter's company, and she was wondering if the company had any information about its films.

The receptionist replied that they had a brochure listing all of their products and she would gladly send one to her. Lori gave the receptionist her mailing address and several days later received a copy of the brochure with page 28 fully resplendent in its display of Robin as Mork.

Lori called me in jubilation. I had her swear out a declaration as to what she had done and how she had come to receive the brochure and took it with me to the scheduled hearing before Judge Harris. Just prior to the hearing, in the hallway outside Department 85, I gave a copy of Lori's declaration with the brochure attached to Henry and went inside the courtroom and deposited another copy with the court clerk.

Henry, seated in the gallery on the opposite side of the aisle from me, read through Lori's declaration. A worried look came over his face.

Before the judge took the bench, the court clerk announced that the judge wanted to see counsel for number 5 on the docket (*Williams v. Garner*) in chambers.

When Henry and I walked into Judge Harris' chambers, Judge Harris exploded. His TRO had been openly and knowingly violated.

Looking at Henry, he said, "Your client, sir, was ordered by me not to circulate this brochure."

He was waving it in the air above his head.

"Your honor," Henry began, but the judge cut him off.

"There is no excuse, sir." He was livid. "Here is what I'm going to do."

He ordered Henry's client to immediately cease printing any more brochures that included the objectionable ad on the bottom half of page 28. He added that Henry's client must come up with a permanent and irremovable patch to cover the bottom half of page 28 on all existing copies of the brochure; to box up every single brochure in existence and have them delivered to my office; and to send someone over to my office to attach the patch to the bottom of every page 28.

"Do you understand?"

Henry replied, "Yes, your honor."

The judge asked me if I had anything to add. I requested that the bond be vacated, to which he agreed, and instructed me to draw up the order for his signature.

Two days later, a U-Haul truck arrived at my office and about 30 boxes of brochures were deposited in our library. Shortly thereafter, three people in wheelchairs arrived, wheeled themselves into our library, and began attaching patches to the bottom of page 28 of each of the brochures. I retrieved one of the brochures and tried to remove the patch. I could not do so without ripping the bottom of page 28 out of the brochure. The *Glasses* film died.

However, nearly five years later, the same *Glasses* resurfaced and that led to another ordeal for Robin which I will explain in a later chapter, but first, do you know anything about card tricks?

That man is the Grand Canyon in the Land of Sphincters
Robin Williams

CHET ATKINS AND FRIENDS AND THE FOUR OF HEARTS

It was May of 1987 and the scene was Uncle Bud's Catfish Restaurant on Old Lebanon Road in the eastern part of Nashville, Tennessee. A young Englishman was working the room, filled with a gathering of some well-known folks and others who were divided up into small groups here and there, enjoying drinks and hors d'oeuvres, and engaged in chatty conversation. He was milling about from group to group, performing sleight of hand card tricks and creating quite a stir.

My wife, Denise, and I were in one of the groups and I was conversing with a small-framed, attractive, dark-haired, pleasant young woman sporting a fringed buckskin vest. With a wide smile, she said she was born Miriam Johnson but was much better known by her professional name, Jessi Colter; think:

"I'm not Lisa – my name is Julie –
Lisa left you – years ago."

Next to her, in black jeans, a black western shirt, wearing a black Stetson, and towering over all of us, stood her husband, Waylon Jennings. Waylon, a client of our law firm, in his rich baritone voice was explaining to Denise why he called me "Hoss." It had to do with being dependable, like a horse. Also in the group, listening attentively to Waylon, was a rather quiet, ruggedly handsome Scottish gentleman with flowing brown hair held in place by a red headband, Mark Knopfler of Dire Straits:

"That ain't workin' – That's the way you do it –
Money for Nothing – and your chicks for free"

Susan Hackney, a television producer and also a client of our firm, approached us with the card trick guy in tow and, after some pleasantries, she introduced him as John Pate. It turned out John was a friend of Mark Knopfler's from the U.K.

Although Mark was usually quite subdued, he was openly proud to have invited John to the gathering and hosted introductions and greetings all around. He remarked that he had met John in London and was simply amazed by John's uncanny ability to stun people with card tricks.

Accepting the cue from Mark, John turned to Denise and asked her to select a card from a deck of cards he fanned out in front of her. She did so and he asked her to show it to everyone, except him, of course. It was the Four of Hearts. He then handed Denise a blue Sharpie marker and asked her to write her initials on the card. We watched as she wrote "MDB" in blue capital letters on the card, her first name being Mary and middle name Denise. She returned the initialed card, face down, to John and he promptly ripped it into four pieces and placed it in his shirt pocket, said that he would be back in a few minutes and walked away.

John returned later, but before I get to that, you may wonder, what were Denise and I doing in Uncle Bud's Catfish Restaurant in Nashville?

ACTUALLY, OUR DAY HAD BEGUN much earlier at the Neely Auditorium at Vanderbilt University in downtown Nashville. We arrived there with Waylon and Jessi and were greeted by Susan Hackney, the television producer. Susan escorted us into the auditorium where she introduced us to one of the finest, most versatile and accomplished guitar players in the world, Chet Atkins, who was wearing a white country gentleman's hat with a wide black band. He was tuning his signature Gretsch guitar, which he set aside to greet each of us with a genuinely warm smile and just-firm-enough hand shake.

Susan and Atkins' manager, Fred Kewley, were producing a television show for Cinemax to be called "Chet Atkins and Friends," and the taping of this tribute to Chet was soon to begin.

A television crew was going about their business of setting up cameras and speakers and carrying out the final stages of getting ready to tape the show.

Chet Atkins was not only one of the world's finest guitar players, often referred to as "Mr. Guitar," he was also a songwriter and record producer par excellence. He had worked for RCA in Nashville and produced the Everly Brothers, Waylon Jennings, and many others, and performed, at one time or another, with nearly everyone who was anyone in the Nashville of his day.

Soon the "Friends" started flowing into the auditorium, and Denise and I took our seats in the audience. In addition to Waylon, Jessi, and Mark Knopfler, there were Phil and Don Everly, Emmylou Harris, Willie Nelson, Michael McDonald, David Pack, and Ray Stevens and, of course, the backup musicians.

I had worked with Susan Hackney and Fred Kewley putting all of the contracts and other paperwork together for the show. After everything was signed, and the show was set to be taped at Vanderbilt, Susan invited Denise and me to attend the taping, and when Waylon learned that we would be attending, he insisted that Denise and I stay at his guest house behind the main residence on his property in Brentwood, Tennessee.

As you might imagine, the show was more than fantastic with all that talent and, being there in person to watch it all made Denise and me feel rather special.

The show opened with Chet doing a solo guitar version

of "Deep Thumb Blues" as only he could play it, followed by an exquisite guitar instrumental duet with Mark Knopfler, the beautiful "I'll See You in My Dreams".

Concluding to a round of applause, Chet stepped aside and Mark broke into "Walk of Life":

"Here comes Johnny - singin' Oldie Goldies -
Be-Bop-A-Lula - Baby - What'd I say"

The Everly Brothers were next, back together since their reunion in 1983, looking wonderfully unchanged, Phil, with a lighter in color and rounder head of hair, Don, just a bit shorter and wider, with darker hair, and both with their guitars strapped over their shoulders and grinning from ear to ear. They sang in their extraordinary, unparalleled harmony:

"Dre-e-e-e-eam - dream – dream – dream –
When I want you - in my arms"

They finished, bowed to thunderous applause, and left the stage, waving.

The applause diminished and Emmylou Harris took center stage. With flowing dark brown hair, deep, bewitching brown eyes, and a wide smile, she sang her signature song, "Precious Memories," a song as beautiful and serene as Emmylou herself.

"Beautiful, just beautiful," Chet said to her when she had finished. "Thank you, Emmylou."

Then the silence was broken and all eyes turned to the guy in the brown sport jacket and wide open white collared shirt, with a well coiffed mop of blonde hair, behind the keyboards to the right. It was Michael McDonald; he changed the mood and got everyone smiling and singing along to his:

"I Keep Forgettin' - we're not in love anymore -
I keep forgettin' - things will never be the same again."

After his final refrain, Denise slowly stopped clapping and

lowered her hands. She turned and was about to say something to me, then poked me instead and pointed to Waylon, as he was walking up to Chet and the microphone.

"This next fella they say is an outlaw," Chet said, chuckling as Waylon approached. "He wasn't much of an outlaw when I first met him, however, back in – when was that?"

"I hope we're not gonna talk about those days, Chet," Waylon said, smiling out at the audience.

"I knew he was going places," Chet said, "when he and I did that first record. Here he is with his personalized Fender Telecaster guitar and black Stetson hat, my friend, Waylon Jennings."

"Thanks, Chet. This one's for you and you know why."

He sang:

"And every time he talked about her –
you could see the fire in his eyes – and he'd say –
I would walk through hell on Sunday –
to keep my Rose in Paradise"

Denise jumped to her feet, smiling and clapping, and before she could sit down, from out of the wings to the left, came a scraggly white-bearded gent, with a red, white, and black bandana wrapped around his forehead, braided pigtails of knotted old gray and white hair over both shoulders, and a red, white, and blue guitar strap around his neck holding up a Martin N-20 nylon-string, beat-to-hell, acoustic guitar named "Trigger," and before anyone could react to his presence, he broke into song with that one-of-a-kind, whiney voice:

"A long time forgotten –
are dreams that just fell by the way"

Waylon shouted, "Willie," and sang in reply:

"The good life he promised – ain't what she's livin' today"

Their duet of "A Good Hearted Woman" that followed,

accompanied by Chet on guitar of course, stole the show in my estimation, at least up to that point, but I admit, I was a bit prejudiced.

The stage cleared, the lights went down, and it felt like the show was about to wind down toward the finale, when Chet stepped up to the microphone, doffed his country gentleman's hat, and staring at it said, "This is my daddy's hat."

The audience became deathly silent as Chet placed the hat back upon his head and dedicated the next song, "I Still Can't Say Goodbye" to his late father.

As he concluded, there was not a dry eye in the audience or anywhere on stage.

Someone dropped a drumstick. Chet turned toward the direction of the sound, and then turned back smiling and invited all of his Friends back onto the stage.

The show closed with a moving finale with everyone, Chet and all of his Friends, playing and singing a rousing rendition of the iconic "Corrina, Corrina."

A huge round of applause and a standing ovation brought the audience to its feet. Susan Hackney was standing next to me and, as the applause subsided, she proclaimed the show a wrap. She then leaned over and told me that everyone would be heading out to Uncle Bud's Catfish Restaurant on Old Lebanon Road and that Denise and I were invited to join. We of course accepted and since we were staying at Waylon's guest house and had ridden to the auditorium with Waylon and Jessi, we rode out to the restaurant with them as well. On the way, we talked about the show and Denise mentioned to Waylon how much she enjoyed his performance in particular. Waylon said, "Darlin', you can come and stay at our house anytime you want. Why you can even bring Hoss with ya."

We all laughed and then, on a serious note, Jessi said, "You know, I think Chet Atkns is one of the nicest men I have ever met."

Denise added, "A true country gentleman."

It started to rain. Small droplets were accumulating on the windshield.

Waylon pulled into Uncle Bud's parking lot and the four of us made our way inside. I remember seeing Phil and Don Everly sitting at the bar next to each other, talking and enjoying what appeared to be Margaritas in schooners. The place was packed with the celebrity performers and production crew members alike all mingling and enjoying themselves. Mark Knopfler came over to listen to whatever Waylon was saying to Denise, and soon Susan Hackney came over accompanied by a young man I didn't recognize.

Looking at Susan and pointing at me, Waylon said, "So I understand Hoss here is your lawyer, too."

"Hoss?" Susan asked incredulously.

Waylon smiled his wily smile and said, "Ask Denise. She can tell you about it."

Susan said, "I'll have to do that, but right now I'd like you all to meet Mark's friend John Pate."

So where was I? Where did I leave off? Oh yeah.

After a short time, John Pate returned as promised, walked right up to Denise and said, "I see you got your card back."

Giving John a look of surprise, Denise mused, "What?"

Slowly he approached her, motioned toward the waistband of her white jeans and said, looking to her and then to me, "May I?"

Denise nodded as did I, and he pulled a card out of the waistband of her jeans. It was the Four of Hearts with the initials "MDB" written on it in blue capital letters. We were all stunned. No one had a clue how he did that. Everyone applauded, and he took a gentle bow. With a self-satisfied smile, he gave the initialed card to Denise for a keepsake, and made his way off to astound others.

Mark said, "Like I told you. The guy is amazing."

After a meal of scrumptious catfish and hushpuppies, some delightful mealtime conversation, and a slice of pecan pie, we rose from our table to say our goodbyes. While Waylon, Jessi, and Denise said their farewells to the others around us, Susan Hackney pulled me aside.

"I really want to thank you for all your help," she said. "So what's your favorite booze?"

"You're welcome, but, what?" I responded, not quite understanding.

"What's your favorite booze, damn it. I am going to send you a case."

"Susan, you don't…"

She cut me off, "Look, you did a great job, especially in your dealing with and protecting me from Fred."

She was referring to Fred Kewley, Chet's manager and her co-producer, who was what my mother would have called, to put it politely, a "real stick in the mud."

"OK, OK," I said. "It's Glenlivet scotch, but I warn you, it's expensive."

"Done," she said and we kissed and went our separate ways.

On the way back to Waylon and Jessi's place in the car, the four of us were still marveling over John's card trick and pondering how he might have pulled it off.

"I think it must have been by sleight of hand," I said.

"It had to be," Waylon added.

"So the card he ripped up and put in his pocket," Jessi said. "That wasn't the card Denise had initialed. He did a switch somehow."

"Right," Waylon agreed. "But he did it so fast, we never saw him do it."

"But what about the card he pulled out of my jeans?" Denise asked.

"Had to be sleight of hand again," Jessi said.

"Yup," Waylon agreed again. "He had that initialed card hidden, somehow, and made us think it was in Denise's jeans, but it wasn't. Very quick, right in front of our eyes, and we never saw him do it." He paused. "I think I'll stick to songwritin'."

The rain had stopped but the driveway to the main house was still wet.

Denise and I said our good nights and headed off to the guest house.

In the morning, we woke up and started our morning routine. The phone rang. I picked it up and heard Waylon's voice.

"Breakfast in twenty minutes, Hoss."

We were met at the front door of the main house by Waylon who smiled, kissed Denise on the cheek, and ushered us into the kitchen, where a barefooted Jessi Colter was at the stove preparing breakfast for the four of us.

We sat down at the table in the dining room, enjoyed delicious eggs and bacon and grits, chatted for a spell and, after we had concluded our meal with a second or third cup of coffee, Waylon turned to me and said, "Let's go into my office, Hoss."

We sat down and, looking at me with his steely gray blue eyes, Waylon said most seriously, "I have been asked by my good friend John Cash to join him and Loretta Lynn on a European tour they call the Wembley Tour some time next spring. I want you to handle all of the paperwork, of course. Mary Lou will give you all of the particulars."

Mary Lou Hyatt was Waylon's personal assistant and she did send me all of the particulars, and I will get to that, but first, some more about playing cards.

The best guitar duo ever
Mark Knopfler and Chet Atkins

Nobody has ever harmonized better than these two guys
The Everly Brothers

Precious Memories from a precious soul
Emmylou Harris

This ain't no dress rehearsal
Waylon Jennings

The Red Headed Stranger with Trigger
Willie Nelson

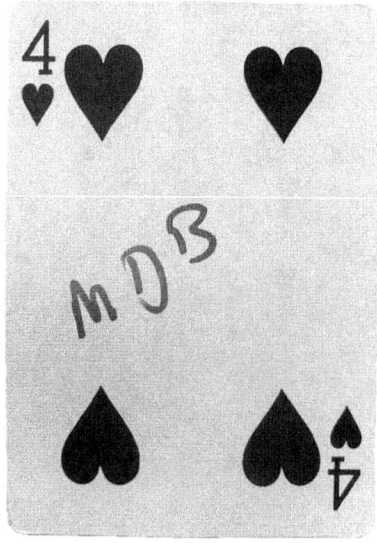

How did it get in her jeans?
Four of Hearts

THE CINCINNATI KID

D o you like to play cards? Do you have a favorite card game? Poker perhaps? Or Gin Rummy? How about Cribbage? And what about Whist? Bridge? Euchre? Old Maid? Go Fish? Crazy Eights? Up and Down the River? Pinochle? Canasta? Chemin de Fer? And on and on.

If you count all the variations of a game as the same game, there are at least 1,000 different card games worldwide and up to 10,000 if you count variations.

Did you know that playing cards were invented by the Chinese over a thousand years ago? Or that the four suits we know today are said to represent the four seasons, summer, fall, winter, and spring, or sometimes the astrological elements of earth, air, fire, and water?

There are thirteen cards in each suit, as there are thirteen lunar cycles each year. There are 52 cards, as there are 52 weeks in a year. And count up all of the symbols on a standard deck of cards and you will arrive at 365, the number of days in a year.

There are two one-eyed Jacks (the Jack of Hearts and the Jack of Spades); a one-eyed King (the King of Diamonds) also known as the Man with the Ax; and the Suicide King (the King of Hearts) with a sword that appears to pierce his head; in a game my daughter taught me, he is also known as the Cock Blocker, don't ask me why.

Growing up, I thought everyone played cards. So, at a very young age, I started playing cards.

The simpler games were taught to me by my older sister and brothers, and the more difficult games I learned sitting on my mom's lap, watching her play various games with my father and friends and relatives. She would point to a card when it was her turn to play and let me play it for her. Later, she would explain why she was playing a certain card and taught me how to shuffle the cards. She even let me deal for her when it was her turn. To this day, I deal with my left hand because, since she was right-handed, I always sat on the left side of her lap, which made it easier for me to deal with my left hand. Fascinated by the games, I picked up on their intricacies as time went on, and I played cards a lot, like that memorable game one night back in 1965 at the Pi Eta Club.

HARVARD DID NOT have fraternities, but rather Final Clubs. One such Final Club was the Pi Eta Club.

In 1963, I had formed a rock band called "The Shifters" with Gerry Margolis, Len Merski, and Pete Lang. Gerry and Len were a year ahead of me in school and were members of the Pi Eta Club. Most of the Pi Eta members were jocks, and all of them were very competitive. Gerry and Len urged me to join Pi Eta and agreed to sponsor me, even though they knew I was not a jock. Never mind, they said. We'll get you in.

The time came for the members to decide whether or not to accept any of the candidates as new members. Gerry and Len told me that when they put my name up for consideration, there was a lot of "who's he" type mumbling and a dragged out pause. The die-hard members were staring at each other, indecisive.

Then Neal Curtin stood up and walked to the front of the room. Neal was a very large and well-respected member of the club, a varsity football player, big as a bear, gentle as a lamb. Teammates said he wasn't naturally mean, but he'd just as soon break you in half as look at you if you pissed him off, or if you were on the other side of the line of scrimmage. But if he liked you, you were golden. As an ally, he was priceless.

Neal spoke softly but firmly.

"Hey, the guy plays mean rock 'n' roll. I want him in." He walked back and sat down.

That clinched it. Nobody was going to oppose Neal's vote. Learning the next day that I had been voted in and how it came about, I sought Neal out.

"Hey, Neal. Thank you, man. I heard about the vote. I really appreciate it."

"Hey, don't thank me. Just so happens my girlfriend likes your band." He laughed.

"Look, plebe. Let me give you a heads up. Some of the guys around here can be real assholes. They're not all super nice like me." He laughed again.

"Keep your wits about you and don't back down. They'll think you're weak. Bob Brink is a prince of a guy and Jimmy Noback is solid as a rock."

Neal next made a reference to a member I will call Steve. Neal continued, "Now Steve. You know Steve. Steve can be a bully at times, but he's also a lot of bluster. I'm just sayin'. But don't give him any room. He'll steamroll right over you. If you stand up to him, he'll actually respect you. Don't get me wrong, on the football field, he's tough as nails. But off the field, he's a different guy. And if he gives you any trouble, I got your back."

IT WAS DECEMBER 1965, and a New England Nor'easter was blowing snow all around the Pi Eta clubhouse, situated on Mt. Auburn Street, just off campus. Gerry and Len had graduated the past June, and my new band, "Oedipus and His Mothers," was hired to play for a dance at the club on a Saturday night. Something in the air said this was going to be an eventful night.

There was a small auditorium in the clubhouse with a three-foot high stage at one end. As we were getting our equipment set up, Bob Brink, the president of the club, came walking towards us. He was not only a jock, but also a scholar. Tall, dark hair, always a smile on his face. Everybody liked Bob, especially the girls. He looked up at me from the dance floor below the stage.

"Let's get this party rollin', guys."

Terry Ney, our bass player, stepped up to the microphone. He nodded to me, on his left, with my Fender Stratocaster at the ready, and then to Dave "Street" Connors on his right, with his Strat, also poised and ready to go, and then back to Rob Cavicchio, seated behind his drum set.

"Welcome, everyone. We are Oedipus and his Mothers."

Terry turned to me, we had done this dozens of times, I came over to the mic and together, from The Rascals' iconic song, we sang:

"One, Two, Three, Good Lovin', ….. Good Lovin'.."

The electric guitars, the electric bass, and the drums pounded out the song and everyone began to dance. It was a good crowd, lots of pretty girls, probably from Wellesley, Pine Manor, Smith, Newton College of the Sacred Heart, maybe even Radcliffe.

Bob danced by with Chrisy, his main squeeze, a cute blonde from Pine Manor. Steve was talking to a dark-haired girl I hadn't seen before. Anyone looking at the stage could see that we were enjoying ourselves. Dave was hitting all of the right stuff with his guitar riffs, Terry was putting on a show, especially for girls around the stage, and Rob sang his back up harmony to my lead like never before. When it came time for a break, the crowd wanted us to keep playing.

"Don't take a break now. Do another Beatles song."

I was on top of the world. My band was playing at my club and I could feel the excitement we were creating. The room was throbbing with rock'n'roll. We all felt the rush that comes from performing in front of an audience that truly appreciates what you are doing.

But all good things come to an end, and after four hours, we closed out the night with the Rolling Stones' "Satisfaction." Slowly the guys and their dates left the auditorium. We packed up our equipment, and I decided to hang around the club for a while. So I bid my bandmates good night, and as they left I went to the kitchen to get a beer.

Steve was in the kitchen. He must have struck out with the brunette. He walked over to me with a beer in his hand.

"Hey, Elvis. So you can play the guitar. Big deal. Can you shoot pool?"

I stopped for a moment and thought about Neal's counsel.

"Try me."

"Oh, look at me shake. "Come on, Minnesota Fats. Upstairs. Eight ball. Ten bucks a game."

He motioned toward the stairs and I followed him up to the pool room. It was a large open room, dark and dank, with a high ceiling, and the only lights were on long chairs that hung from the ceiling, each one centered over a pool table. There were four pool tables. Steve and I went over to the only one that was unoccupied, and he started racking the balls.

Steve was at least six-foot-three, 275 pounds, and played defensive end on the varsity team. He was All-Ivy and All-East, a real beast of a guy. He was wearing a sweatshirt with the Harvard "Veritas" crest in the middle and the words "Property of the Harvard Athletic Association" printed on it. He came from South Boston and had a swagger about him, a "don't mess with me" attitude. Sandy reddish hair and biceps as big as my calves. Years later he would be drafted by the New York Jets and play NFL football on the same team as Joe Namath, and would eventually sport a Super Bowl ring.

But right now Steve was losing to me at Eight Ball and was not a happy camper. He watched grimly as I ran in the eight ball to close out and win the game. He banged his cue on the table.

"That does it." He threw a ten dollar bill on the table. I'm done."

"One more game?"

"Nah."

We put our cues back in the cue rack. Bob Brink came over to us.

"Would you guys be interested in a little poker game?"

"Yeah, sure. What's up?"

"We're putting a game together in the card room and need a fifth and a sixth. It's table stakes. Cash only. Are you in?"

Steve and I looked at each other, we both nodded yes and followed Bob to the card room.

I had the money from the band gig and I had cashed my Navy check earlier that day. I figured I was well-heeled enough for the game, especially if I got lucky. If not, I told myself, you can lose three hundred and call it a night.

Steve and I sat down at the round, green, felt-topped poker table. I was sitting across from Bob with two guys to my right and two guys to my left. Everyone knew everyone. My especially good friend, Neal Curtin, was the guy sitting two guys to my right and Steve was sitting two guys to my left. The other two guys, one to my right and the other to my left, Ron and Dan, respectively, made for six players.

Ron was the only guy I knew with a tattoo. It was a snake, and it was on the left side of his neck, facing me. Dan was very quiet and very serious but one hell of a linebacker.

The game continued well past 3 am. It was dealer's choice and most of the guys dealt five or seven card stud.

I loved to hear the ruffling sound as the cards were shuffled and noticed that each player-dealer had his own unique style of preparing the cards for the deal.

Beers were available from the club kitchen, and the room was beginning to cloud up with tobacco smoke.

The cards were clicking as they were dealt, obviously a new deck.

Steve and I had both been winning and accumulating a significant stash. I had a stack of bills in front of me, as did Steve. I figured us for about the same amount of money.

Around 4:30 am, Bob announced that the deal would go around the table one more time, and he would deal the last hand.

Everyone took their turn dealing and the deal got back around to Bob.

"Seven card stud, gentlemen, straight up, nothing wild. Ante a dollar."

Everyone threw a dollar into the pot in the middle of the table.

Six dollars in the pot.

Bob dealt two cards down to each of us. Like everyone else, I secretly looked at my hole cards. I didn't pick them up, but rather turned their edges up just enough to see them. I had the Jack of Clubs and the one-eyed Jack of Spades.

I turned the edges back down and showed no reaction.

Next Bob dealt one card up to each of us. Part of playing poker well is noting every card visible on the table. Neal had the Queen of Hearts, I had the Six of Diamonds, Steve had the Queen of Clubs, but there were no Kings or Aces showing on the table.

"First Queen bets."

Neal threw a dollar into the pot and said, "I bet one dollar for my 'mop squeezer'."

Ron looked at his hole cards, called the bet, and threw in his dollar.

I called also and deposited my dollar.

Dan said nothing. No surprise. He just threw a dollar in the pot.

Then it was Steve's turn.

"Here's your dollar and I raise five dollars."

Steve very deliberately placed six dollars in the pot, one at a time. He must have a pair, probably Queens.

Everyone called the five dollar raise. No one was going to fold the last hand of the night at this point.

Forty-two dollars in the pot.

Bob next dealt one card face up to everyone.

I had the Four of Spades, Dan got the Ace of Clubs, and Steve received the Queen of Diamonds to go with his Queen of Clubs.

"The pair of Queens bets," Bob said. That pair was the highest hand showing on the table.

A dog was barking outside somewhere.

Steve threw 10 dollars into the pot.

"My Queens bet 10 dollars."

Bob called the bet.

Neal folded his hand, including the Queen of Hearts, and threw his cards into the dead pile.

I looked at Ron to see what he was going to do. His snake looked back at me.

"I fold," he said.

The bet came to me.

I put 10 dollars in the pot.

"I call."

Dan paused and slowly threw ten dollars into the pot, without a word.

That left four of us in the game, Bob, then me, Dan, and Steve.

Eighty-two dollars in the pot.

Bob dealt the third up card to me, the other one-eyed Jack, the Jack of Hearts. I had three Jacks, but nobody could know it but me.

Steve received the Ace of Spades.

Bob said, "The Queens still bet."

That dog was barking even louder now.

Steve looked smug and arrogant.

"My Queens are good for another ten dollars."

Bob threw his cards into the dead pile.

"Too rich for me." He looked dejected. No one likes to fold the last hand.

Dan stubbed out a cigarette in an ashtray, pushed back in his chair, and took a sip of his beer, waiting for me.

At this point, I am thinking. I have three Jacks, but only one is showing. That is definitely a plus. Neal folded a Queen, so Steve probably does not have three Queens, but rather I think he is holding two pair, most likely Queens and Aces. I decide to press the bet.

"I'll see your ten and raise you ten."

Dan looked at my up cards and then looked at me, as if to say, "What are you betting on?" He threw his cards into the dead pile.

Steve smiled.

"Here's your ten, smart ass, and 20 more."

He sneered at me as he threw his money into the pot.

I didn't hesitate one second. I threw a 20 into the pot.

"I call."

One hundred-sixty-two dollars in the pot.

I surveyed my remaining stash, very carefully. I thought of Kenny Rogers.

"You never count your money when you're sittin'
at the table."

I was still OK and had some more cash in my pocket.

Now it's just Steve and me.

Bob slowly delivered the last up card to each of us. No one left the table. In fact, the group of players looked like it did at the start of the game, just like that painting of six dogs sitting around the poker table. I vowed to buy that painting and hang it on a wall in my office some day.

I get the Nine of Clubs, no help. Steve gets the Two of Hearts, no apparent help.

We each have six cards now, two down and four up, and the last card will be dealt down.

Steve's hand looks like this:

Down card, Down card, Queen of Clubs, Queen of Diamonds, Ace of Spades, Two of Hearts

My hand looks like this:

Down card, Down card, Six of Diamonds, Four of Spades, Jack of Hearts, Nine of Clubs

Steve bets twenty dollars more. Is that a sign of weakness? Or is he feeling me out? I call his twenty.

Two hundred and two dollars in the pot.

Looking at my exposed cards, Steve smiles and must think I am an idiot. I do not even have a pair showing. Bob, looking at my cards, is also wondering why the hell I would call.

"Last card, fellas, down and dirty."

Neal takes a slug of his beer. You could feel the tension building. One more card to go. It looks like even Ron's snake is paying attention.

Bob gives each of us a down card in turn and the table goes very quiet. Neal moves a little in his chair. Dan is motionless and speechless. Bob gathers up the dead pile and folds those cards in with the remaining balance of the deck in his hands. No more cards will be dealt. This is all she wrote.

Steve glances quickly at his last down card and I see no reaction. Rather, before Bob can even say "Queens are still betting," he picks up all of the money in front of him, peels the bills off one by one while counting, and then plunks them into the pot.

"I am going all in." He is oh so smug. "I bet $100."

Three hundred and two dollars in the pot.

I read Steve's actions to mean his hand was made in six cards. His last card did nothing to improve his hand. He probably has a full house, at best. He can't have four Queens. Neal folded the fourth Queen earlier. He can't have four Aces. Dan folded the Ace of Clubs. He has either three Queens and two Aces, or three Aces and two Queens. Either way, a very strong hand and, either way, better than my three Jacks. Or maybe he doesn't have a full house and he's bluffing. What should I do?

Even if my last card is a Six or a Four or a Nine, giving me a Jacks over full house, that's not good enough to beat Queens over Aces or Aces over Queens, if he has them. I guess I have to fold. It all depends on this last card. I don't want to fold, but I am prepared to fold. Only a fool would call his all-in bet with Jacks over, but I really don't want to fold.

The dog has stopped barking.

Everyone is staring at me. I can feel Steve's eyes on me, but I do not return his gaze.

What if this last card is a Six or a Four or a Nine? What if it is not? What if he doesn't have a full house?

Bob taps his fingers on the table.

"What'll it be, Clair?"

Steve is all grins.

Dan scoots his butt back up into his chair. He's completely engrossed in the drama. He probably wishes he were still in the game.

Slowly, I start turning up the edge of my last down card, secretly, just enough of it off the felt so that I see what it is and, staring up at me, is the Jack of Diamonds. Yes, the Jack of Diamonds. I flash on Steve McQueen and *The Cincinnati Kid*. The Jack of Diamonds. Unbelievable. I have four Jacks. He cannot beat me.

I look up and try desperately to remain deadpan. I survey the stash in front of me and mentally count it. Then I pull the last of my cash from my pocket, stare at it, and mentally count it.

Everyone, especially Steve, is wondering, "What is he doing?" Now I feel like Edgar G. Robinson in *The Cincinnati Kid.*

I look at Bob and then at Steve. I smile. I see meanness, almost hatred, in Steve's eyes, as if he's saying: "You may have beaten me at pool, but I got you now, you bastard."

I am relishing this moment.

"Here is your 100." I place a stack of bills into the pot.

"And I raise you 200 more." I place another stack of bills into the pot.

I sit back, remaining as calm as possible.

Five hundred and two dollars in the pot.

"What?" Steve snorts. "You're fucking bluffing, you bastard. You can't do that. You know I bet all the money I have. Fold your fucking bull-shit hand."

I smile. I know he wants to kill me. Nobody says anything. Bob breaks the silence.

"This is an all cash game, table stakes, Steve. You knew that going in."

"But, this is bull-shit."

"You either call the bet or fold. That's the rule, and you know it."

Neal leans forward, staring at Steve, and says.

"Yeah, that's the rule."

"But I have no more money left," Steve cries out. "And I have the winning hand."

Somewhere a clock chimes five times.

Steve is now pleading.

"Ron, Dan. Come on. One of you guys has got to bank me here."

Ron sits back.

"Not on your tintype."

Dan says nothing.

"Okay, fuck it. Fuck you all." He reaches into his pants pocket. He is steaming.

"Here are the keys to my 'Vette. It's worth far more than two hundred bucks."

He throws his car keys into the pot and stares me down.

"I call your fucking two hundred dollars."

I don't flinch. I have four Jacks.

Bob looks at me.

"This is a cash only game, as I announced at the beginning," he says. "But I will leave it up to you, Clair. Will you accept the keys as a call to your two hundred dollar bet?"

I look at the other faces around the table, and then at Steve, and back to Bob.

"I think I *have* to accept them. Yes, I accept them."

Steve stands up, turns over his three down cards face up on the table and bellows.

"Queens full over Aces, asshole."

All eyes are on his cards. Then they turn to me.

I remain seated and then, to stunned faces all around, especially Steve's, I turn over the three Jacks that have been hidden in the hole. Neal smiles, Ron puts his hands over his face in disbelief, Dan grins, and Bob's eyes are as wide open as I have ever seen them. Again, I feel like Edgar G. Robinson. I look straight at Steve.

"I'm afraid that's not good enough, my friend. I have four Jacks."

The air in the room is as thick as fog. You could cut it with a knife. Time stands still.

Steve reaches for his car keys, but Bob grabs his hand.

"A bet is a bet, Steve. You lost."

And with that, Bob pushes the entire pot, including the car keys, over to me.

Neal stands up.

"If I hadn't been here, I would not have believed this."

Ron reaches out and slaps me on the back. Dan says nothing.

Steve turns his back, storms out of the room, and stomps down the stairs, while shouting out cuss words and threats of violence.

Blank faces all around.

I stuff my cash winnings into one pocket. I jiggle the car keys in the air in triumph and then put them in my other pocket.

Everyone is watching me but no one is saying anything or moving. They are all just standing there, still absorbing what just happened, still in disbelief.

I really can't believe it either, but slowly it all starts to gel, and I rehear Steve's cussing and threats and decide to stick around for a while.

Finally, the five of us meander down the stairs. Someone says, "Should we have one for the road?"

"Not me."

"I'm gonna hit it, guys."

"Nice hand, Clair."

I grab Neal's arm and ask him if he would be so kind as to accompany me back to campus.

"Let's have a beer," he says. "Then you and I can make our way back to Eliot."

Fortunately we did not encounter Steve on the way back to Eliot House. Thanking Neal for accompanying me, I turned in for the night.

Sometime after 1 o'clock in the afternoon, my roommate Pete woke me up and said he was going down to lunch. He asked me what kept me out all night. As I was explaining the events of the previous evening and morning, there came a knock on the door.

I went to the door, opened it, and there in the hallway was an older man, who looked to be in his fifties, with a mean look on his face, and Steve sheepishly standing behind him.

I was petrified.

"Are you Clair Burrill?"

"Yes, sir."

"Did you play poker last night with my son, Steve?"

"Yes, sir, I did."

"Do you have the keys to his Corvette?"

"Yes, sir, I do."

"What was the amount of the bet that Steve called with his keys?"

"Two hundred dollars."

"Here's $200." He thrust two $100 bills toward me.

"Go get the keys."

Going into my room, my mind was spinning. I do not have the title to the car; they will never give it to me; I don't even know where the car is; I can never say I won it in a card game, technically an illegal card game at that; I have no choice.

Returning with the keys, I gave them to Steve's father and he handed me the two one hundred dollar bills. Then he turned to his son.

"Don't you ever do anything that stupid again. And don't you ever play cards with this guy again. You hear me?"

They turned and walked away and I closed the door.

Steve and I ran into each other numerous times thereafter, on campus and at the club, but we never played cards or pool again, and although we did speak to each other from time to time, it was not about cards or pool.

I am glad that Steve made it to the NFL, played on the same team as Joe Namath, and earned a Super Bowl ring, but I will never forget playing cards with him that night, and I will always remember the Jack of Diamonds. And, for similar reasons, as you will learn in a bit, I will always remember the Seven of Clubs. But first, let's take a trip to Montevideo.

The Jack in the hole
Jack of Diamonds

MYRON AND RONNIE IN MONTEVIDEO

I attended Harvard on a Navy ROTC scholarship. In my Unit, we were referred to as midshipmen, just like the attendees of the U.S. Naval Academy at Annapolis, advancing from Fourth Class Midshipmen in our freshman year to First Class Midshipmen in our senior year.

Also like Annapolis midshipmen, we were required to report for Navy duty, so-called summer cruises. For my first summer cruise, I reported to the U.S.S. John W. Weeks, a destroyer homeported in Norfolk, Virginia. I was assigned to the Deck Division, working, eating, and sleeping the same as the enlisted sailors on board.

The following summer, I spent half of my required time with the Marines in Little Creek, Virginia, and the other half in flight training in Corpus Christi, Texas.

This story begins, however, with my last summer cruise in 1965, touted to be the best summer cruise.

I was scheduled to fly to Europe to board an aircraft carrier operating in the Mediterranean. I would be billeted with the junior officers, and the ship would be putting into various Mediterranean liberty ports. I was looking forward to it.

Then, unfortunately, LBJ sent the Marines into Lebanon and all midshipmen cruises to the Mediterranean were canceled.

Instead, I was ordered to report to the U.S.S. Wasp, an aircraft carrier stationed where else? – in Boston – practically my hometown, on the other side of the Charles River from Cambridge. This could not have been worse news. I could not accept the fact that I would be spending my summer in Boston instead of cruising the Mediterranean.

I was devastated and went to see my NROTC supervisor. He was sympathetic and told me there were so-called "foreign exchange cruises" available to qualified midshipmen.

He asked, "Do you speak any foreign languages?"

I said, "I have taken two years of Spanish."

"Aha, you are fluent," he said. "I will put your name in for all available foreign exchange cruises with English and Spanish-speaking navies."

He did, my orders to the Wasp were canceled, and I was ordered to report to Colonel R. G. Hutchinson, USMC, the U.S. Naval Attaché in Montevideo, Uruguay.

I left JFK bound for Montevideo in early June 1965. It was hot and humid in New York, but it was wintertime in Uruguay, so I packed my winter uniforms.

The flight was long, I slept a lot, and when I finally de-planed in Montevideo, I was met by a sergeant attached to the U.S. Army Mission. He took me to a small hotel in downtown Montevideo and on the way told me that two Annapolis midshipmen, Myron Hura and Ronald Wesley, were staying at the same hotel.

I woke early the next morning, laid out my dress blue uniform, and called down to the front desk.

A clerk answered, "Hola y buenos dias."

"¿Habla usted Inglés?" I asked.

"Yes, of course. How can I help you?"

I told the clerk I was trying to reach two guests of the hotel who checked in yesterday, both Norteamericanos and perhaps in military uniforms. She said they were staying in the same room and would connect me.

The phone rang twice. A male voice answered. I asked if Myron or Ronald were there.

"This is Myron. Who is this?"

I gave Myron my name, told him I was an ROTC midshipman in Montevideo on an exchange cruise and asked if he was from Annapolis. He said that yes, both he and his shipmate Ronnie were down for the same cruise. We agreed to head over to report to Colonel Hutchinson together.

The three of us met in the lobby, in dress blue uniforms, introduced ourselves, and jumped into a cab. In perfect Spanish, Myron conversed with the cab driver as we were taken to the U.S. Embassy.

Colonel Hutchinson's office was on the second floor. His secretary said the Colonel was expecting us and to go right in.

Colonel Hutchinson was a true U. S. Marine Colonel, squared away in every respect. We stood at attention, side by side, and waited for the Colonel to speak.

"At ease, gentlemen," he said, "and welcome to Montevideo."

We relaxed only slightly.

"I looked at your orders and I am a little puzzled. Straight up, I really do not know what I am going to do with you. The Uruguayan Navy doesn't go out on maneuvers this time of year. As you no doubt noticed, it's winter down here."

"Yes sir," we said in unison.

"Under the circumstances," he went on, "I'll tell you what I am going to do. I am going to give you a week to get acclimated to Montevideo. You speak Spanish, right?"

Myron and I answered at the same time. Myron said, "Sí" and I said "Yes."

The Colonel smiled and said, "Apparently one of you does."

He went on, "I want you to come back to my office in one

week, same time, and, in the meantime, I want you to lose the uniforms, nothing but civies from now on. We do not wear the uniform in public. So when you come back, come in civies, any questions?"

We snapped to attention and said, again in unison, "No sir."

"Alright then, you are dismissed."

We did an about-face and exited the office.

In the cab on the way back to the hotel, I asked, "Did you guys bring any civies? I didn't."

Ronnie said, "I brought one pair of jeans and one sweatshirt."

Myron said, "Ditto, that's what we were told we could bring."

Then Myron spoke to the driver, again in perfect Spanish, and we wound up at the Uruguayan equivalent of a department store. We bought pants and shirts and heavy overcoats.

We went back to the hotel, changed clothes, stowed our gear, and met in the lobby lounge. We ordered some coffee and began to chat.

Ronnie was from Iowa. He had a steady girlfriend who was a sophomore at the University of Maryland, and his hobby was ham radio. He was a devout Baptist and read the scriptures every day.

Myron was born in Ukraine. During World War II, his family fought their way out of Ukraine, across war-ravaged Eastern Europe, and wound up in Argentina, where he received all of his secondary education; hence, he spoke fluent South American Spanish. In fact, he spoke five languages, including Russian and English. He was also an All-American soccer player at Annapolis.

I asked, "So what do you guys want to do for the next week?"

Ronnie said he was going to look for ham radio operators and planned to get into a cab and ride through residential areas, looking for ham radio antennas on rooftops.

Myron looked at me and said, "Let's grab some lunch, and, Ronnie, we will catch up with you later. Good luck with your antenna hunting."

Myron and I became close. We hit it off right from the start and for the next six days did what I think most 21-year-old red-blooded young men would have done under the circumstances. But our fun time was about to come to a screeching halt, thanks to Ronnie.

The week flew by and we were back in Colonel Hutchinson's office, in civies.

The Colonel said, "Gentlemen, I still do not know what I am going to do with you."

Myron and I smiled. Then Ronnie said, "Sir, I have an idea. Why don't we go to the Uruguayan Naval Academy? Foreign naval academy students attend Annapolis and this is an exchange cruise."

"Great idea," the Colonel said, showing a sign of relief. "I'll set it up and my secretary will contact you with the details. You are dismissed."

Same snap to attention, about-face, and exit.

When we got down the stairs to the first floor, Myron turned on Ronnie.

"You jackass, Ronnie," Myron said. "You may as well have said, 'I got an idea. Why don't you put us in jail?'"

Then turning to me, Myron said, "Wait until you see this place. We are fucked."

We reported to the Uruguayan Naval Academy, the Escuela Naval, and it was bad news. Instead of a warm hotel room, we were bunked in a concrete dungeon. With no heat. The place was supposed to be heated by electricity, but a severe electrical power shortage due to a killer drought meant the country's major hydroelectric dam wasn't producing enough electricity. To conserve electricity, power was cut off to most government facilities, including the Escuela Naval. Yes, we were fucked. I slept in my overcoat.

I could see my breath at all times, even in bed while trying to sleep, and we had swimming drills in an unheated pool. I was so cold, I couldn't drown.

The government also ordered all clocks moved ahead three hours to preserve sunlight and many shops and restaurants used kerosene lanterns to stay open after the sun went down.

One whole horrible week passed in that hell hole and then, Hallelujah!! We were summoned to Colonel Hutchinson's office. There was going to be an all-hands-on-deck party at the home of the Army Attaché, and the Colonel insisted that we attend.

The party was a welcome reprieve from what Myron and I were calling "Escuela del Infierno," the school from hell. All U.S. military and government personnel in Montevideo were in attendance, drawn by the good food and drink. As newcomers, we attracted a lot of attention.

An attractive young woman with blazing red hair was actively engaged in conversation with a guy across the room. Myron approached and started talking to them. After a while, the guy gave Myron a smirk and moved away. The young woman tossed back her head of stunning red hair and laughed. Smiling, Myron took her empty glass and headed toward the bar. I stopped him and asked, "Who is that?"

"That, my friend, is Sally, and she just may be our blessed savior."

"What?"

"Sí, mi amigo. I think I have just met our ticket out of Escuela del Infierno."

"No shit?"

"Sally, you will be happy to know, is the secretary to no one other than our host, Colonel Robert L. Masters, the Army Attaché. Sally is a savvy military brat with a lot on the military ball. She told me there is a supply flight, an Air Force C-130, that flies out of Panama City, Florida, that makes the rounds of South America, stopping in every capital city."

He paused, looked over at Sally, pointed to her empty glass, gave her an "I'm getting it" type of gesture, and continued.

"This C-130 picks up and drops off supplies and mail for the U.S. military personnel stationed throughout South America, and guess what?"

"What?"

"There are six seats on the plane."

"So."

"There are only three of us, dummy. And yes, we would have to include Ronnie."

"Include Ronnie, for what?"

"Sally says that the seats are rarely used, the plane is due here in Montevideo the day after tomorrow, the next stop is Asunción, Paraguay, and she thinks there is no reason why we can't be on it. And, of course, we can't leave Ronnie out."

"You have got to be kidding, but what about Colonel Hutch?"

"Sally says she will plant the seed with her boss, Colonel Masters; he and Hutch are tight, and Hutch can then kill two birds with one stone."

I saw the light, "He can get us out of his hair and we get out of Escuela del Infierno."

"Roger that, Einstein."

"Is she with that guy she was talking to?" I asked.

"No, and she is not with anyone else, so I'll see you tomorrow."

The next day, we were summoned to Colonel Hutchinson's office.

"Gentlemen," he began. "I have come up with an idea that I think you will like. I decided that, since you are here in South America for such a short time, you should see some more of it, not just Montevideo. So I am cutting you some orders to get on tomorrow's supply flight to Asunción, Paraguay. How does that sound?"

Myron, not at all surprised, said, "Thank you, sir."

I said, "That sounds great, sir."

Ronnie said, "But what about the academy?"

I wanted to choke him.

"I'll take care of the academy," the Colonel said. "Now get your things in order and your butts out on the tarmac at 0600 sharp tomorrow. My secretary will give you all the dope you will need, and have a Foxtrot Golf Tango." He smiled. "Oh, and one more thing," he said. "Burrill, I overheard you mention at the party at Colonel Masters last night that you play the guitar."

"Yes sir. You heard correctly."

"I play guitar as well, and in Asunción, they make the finest hand-tooled leather guitar cases in the world. You may want to pick one up for yourself."

"Yes, sir."

"The last time I was up there I ordered one for myself. My good friend, Colonel Samuels, the Army Attaché there, has it. So when you get there, I want you to get in touch with Colonel Samuels and tell him I sent you personally to retrieve my guitar case for me."

"Yes, sir. I will be sure to do that."

"Okay, then. You gentlemen are dismissed."

We left his office in our usual fashion.

The next morning at 0600 sharp, Myron, Ronnie, and I were standing on the tarmac. The C-130 had rolled to a stop. We presented our orders to the flight chief and he directed us to our mesh seats on the port side of the fuselage. We were on our way to Asunción and, as it turned out, to points beyond.

WE CAN'T FIND KEITH

As I mentioned, while they were still on the 1975 Tour of the Americas, the Stones performed at the Memorial Stadium in Memphis, Tennessee, on the Fourth of July. The next day I received my second urgent call from Peter Rudge.

"Clair, we can't find Keith. Someone said he rented a car and he and Freddie are headed toward Dallas. We are playing the Cotton Bowl there tomorrow. I fear the worst."

"Did you call Bill?" I asked him.

Bill was Bill Carter, an attorney from Arkansas. He was the go-to guy for just about every possible shenanigan the Stones might pull off or try to pull off or think of pulling off. He had been a Secret Service agent, and legend had it that he was instrumental in getting Keith, a self- proclaimed addict, into the country for the Stones tours.

It was no secret that controlled substances might have been involved in the supposed road trip (pun intended), especially since Freddie, the alleged bagman, was thought to be involved.

"Yes," Peter said. "Bill was in Memphis. I have reached out to him, but haven't made contact yet."

"I'll see if I can get hold of him," I said.

I did get in touch with Bill and he told me that he had learned that, indeed, the boys, including not only Keith and Freddie Sessler, but also Ronnie Woods and Jim Callaghan, had rented a brand-new yellow Chevy Impala and were headed to Dallas, but, unfortunately, they were detained by the police in Fordyce, Arkansas. They apparently stopped at a diner there, the 4-Dice Restaurant, for lunch and didn't exactly blend in with the local folks. Bill said he was on his way to Fordyce as he spoke. I told him I would call Peter and let him know.

Now what happened next depends upon which account you read or listen to.

Bill Carter's account is set out in his book, *Get Carter*. Keith's account is in his book, *Life*. Ronnie Wood's version is in his book, *Ronnie*. And nearly everyone who was in Fordyce at the time, or anyone else who might have been otherwise involved, has his own story.

What appears in all accounts is that Keith was charged with reckless driving and possession of a concealed weapon, a hunting knife, and Freddie was charged with possession of a controlled substance. What also appears is that Keith paid a fine of $162.50 for reckless driving and all other charges were dropped. Also a fact is that in 2006 the then-Arkansas Governor, Mike Huckabee, pardoned Keith of the reckless driving charge and Keith says he never asked for the favor.

Bill Carter's account of what happened is definitely the accurate one. He says no matter what anyone else might say, the police botched the arrest and the search, and the judge knew it, as well as the prosecuting attorney.

Keith's account, on the other hand, is full of somewhat questionable embellishment, according to Carter and others, including Ronnie. And interestingly, Keith chose the Fordyce situation for the opening chapter of his book, notwithstanding all of the other craziness in his life, like the jam sessions with other guitar legends, the rivalry and love-hate relationship with Mick Jagger, the booze and drug-fueled benders, the sold-out shows,

Altamont, etc., etc. Nevertheless, Keith opens his book with this. (Keith Richards, James Fox, "Life", chapter one, page 1)

> *"Why did we stop at the 4-Dice Restaurant in Fordyce, Arkansas, for lunch on Independence Day weekend? On any day? Despite everything I knew from ten years of driving through the Bible Belt. Tiny town of Fordyce. Rolling Stones on the police menu across the United States. Every copper wanted to bust us by any means available, to get promoted and patriotically rid America of these little fairy Englishmen."*

Keith would have you believe that the car was loaded with drugs, including those hidden in the door panels; that the trunk was full of booze; that he and Ronnie spent forty minutes in the john of the restaurant, doing drugs, and causing the 4-Dice staff to call the cops; that the police chief was vindictive, etc., etc. But as I say, Bill Carter and Ronnie Woods debunk most of that.

For sure, Keith did have a hunting knife and Freddie, no doubt, possessed a controlled substance or two.

So where is the knife today? No one knows. What about the car? After the smoke cleared, Bill Carter arranged to have the boys flown to Dallas, so where's the yellow Chevy? Keith says they left it in a garage, still full of dope.

Joe Pennington, a deputy sheriff who was involved with the search of the car, said there was a small packet of cocaine, a spoon, and a hunting knife, and that was all. Joe's son, Allen, retained the spoon. It remains the only artifact of this crazy event.

Bill Carter said that the tale, no matter who tells it, is pretty unbelievable.

But here's a different story.

It is my favorite version of the tale, no matter how apocryphal.

KEITH AND FREDDIE rented the car and, although being warned by Bill Carter not to drive across Arkansas, they did so anyway.

Why not? What could be more challenging? And besides, Keith was a Rolling Stone.

In the early morning hours of July 5, 1975, Keith and Freddie drove into Fordyce, Arkansas, population 3,751, and spotted an all-night diner. Cleverly, it was called the 4-Dice Restaurant. They went inside to get something to eat. They did not exactly fit in with the locals and the proprietor called the one and only constable within fifty miles to come over and take a look at these guys.

"They just look like they musta done sumpin' wrong," she said to the constable. "And they been in the restroom together, laughin' and smokin' sumpin' that I don't think is tobacky. You know what I mean?"

While the boys were eating their breakfast, the constable appeared and did a complete search of the yellow Chevy with Tennessee plates out in front of the diner. He entered the 4-Dice, spotted the boys, came over to them, and said, "You boys ain't from around here are ya?"

Keith said, "You got that shit right, Einstein" and turned back to his steak and eggs. Freddie laughed.

"Stand up, smart ass," the constable demanded. "And turn around."

Hesitantly, Keith stood, smiling all along.

"Seems to me someone smells like dope around here. You boys wouldn't have any dope on ya, would ya?"

"We don't do dope, Sherlock," Keith said. "Just crack and horse and meth." Freddie laughed again.

"Well, we'll see about that. Empty yer pockets on this here table."

Keith emptied the contents of his pockets on the table, and amid the car keys and other personal things was a small packet of a white substance. He stared at the constable who rummaged through the stuff on the table, and singling out the packet, said,

"I'm gonna hafta take this little item into evidence, boys." He put the packet into a plastic bag. "And you boys can join me in my vehicle for a little trip over to our local hoosegow."

It must have been about this time that I got the call from Peter and eventually got in touch with Bill Carter, because, as this version of the story goes, Bill was already on his way to Fordyce.

The Honorable Thomas Wynne, a judge in Dallas County, Arkansas, was sound asleep when he was rudely awakened by a pounding on his front door. It was the constable and the boys, accompanied by William Neal Carter, Esq. The judge answered the door in his nightshirt.

"I am terribly sorry to wake you, your honor," the constable said. "But this here lawyer says he demands to see you, right here and now, cuz' his two clients here gotta get to Dallas, Texas, by nightfall for some kinda concert."

"It's OK," constable," the judge said. Then turning to Carter he went on, "What's this all about, Bill?"

"Good morning, your honor. I hate to disturb you, but this is a matter of some significant urgency. I am sure your honor has heard of the rock 'n' roll band called the Rolling Stones, and this young man," he said pointing to Keith, "is one of the principal members of that band, and ..."

The judge interrupted, "God's sakes, Bill. I may be a hillbilly judge, but even I have heard of the Rolling Stones. Now y'all come inside."

Everyone crowded into the judge's kitchen and Bill took a seat at the kitchen table across from the judge. Bill had with him one of those aluminum briefcases that was especially light and convenient for traveling. He placed it on the floor next to his chair. Everyone else remained standing.

"The fact of the matter here, your honor, is," Bill began, "that Randy, good constable that he is, conducted a warrantless search of my clients and their vehicle when all my clients wanted to do was to enjoy some steak and eggs over at Mama Holt's place."

"Now there's no reason to make a federal case out of this, your honor," Bill went on. "I just want to know how much the fine is, so my clients can be on their way to Texas."

"Hold on just a minute," Judge Wynne said. "Randy, did you go and search these boys and their vehicle? Without comin' to me first?"

"Well, I…"

"Dammit, Randy."

"Judge, I hate to be pushy," Bill said. "But we really have to be on our way. About the fine?"

With that Bill picked up his aluminum briefcase and placed it on the table.

"Now Bill," the judge said. "You know I have to consider all of the legal ramifications and cogitate on the seriousness of the circumstances…"

Bill opened the briefcase.

Looking into the briefcase, the judge paused and said, "Having considered all of the premises, it is the decision of the court that this matter be concluded and the court stands adjourned."

Bill put the boys on a plane to Dallas.

As I say, Bill Carter's account is undoubtedly the accurate one, but I really like this version, apocryphal or not.

AFTER DALLAS, the tour moved on to Los Angeles with five show dates at the Forum. I attended every one of them with a backstage and all-access pass. It was there that I finally met Peter Rudge in person; he introduced me to Mick, Keith, Bill, Ronnie, and Charlie, not individually but as a group while they were relaxing in their dressing room.

"Hey, guys," Peter said. "This is Clair Burrill, the guy who shut down the buggers with the knockoff stuff in Kansas City."

Several of the Stones looked up and nodded, and one of them said "Nice job," and that was that.

I still have my tour file and it includes a list of the songs that the Stones performed on that tour, and I can still hear them playing in my head. The Stones generally performed 22 songs at each performance, with encores in New York and Los Angeles. The songs included "Honky Tonk Woman," "Brown Sugar," "Gimme Shelter," "You Can't Always Get What You Want," "Wild Horses," and "Jumpin' Jack Flash," to name a few, but noticeably absent were all of the pre-1968 songs, including "It's All Over Now," "Time Is On My Side," "The Last Time," "I'm All Right," "Play With Fire," "Under My Thumb," "19th Nervous Breakdown," "Paint It Black," and most notably "(I Can't Get No) Satisfaction," because, as you will recall, these songs remained owned by Allen Klein.

After Fordyce, there was no need to use any other lawyers on the tour, and after the tour finally wound up with the Buffalo show on August 8, I called John in Kansas City and thanked him again for his great work. I said I understood that his firm had been paid in full by Sunday Promotions.

He confirmed to me that, yes, indeed, they had been paid and thanked me for choosing him and his firm, and asked, "When are the Stones touring again?"

We both laughed and he added, "By the way, what do you want me to do with the lawsuit and all of the stuff the marshals seized?"

"Well," I said. "The Tour of the Americas is over, the logo is history, and those who wanted memorabilia bought the real stuff from our client, so let's dismiss the case and give the knock-off stuff back to the defendants. It's virtually worthless and I am sure the judge and the marshals would just as soon get it off their plates and out the door."

"OK, sounds good and will do. And thanks again."

Except for the brief introductory hello backstage at the Forum, I didn't have any interaction with Mick Jagger, but that would change.

We found him
Keith Richards

RECORD PLANT

W hen I joined the firm in Los Angeles in 1975, the first client I worked for and actually met in person was Chris Stone, one of the two owners of The Record Plant Recording Studios, Inc., known affectionately as The Plant, the premiere recording studio in the western United States. The other owner was Gary Kellgren. Chris was a business maven and Gary was a recording engineer without equal. Anyone who was anyone recorded at The Plant from the day it opened its doors in 1969.

Representing the Record Plant was great fun. I used every excuse I could think of to go there, meet with Chris for whatever reason, and tour the place. I always ran into somebody who was recording their latest creations. In my early days, it might have been Alice Cooper, Leon Russell, or Rod Stewart. Later on it might be the Stones, the Beatles, or Stevie Wonder.

I hadn't been working for the Record Plant for very long when some bad things started to go down. Chris and Gary had a falling out. I was legal counsel to the corporation and could not represent either of the two owners individually. To complicate matters, they had signed an unusual agreement drafted by a former business attorney. The agreement declared that, starting out, it was agreed that Chris owned a greater share but that, over time, both he and Gary would wind up equal shareholders. The agreement contained a formula that was supposed to achieve that end.

I reviewed the agreement and came to the conclusion that, regardless of what the intention may have been, the formula would never result in the two of them being equal. It can be described as follows:

Assume you are facing a wall ten feet away and the formula states that you are to approach the wall, each time advancing half the distance between you and the wall. Question: Do you ever get to the wall? Answer: No. Although you will get very, very close to the wall, in fact, you will never get there.

Now consider that Chris has 100 shares and Gary has 50 shares and Gary is entitled, upon the occurrence of certain events, to be issued half the number of shares separating their holdings with the intention, presumably, that one day they both will have 100 shares. But they never will.

So who is the majority shareholder? It was Chris at the beginning and always would be Chris. Gary's attorney argued that the intention was for the two of them to become equal, that the agreement contained an obvious mutual mistake.

Rather than litigate that issue, the decision was made to find a buyer and sell The Plant. Chris and Gary would sell "all" of his respective holdings to the buyer with the result that, regardless of the number of shares they each owned separately, the buyer would wind up with 100%.

Finding a buyer was not easy, but eventually one was found and the negotiations began. Chris and Gary had their own attorneys, and I participated as corporate counsel. I shuttled back and forth between conference rooms. In room one I met with Chris, his attorney, and the buyer's attorneys. Then off to room two to meet with Gary, his attorney, and the buyer's attorneys, until two separate agreements had been separately negotiated to the satisfaction of Chris, Gary, and the buyer.

Late one Thursday afternoon, in 1977, the two separate agreements were finalized in principle and a pre-closing closing was held, getting all of the requisite documents in place for a formal closing the next morning.

I returned home late that Thursday evening and felt much relieved that, after months and months of work, the dispute was over, the problem was solved, and the deal would close the next morning. But it didn't happen.

I awoke that Friday morning and was getting dressed when the phone rang. It was Phil, Chris' attorney. He said, "Clair, there will be no closing today."

"What, why not?"

"Gary drowned in his swimming pool last night."

When I got to the office, I learned that Gary was not alone but that a young woman, Kristianne Gaines, drowned in the pool with him.

The coroner ruled it a double accidental drowning, but rumors circulated suggesting all kinds of crazy theories. Lovers double suicide?

Ronnie Wood, guitarist with the Rolling Stones, opined that Gary probably died of electric shock trying to fix his underwater speakers and that Kristianne drowned trying to save him. But her friends said that was doubtful because Kristianne did not know how to swim.

Needless to say, the deal for the sale of the Record Plant fell through.

After this tragic event, the Record Plant was owned, again in some disputed quantities, by Chris, Gary's widow Marta Kellgren, and Gary's estate, and relations were now not only strained but more numerous. Did it all get sorted out? Of course, but that's another story.

BILLY

Wilbur Meshel, better known as Billy, was the second client I met in person. We had lunch together at the Hamburger Hamlet, across the street from my Sunset Boulevard office. He was the head of a successful music publishing company. I learned he had written some songs himself and that he had a connection with the recording group called The Elegants (think "Little Star").

A smallish, wiry man, with a sharp mind and a dry sense of humor, Billy loved jokes—telling them and hearing them almost as much as he loved wine and cigars, not to mention a good scotch. Everything about his appearance was neat as a pin, including his haircut and manicured fingernails.

We dove right into conversation. It became obvious very quickly that Billy knew music like a second language. He lived it and breathed it. I listened as he went on about the songwriters he had signed to his publishing company and the hits they had written. It was a long list. I knew it was going to be fun working with him.

Billy next steered the conversation to more personal stuff.

"Are you married?" he asked.

"Yes, my wife's name is Denise and we have two daughters, Leigh and Kate."

"I have a wife and two kids also," he said. "My wife's name is

Roberta and she is a 'killer.' You will have to meet her, I mean, she is a 'killer'."

I didn't quite know what he meant by that, but as time passed, I came to fully understand it for two reasons.

First, Billy used the term a lot over the years that I knew him and in a lot of different contexts. For example, at another lunch years later, at Le Dome Restaurant Brasserie on the Sunset Strip, he picked the wine. He always picked the wine. As I said, wine was a passion of his, as well as cigars.

The sommelier came over to our table.

Billy asked me, "Do you like Chardonnay?"

I said, "Sure," trying to hide my wine ignorance.

"How about a Far Niente?" he suggested.

In truth, I had no idea. I would not have known the difference between a Far Niente and a Near Niente for that matter.

He ordered a bottle of Far Niente Chardonnay 1982 and the sommelier nodded his approval.

"Excellent choice, sir," he said as he withdrew.

Billy expounded upon Far Niente.

"The name comes from an Italian phrase meaning 'without a care' from a more carefree time, I would say, in the 1880s. The winery is in Oakville, California. If you haven't done so, you and Denise must make a trip to the wine country. Wait 'til you taste it. You are going to love it. It's a 'killer'." And it was.

The other reason I came to fully understand what a "killer" was, in Billy's vernacular, is that I met Roberta, a warm and gentle soul with a heart the size of Nebraska. She spoke in soft tones that caused one to listen closely and, hearing her words of wisdom, caused one to listen even more carefully. She indeed was a "killer."

Later on, years later, after many lunches and dinners and meetings and good times, Billy and Roberta and Denise and I would make road trips into the wine country around Santa Ynez,

California. On the way up, we would stop at their favorite pizza place near Ojai. Of course, the pizza was a "killer."

Roberta would drive, Denise would ride shotgun, and Billy and I would sit in the back seat and tell stories and jokes. I can still hear him laughing.

For his 80th birthday, Roberta and her children created a birthday book and asked Billy's friends and relatives to make contributions to it. Denise entered:

"Happy Birthday, Billy! You're a man of knowledge, many talents and interests and just an all around fun person to spend the day with! Clair and I have so enjoyed our dinners, day trips and excursions with you and your lovely wife, Roberta. Our conversations are the best! We're looking forward to our next adventure with you!"

I wrote:

"I shared many jokes with you over the years and some of them I know are your favorites. Instead of running on with a bunch of them, to test your memory, I decided to give you just the punch lines to include in your book. You could call it: Punch Lines from Clair. Hey Billy, do you remember the jokes?

1. When St. Peter returned, the gates were gone.
2. So how did you die? I froze to death.
3. For those of you on the left side of the aircraft, Lufthansa would like to thank you for flying Lufthansa.
4. So what about my wife and kids? Well, they were up on the roof.....
5. Tonto, you dumb shit, someone stole our tent.
6. It's because I am pissing in your boot, you peasant.
7. You stay out of this. I'm talkin' to that little shit on your lap.

And the coup de grace

8.   Oh, beggin' your pardon, Father, I thought you said goat.

Enjoy."

I could write on and on, but suffice it to say, I miss him.

Billy introduced me to many songwriters and performers who became clients of mine. It was a terrific relationship that I treasure to this day. It was Billy who introduced me to Bob Merrill, né Henry Levan, a songwriter so prolific, anyone reading this would recognize most if not all of his hundreds of songs. Shortly after the introduction, Bob became a significant client.

What a killer!
Billy Meshel

MARCIA WITHERS

By this time, I had been practicing law in the entertainment business for a while and had seen and done a lot, but this next situation sticks in my mind for several reasons that I think will become obvious as you read on.

Gary, the CPA who referred Neil Giraldo to me, albeit indirectly, also referred William Harrison Withers, Jr., better known as Bill Withers, and his lovely wife, Marcia, to me.

Marcia, a tall, elegant lady, always polite, soft spoken, and stylishly dressed, ran the show, taking care of everything necessary to run a successful music publishing and production company.

Bill, tall himself, mild mannered and wise, always carried himself with noticeable dignity and never failed to make you feel comfortable around him. He had a slow delivery, but when he spoke, people paid attention. He was witty and smiled cunningly whenever he hit you with a bit of sarcasm or irony. He was a punster, too, but he had steely eyes that would hold your gaze when he wanted you to know he was being serious.

He was the genius songwriter and performer who gave us such classic hits as "Lovely Day," "Grandma's Hands," "Use Me," "Lean On Me," "Just the Two of Us," and, of course, the creme de la creme, "Ain't No Sunshine."

It was truly a pleasure working for these genuinely decent and intelligent people.

But, as for most of us, even for Marcia and Bill, there came a time when something not so pleasant popped into their lives.

Once again, it relates to the 1970s, when Bill was cranking out hit after hit. He was fortunately able to go into the recording studio, surround himself with talented musicians, and put down the sounds that he had in his head the way he wanted them to sound. He was working on his second album when he asked a talented keyboard player, Michael, to join him in laying down some tracks in the recording studio. And as things progressed, Bill recognized Michael's contributions not only on the keyboard, but as an arranger. So Bill, prince that he was, did Michael a solid for his special contributions to the sessions; he gave Michael one of his producer royalty points.

Bill didn't have to do that, of course. Michael had signed on as a side man and agreed to accept a flat fee. But Bill insisted, and a contract was drawn up between Bill's company and Michael, memorializing Bill's gratitude to Michael and granting Michael a one-point royalty with respect to the five recordings on which Michael had provided his musical and arranging services. And that was that.

Everything was cool until nearly 35 years later, in 2010, when I received a call from Marcia telling me that, out of the blue, she had received a letter from an attorney representing Michael. She said it was a terrible letter making all kinds of claims and demands. I asked her to send the letter to me.

After I read it, I asked her for a copy of the 1975 agreement wherein Bill gave Michael the one royalty point.

The letter from Michael's lawyer claimed that Bill wasn't paying Michael with respect to the exploitation of one of the tunes from the 1975 album, "Lovely Day." The lawyer claimed that "Lovely Day" had been used in a television commercial, and Michael had not been paid for that use.

There are many ways to exploit music. Music can be recorded, of course. It can also be sold in sheet music form. It can be performed live in a club or at a high school. It can be dramatized on a Broadway stage. And it can be synchronized with visual images, in movies and television programs and television commercials. And, of course, today it can be streamed and downloaded on computers and cell phones and other devices. And each one of these different uses is considered separate and unique, and therefore each requires its own license in writing.

Having read the letter, I turned to the contract between Bill's company and Michael and read it carefully. It stated clearly that Michael was to be paid his one royalty point for uses of "Lovely Day" "on records," but there was no mention of any payments for any other uses. Technically, legally, Michael was not entitled to anything for any uses of any of the five songs he had worked on other than as they were exploited "on records." In other words, legally, and of the most significant importance in this scenario, Michael would not be entitled to any payments for any uses of any of those songs in television commercials.

I explained this to Marcia and Bill and suggested that I call Michael's lawyer.

The first thing I asked him when I called was if he had read the contract. Of course, he said yes. So then I asked him where in the contract it said anything about Michael being entitled to any payments for uses of the song in television commercials.

He said, "It doesn't have to be in the contract, because it is a standard custom and practice in the recording industry to pay for all uses."

I said, "Ah, nice try, Jack, but that ain't gonna fly. A contract is a contract."

He said, "See you in court."

Just like that and, before I could say Jack Robinson, he filed a complaint in court claiming payments to Michael were due based on the standard custom and practice in the industry. So I filed an answer that basically said "go pound salt," a contract is a contract, and the legal battle began.

Bill and Marcia were concerned. Bill told me that he couldn't believe Michael would do such a thing after what he did for Michael. Marcia was sure that his lawyers put him up to it. Regardless, they were in a lawsuit and were not happy about it. Bill looked at me and said, "You know, on the one hand, I can see why he might feel slighted, but he sure went about it the wrong way. What's wrong with his picking up the phone and giving me a call?"

I asked, "You want me to see what they might accept in settlement, to make this go away?"

"Not yet, let's see what happens as we move on down the road and he has to keep paying his lawyer."

The skirmishing and legal maneuvering soon began. Bill clearly had the upper hand with the wording in the contract, and, the next thing we knew, I received a notice that Michael's lawyer had withdrawn and had been replaced by a new lawyer; I'll call him, Matt. Matt came on aggressively, trying to suggest that he was a far better lawyer than the first guy, but he soon realized that there was no getting around the words in the contract and, after a month or so, he withdrew also.

Enter lawyer number three. I'll call him Mr. Jones. A short man with horn rimmed glasses, Jones was all business. He, with his big firm behind him, launched immediately into full scale discovery mode. He was going to bury us in paper. I figured his firm had taken on this case on a contingency fee basis, probably figuring that Bill Withers had plenty of money and, when push came to shove, Bill would offer to settle. The odds were with Jones because, as in nearly all cases like this, sooner or later the defendant comes to the realization that it's all a matter of dollars and cents. Pay the plaintiff something to get rid of the case and avoid a trial that will cost far more.

Among other things, Jones sent me notices for the depositions of both Marcia and Bill, with Marcia going first. Marcia's deposition, under oath of course, was conducted in my office with Jones doing the questioning and everything being taken down by a stenographic court reporter.

The witness being deposed must answer every question he or she is asked unless, and only unless, the question calls for an answer that is privileged. If it is privileged, the witness' lawyer can instruct the witness not to answer the question, asserting the privilege. There are several privileges, the most common one being the Fifth Amendment privilege against self-incrimination. Other privileges include the attorney-client privilege, the doctor-patient privilege, and the husband-and-wife privilege.

Unfortunately for Mr. Jones, Marcia and Bill were entitled to the husband-and-wife privilege. Remember, Marcia ran the business affairs, and Jones was questioning her about the operation of the business, the payment of royalties, and so forth.

Jones inquired, "Did you have conversations with Bill Withers about the payment of royalties to Michael?"

"Yes."

"Please tell us the substance of those conversations. What did you say to him? What did he say to you?"

I interrupted immediately. I was not going to give Mr. Jones any quarter.

"Objection," I said. "Your questions call for information that is privileged. I instruct the witness not to answer."

This drove Jones bonkers. He stood up, took his glasses off, tossed them on the table, and said. "What?"

"The husband-and-wife privilege, counselor. I instruct her not to answer."

Jones stumbled. He was perplexed. He paused in thought. The court reporter coughed and adjusted herself in her chair. Marcia remained quiet and still to my left.

Then Jones said, "I am asking the court reporter to mark the record here; I will be taking this matter before the judge to get a ruling."

I said, "Be my guest."

The deposition proceeded and Marcia did not respond to any of Jones' questions about her conversations with Bill. She answered very well all of the other questions and the deposition eventually came to an end.

We were "off the record," and the court reporter was packing up her equipment when Jones leaned across the table toward Marcia and said, "I just want to tell you, Mrs. Withers, that I admire your husband and his work very much. When I was dating my wife-to-be back in Oklahoma, our song was "Just the Two of Us."

He handed Marcia a CD.

"If it's not too much of an imposition, could I ask you to please ask your husband to sign this for me?"

Before she could respond, I reached over and put my hand on Marcia's to politely silence her and looked across the conference table at Jones.

"I'm instructing the witness not to answer that question."

Marcia looked at me in total surprise, as did Jones. I paused for a beat. No one moved or said a word. My grin gave me away and Jones and Marcia and the court reporter all broke into laughter. Taking the CD from Jones, Marcia graciously said, "Of course."

You will recall that Jones had also served a notice to take Bill's deposition on a future date. To be continued.

I am instructing her not to answer
Bill and Marcia Withers

MARTY KLEIN AND
THE SHMENGES

It's time to check in on John Candy again.

SCTV took off and became a staple for late night viewers on NBC. John Candy was a huge hit with his many memorable characters, including Mr. Mambo, of course, and Dr. Tongue, William B. Williams, Johnny LaRue, and, the incomparable, Yosh Shmenge. Yosh played the clarinet and, together with his accordion-playing brother, Stan Shmenge, portrayed by Eugene Levy, made up a zany send-up polka band duo, the Shmenges, performing as The Happy Wanderers.

John's star was rising, which made him ripe for the talent agencies to swoop in and make their rush at him.

John asked me to join him in Toronto when the first plague of talent agent locusts was about to descend. The first agency sent six agents, which turned out to be the wrong move. We sat in a large conference room in a downtown hotel. There were two young women, three young men, and one older woman, who was in charge.

I think the younger people were there because they would be more tuned into SCTV and its humor that poked fun at television programming in particular. One after the other, they fawned over John, saying things like, "I really like Dr. Tongue," and "How did you ever come up with, Harry, the guy with the snake on his face," and "My favorite is Mr. Messenger."

John was polite, but it was too much, and it seemed to go on forever. I saw that John was trying to hide his discomfort. I found the right moment and addressed the boss lady politely saying, "John has another appointment and..."

She cut me off, "But of course; well, this certainly has been a most interesting chat, and we all hope that you will give us a chance to work for you, John. And Clair, I will give you a call when you get back to L.A."

There were glad hands and thank yous all the way out the door. John and I went directly to the bar, sat down at a table, and ordered drinks.

John said, "Do you believe that? Holy crap, do they really think I would want to be represented by a gang of brownnosers?"

I said, "Welcome to Hollywood."

"Geez," he said, "I feel like I need a shower."

I did receive the call from the boss lady. Among other things, she said that she might be able to send some clients my way. I ignored that and told her, politely, that John was going to talk to some other agencies before making up his mind about representation.

"Of course," she said, "and please let me know if there is anything else we can do for John...or you."

There was another en masse meeting with another agency, with the same rigmarole.

Then one day I received a call from Marty Klein, the head of the Agency for the Performing Arts (APA), who represented Steve Martin, Rodney Dangerfield, and other comedians. Marty said that he and his partner, John Gaines, would like to take me to lunch.

Marty suggested the Le Dome restaurant on Sunset near

both our offices, and we decided to meet at his office and go over together.

Marty's office was comfortable and well appointed, nothing gaudy or glitzy. As he greeted me, I couldn't help noticing his unusual voice, hard to describe. It had a high-pitched ring to it.

John Gaines joined us. John was tall and slender and colorfully dressed in a flowery silk shirt with billowing sleeves and a flaming red ascot. Marty talked briefly about becoming an agent and working with comedians. John spoke of his work in the movie business. I judged Marty to be in his early forties and John a bit older.

We went to Le Dome in Marty's car, and it was clear that Marty and John were regulars from the way we were treated from the parking valet to the maitre d' to the waiters. We sat at Marty's right corner table on the terrace. Marty ordered a Stoli martini, John ordered a glass of Chardonnay, and I echoed John's choice.

Midway through our lunch, Elton John walked onto the terrace. He was met with darting eyes and nodding heads from dining patrons and a wave of attention from the wait staff. He came right over to our table; there was an obvious attraction between Elton and John Gaines. They grinned hellos at each other. Elton was dressed even more flamboyantly than John, with frills and bangles and star spangled glasses. Marty introduced me as John Candy's lawyer.

"I *love* John Candy," Elton said, with a high hand wave, and left for his table.

When he was out of earshot, I asked, "Do you guys represent Elton?"

"No," Marty said, "but we want to."

He and John smiled at each other and I said, "No doubt."

Marty set down his martini and said, "When you get a chance, not now, but later, turn around. That's Bernie Taupin sitting with Elton. They are probably writing their next hit song." He chuckled.

Marty picked up the tab and, as we were about to leave, he suggested that he and John fly up to Toronto and take me and John Candy to dinner. I said it sounded good to me and I would check it out with Mr. Candy.

I returned to my office and called John, who was at the studio in Toronto working on SCTV. I told him of my lunch with Marty Klein and John Gaines and that they wanted to fly up to Toronto and take us to dinner.

John asked, "Do you like these guys?"

I said, "Yes, and I think you will too."

"Then let's do it."

"Okay, I'll set it up."

The dinner was a success from every point of view, no glad-handing, no fawning, but rather, getting to know you and straight-forward business. Marty and John focused on "this is what we can do for you." John was impressed.

At an appropriate moment, I mentioned that John had a loan out corporation called Frostbacks Productions.

Marty asked, "What is it called?"

John said, "Frostbacks Productions. You know, people who come up over the border from Mexico to work in the states are called Wet Backs, right? Well, then, us guys who go down over the border from Canada to work in the states must be Frostbacks."

Everyone laughed.

John was at ease. We were on his turf and he was being himself. Marty and John were the complete opposite of the other agencies' overbearing behavior. I sensed an obvious fit, which John confirmed to me on the way back to his home.

"So how did it go?" Rose asked.

"These are the guys, Rosie," John said as he kissed her. "We are going to be represented by APA."

When I got back to L.A., I called Marty and thanked him again for dinner and asked him to send over his proposed agency contract. He was very pleased and the contract arrived by courier within the hour.

I went over the contract with John and told him that, in addition to a few minor changes, I was going to request one major change. I explained that it was a tradition in the agency business to have all monies destined for the artist be sent to the agency, and upon receipt, the agency would deduct its commission and then remit the balance to the artist. I told John I intended to have all of his money sent to Frostbacks and Frostbacks would then remit APA's commission to APA.

John said, "I like it. Go for it. And I guess this is why you get the big bucks."

We laughed.

Marty was not too keen on my request but gave in, I think, because he saw big things for John down the road. He was right.

John signed two copies of the revised contract with APA and I took them with me to the Polo Lounge at the Beverly Hills Hotel where I was meeting Marty and John Gaines for lunch. Marty co-signed both copies and gave one back to me. Marty and John then laid out their plans for Mr. Candy for the ensuing weeks and months. I was again impressed with these guys and Marty put the capper on the lunch meeting when he said, "Just remember, Clair. It's called 'show business,' not 'show art'."

John Candy, like so many other comedians and all of his cohorts in crime on SCTV, made people laugh by poking fun at anything and anybody, not in a malevolent way, but a mischievous way.

In that vein, John shared a few secrets with me, including some about the Shmenges.

John had a personal friend, no one in the entertainment business, just a close friend from boyhood. The friend had a knack for coming up with crazy, fanciful words and phrases that just popped into his head. On one occasion when the friend thought

John was being a bit of a yokel, he said to John, "You are such a shmenge."

Of course, there is no such word, but the sound and the connotation of it stuck in John's brain. He remembered it and put it to use when he and Eugene Levy created the Shmenges.

If you were to ask any followers of the Shmenges to describe Yosh and Stan, they would say they both wore Bavarian outfits and had noticeable facial moles, Stan had one prominent gold front tooth, and they spoke in hilarious, nasally, high-pitched voices. If you listen closely, you can hear their intro to the "Cabbage Rolls and Coffee" polka:

"Hello, I'm Yosh Shmenge." "And I'm Stan Shmenge." "And we are The Happy Wanderers."

Sitting in the back of a limo one evening, eating pizza with John, I asked him about the Shmenges' voices. He told me it was his idea.

"Marty Klein," he said. "I wanted us to sound like Marty Klein."

"Oh my God," I said, making the connection. "Do you think *he* knows?"

"Well for God's sake, don't tell him," John blurted out. Then he smiled and took a bite of pizza.

Marty Klein and John Gaines did a fine job representing John Candy over the years. Then tragically, in 1992, Marty Klein suffered a massive heart attack and died at age 51 and John Gaines succumbed to AIDS four weeks later at age 54.

I never did tell Marty about the Shmenges' voices.

I'm Yosh Shmenge
John Candy

THE BOONDOGGLE BEGINS

The C-130 touched down on a runway at a Paraguayan military base. Myron, Ronnie, and I disembarked. We were standing on a runway, in the middle of nowhere. We stared at each other. Now what? No taxis, nothing.

I walked back to the plane and asked the flight chief how far it was to town. He said about thirty miles. Great.

Then, coming around from the other side of the plane was a drab green military truck with a distinctive white star on the door. It pulled up alongside the aircraft, a hatch opened, and two of the plane's crew began offloading and on loading sacks of stuff with two guys in the truck.

The driver of the truck got out. His uniform indicated he was a U.S. Army Sergeant. I had an idea and approached him.

"Sergeant," I said.

"Yes sir," he replied politely.

"Do you happen to know a Colonel Samuels?"

"Yes sir, that's my CO. Why?"

"Well, I hate to bother you, but I am here on a special personal mission under orders from Colonel Hutchinson in Montevideo, my CO, to report to Colonel Samuels." I pointed at Myron and Ronnie. "Do you think you could give us a lift?"

He agreed. It was a good thirty miles until we turned into a driveway leading to a building with an American flag flying above it. The sergeant said Colonel Samuels' office was to the right just inside the front door.

The three of us got out of the truck and the sergeant drove off.

Myron looked at me and asked, "What the hell is going on?"

I explained what I had done and what I was about to do, and Myron and Ronnie decided to wait outside.

I went in and to the right was a young lady sitting at a desk in front of a door upon which was printed:

Colonel Artemis J. Samuels
Commanding Officer

"May I help you?" she asked politely.

"Yes ma'am. My name is Clair Burrill and I am here under orders from my Commanding Officer in Montevideo, Colonel Hutchinson, to report to Colonel Samuels on a special personal mission."

She said Colonel Samuels was on the golf course and would not be returning today. She asked where I was staying, and I told her my two colleagues, waiting outside, and I had never been to Asunción before. She suggested that we stay at the Hotel Guarani.

She picked up her phone and asked someone to bring the Colonel's car around to the office.

"Corporal Mitchell will take you to the hotel," she said. "I will tell the Colonel you are staying there."

I thanked her and went back to join Myron and Ronnie.

The Guarani was a grand hotel with a spacious lobby and walls covered in exquisite murals.

As Myron had taught us during that first week on our own in Montevideo, Myron and Ronnie went to the front desk, toting our three bags, and checked into one room with twin beds. Meanwhile, I wandered over to the concierge and exchanged US dollars for Paraguayan Guarani.

Once in our room, we took a mattress off one of the beds and placed it on the floor. We each flipped a coin and the odd man got the bed. The other two did a heads or tails call, and the winner got the mattress on the floor. The loser would sleep on the box spring.

The good news is we split the price of one room three ways. The bad news is nearly every time Ronnie got the bed. He claimed it was because he was closer to God.

The phone rang. Myron answered it.

"Yes sir. He is here. Yes sir, I will put him on the phone."

Handing me the phone with his hand over the mouthpiece, he said, "It's Colonel Samuels."

"This is Clair Burrill," I said.

"Well, Mr. Burrill. This is Colonel Samuels and I want to know who the hell you think you are?"

"Yes sir, I..."

"Don't interrupt me. You commandeered my sergeant and truck, and then you had the balls to commandeer my private car and driver. I want an explanation and I want it now."

"Yes sir."

"I'm listening."

"Sir, I am a US Navy midshipman on a foreign exchange cruise with the Uruguayan Navy and my commanding officer is Colonel Hutchinson in Montevideo. He cut me orders to come to Asunción and asked me, as a personal favor, to report to you and pick up his custom-made leather guitar case and bring it back to him."

There was a long pause. Then Colonel Samuels said, "Well, I'll be damned. That sounds like Hutch alright." He laughed. "And he asked you as a favor to report to me and to pick up his goddamned guitar case. I'll be damned. I'm coming down there. Stay put, you hear?"

"Yes sir," I said and hung up the phone.

Myron asked, "What just happened?"

I told him he was about to meet United States Army Colonel Artemis J. Samuels.

The Colonel arrived in twenty minutes and met Myron and me in the bar. Ronnie was in the shower.

A barrel-chested man who looked like a center linebacker for the Chicago Bears walked into the bar carrying a guitar case. I extended my hand and introduced myself. He shook my hand and nearly crushed it. I introduced him to Myron.

He handed me the guitar case, we found a table, he called a waiter over, and we ordered drinks. He wanted to know everything about us and our cruise and our relationship with Colonel Hutchinson. He was honestly interested.

After a second round of drinks, Myron mentioned that he grew up in Argentina before his family moved to the states. The Colonel asked him if he played soccer there. I intervened to mention that Myron was an All-American soccer player at Annapolis. The Colonel was impressed. He was an avid soccer aficionado and spoke of his favorite Paraguayan team, Club Nacional.

"As a matter of fact," he said. "Nacional will be playing Club Cerro Porteño this Saturday. You guys must come to the game and to my place afterward for a barbeque."

After he left, Myron and I raised our glasses and toasted our good fortune.

Two comely local young ladies cruised by, and Myron said something in Spanish that I didn't catch, which caused them to stop in their tracks and turn around. Myron said something else, and they smiled and sat down at our table. Myron introduced me to the girls and ordered drinks for them. By the time we returned to our room, we were half in the bag. As we entered, we were laughing quite loudly, which disturbed Ronnie, who was sitting up in bed reading the Bible. He made some comment about how rude and depraved we were, which prompted me to ask, "Hey, Ronnie. What the fuck do you do for a good time?"

He responded, "I'll have my good time when you two are in hell."

He shut off the lights and we all crashed.

ARRIVING AT THE COLONEL'S HOME, we met his wife and his twin, very attractive, twenty-year-old daughters, Jeanene and Janette, on break from college at Ole Miss. We all went to the soccer game. Myron and I sat on either side of the twins, whom I could not tell apart. When I went to the concession stand, they deliberately switched seats. I came back, sat down, and called Jeanene Janette until they finally switched seats again. Everyone laughed, including me, but Myron laughed the loudest which led me to believe he orchestrated the switch.

The barbeque was asado a la parrilla, with different cuts of beef and pork, sausages, and corn. It was delicious.

The evening wore on and soon it was time for us to head back to the hotel. Colonel Samuels called us a cab and walked us to the door. We thanked him for his hospitality.

"So where are you guys headed next?" he asked.

"We'll be returning to Montevideo on the next flight back," Myron responded.

"Nonsense, I think you should catch the other flight and go up to Rio. Have you been to Rio?"

"No sir."

"Well, you can't miss out on that. I will cut you some orders and you can report to General Waters, the Army Attaché up there, and you can tell him that I sent you on a personal mission," he laughed. "No guitar case involved, just tell him I thought you should see Cristo Corcovado."

He also said he would send a telegram to Colonel Hutchinson telling him his guitar case would be delayed, that it would be coming to him via Rio de Janeiro. He assured us Hutch would understand.

He did cut us orders, he did send the telegram, we did go to Rio, we did see Cristo Corcovado, and much more.

GO GET "EM HOSS

Waylon Jennings' assistant, Mary Lou Hyatt, sent me information relating to the Wembley Tour, scheduled for the Spring of 1988 at various European venues, including, of course, the Wembley Arena in London. The headliners were Johnny Cash, Loretta Lynn, and Waylon. The UK promoter, Mervyn Cohn, arranged the tour, and his reputation as a tough cookie preceded him.

I received the proposed tour contract from Mervyn's attorneys, negotiated all of the details, and ultimately arrived at an agreement acceptable to Mervyn and Waylon. It was signed and exchanged well in advance of the scheduled tour kick off date.

Then, with the tour to commence in roughly two months, I received a call from Mary Lou informing me that Waylon was not going to participate in the tour. She said that Waylon told her he was not going to go to Europe, and he certainly was not going to take Jessi and Shooter (his son) to Europe, where some crazy Arab terrorists were shooting up airports.

"But he is under contract," I said.

"I know," she said. "But he is not going and wants you to deal with it."

I had a short phone conversation with Waylon wherein I did what I could to explain the probable consequences of his decision, that Mervyn would undoubtedly claim "breach of contract," but the conversation ended with Waylon saying to me, "I ain't goin,' Hoss."

It was not going to be my favorite phone call, but I called Mervyn's attorney. I informed him that Waylon would not be participating in the tour. I explained his reasons and defended his decision on the ground that the contract was "frustrated." In other words, the contract was no longer capable of being performed because outside events were making performance impossible, outside events beyond either party's control. It should come as no surprise that Mervyn's attorney did not buy my argument. And no matter how often and vehemently I insisted that Waylon was perfectly justified in canceling his participation, he was just as adamant that Waylon was not justified and threatened a lawsuit.

The yelling and screaming and legal positioning ended with the old challenge, from both sides, "See you in court."

The weeks came and went, and the tour proceeded without Waylon.

Mervyn's attorney called and told me he would be sending me a courtesy copy of the complaint he was about to file against Waylon for breach of the tour contract.

I dialed Waylon's private number. I told him I had some bad news and some good news.

"What's up, Hoss?" he asked.

"Well, the bad news is I was just informed that Mervyn is going to file a complaint against you for breach of contract for your not participating in his Wembley Tour, which you and I both know was inevitable."

"What's the good news?"

"The good news is that when I negotiated the contract, I insisted, and Mervyn agreed, that any and all disputes arising out of the contract would be litigated in Nashville."

"Go get'em, Hoss."

The case was indeed filed in the Davidson County Circuit

Court in Nashville. I knew we had a leg up if we ever got to trial in front of a Nashville jury. But of course we hoped we would never have to go to trial under the circumstances of a somewhat shaky defense.

We will never know what might have happened, because, like most cases, this one settled. The exact terms of the settlement are confidential. When those terms were finally agreed to by all concerned, I flew to Nashville with the settlement agreement in hand and took a cab to Waylon's home in Brentwood.

Jessi Colter, Waylon's wife, met me at the door and said Waylon was in his office.

By this time, Waylon and I had become close. He, of course, knew that I was coming and why. Knocking on his open office door, I greeted him with, "Hey, Willie, I mean Waylon."

He looked up from his desk with a face full of snarl and squinty eyes and growled, "You're gonna die, Hoss."

"OK, sit down and tell me the whole enchilada, the whole 'who shot John'."

I explained the settlement terms in detail and, as I said, they are confidential, so the only thing I will say here is that as part of the settlement, Waylon agreed to participate in a "replacement" Wembley Tour the following Spring with Tammy Wynette and Buck Owens.

Having listened to my explanation attentively, Waylon sat still for a moment, pensively absorbing everything I had said. Then looking up from the settlement agreement I had set in front of him, he said, "I'll sign this, Hoss, on one condition."

"What's that?"

"You are goin' along. I don't trust Mervyn Cohn and I want you there with me, the whole time. Deal?"

"Deal."

He signed it, handed it back to me, and that's how I became

what I called the 13ᵗʰ member of the band, like the 13ᵗʰ doughnut in a baker's dozen.

The tour kicked off in Amsterdam with Buck opening, Tammy doing the second set, and Waylon closing. For each performance, the three of them would switch off and alternate their sets.

The next stop was London with performances at the Wembley Arena where Waylon would be opening the concert on the first performance date. It was the day before, and we were all at the arena; Waylon's band members and roadies were setting up equipment and getting ready for sound check. Waylon was relaxing in a chair in front of the stage, in his Fila leisure wear and his signature black Stetson, of course.

Mervyn's accountant had made arrangements to meet with me at the arena to go over payment details and related matters. While he and I were talking, a short man in a business suit entered the arena floor from a distant door. The accountant pointed to him and said, "That's Mervyn."

Mervyn walked up to Waylon and extended his hand. Waylon, gentleman that he was, stood up and shook Mervyn's hand, even though he did not know who the man was, never having seen or met him before. And at that very instant, I snapped a picture of the two of them with my camera, and in the same instant, I heard Mervyn introduce himself and couldn't help but notice that Waylon looked like he wanted to wash his hand. I held my breath.

Fortunately, before anything else could happen, Emmit, Waylon's road manager, called out to Waylon that everything was ready for him to take the stage and Waylon excused himself and mounted the steps up to the stage where Jerry "Jigger" Bridges, Waylon's lead guitar player, handed Waylon his Telecaster. A couple of E chord arpeggios on the Telecaster, echoed by Ralph "Mr. Moon" Mooney on his steel guitar, a rappity-rap-rap on the drums from Jeff Hale, and the strains of "Mamas Don't Let Your Babies Grow Up to be Cowboys" soon filled the Wembley Arena.

Mervyn listened, smiling, then at the beginning of the second chorus, he collected his accountant and the two of them nodded, applauded politely, waved their goodbyes, and headed out, never to be seen again for the duration of the tour.

The sound check rehearsal ended and I headed to a back stage door toward a tour bus waiting to take us all back to our hotel. Before getting to the bus, my attention was drawn to a large van with television call letters printed on the side panel. I stopped and watched as several men started unloading cables, large television cameras, and other equipment out of the back of the van.

I walked over toward the van and approached a guy who looked like he was in charge.

"So, what are you planning to do here, with all this equipment?"

"Right you are, we're settin' up for the telly."

I told him that's what I thought and that he couldn't do that.

"And who might you be, sir, to be sayin' such?"

I told him I was the tour lawyer, that I negotiated the tour concert agreement with Mervyn Cohn the tour promoter, and asked him if Mervyn Cohn was the guy who hired him.

"I don't know any chap named Mervyn Cohn. All I know is that I was told by me boss to come round and get set up the concert for the telly."

I told him I understood, but if he was going to do that, there was going to be a big problem. In fact, I told him, if you do that, you are definitely going to have to come back and tear it all down and pack it all back up again.

The bus driver tooted the bus horn, and I waved an acknowledgement to him as if to say, I'll be there in a minute.

The TV foreman turned to his workers and said, "Hold on, chaps. We may have a bit of a problem here."

I said, "Look, may I suggest that before you do anything else, you go call your boss and tell him what I have told you, and see if he wants to call me."

I pulled out my business card, wrote down the name and phone number of the hotel we were staying at and my room number, and gave him the card. I said, "I am sorry, but I can't let you take any of this equipment into the arena."

An arena security guard standing nearby had been watching and listening to us. I motioned for him to come closer. As he started toward us, the foreman called out to his crew to put the stuff back in the van.

"OK, Gov'na. I'll ring up me boss, and if he has a problem, he will ring you up. Have a nice day." He walked back toward the van.

I turned to the security guard, introduced myself, gave him one of my business cards with the same information written on the back, and said, "As I think you may have heard me say to the TV guy, this concert is not allowed to be televised. So if that guy and his crew, or anyone else comes back here thinking they are going to televise or record the concert, please give me a call, OK?"

"Right you are, Gov'na. You can rest assured. 'Twon't be anybody allowed into the arena for any recording. Mark it."

I thanked him and bid him goodbye.

As I mounted the steps into the bus, I received a round of applause and, from his first-row seat just behind the door, Waylon said, "Well, I guess you earned your keep, Hoss. Glad I insisted you come along."

As in Amsterdam, the concert performances at Wembley were sold out and audiences' reactions brought on encore after encore. The concert was not televised.

When it came time to leave our London hotel and move on to the next tour venue in Bournemouth, on the English Channel, Waylon came to me and said that he and Buck and Tammy and others had decided not to make the trip to Bournemouth on the personnel bus. Rather, they had hired a mini-bus to take a detour that would include a visit to Stonehenge. He apologized, saying there was room for only twelve people on the mini-bus and unfortunately I could not be included. I, of course, said I understood.

By this time I had become very friendly with Jigger Bridges and Jeff Hale. Mary Lou had correctly predicted that would happen, and I went to them and asked if they would be interested in seeing Stonehenge. They both said yes, so I went to the concierge desk at the hotel and hired a car and driver to take us there and then on to Bournemouth. Word got out, and Keith, Waylon's bass player, joined us for the side trip.

Early the next morning, Jigger, Jeff, Keith, and I met in the lobby of the hotel. While standing around getting anxious to be on our way, Jigger noticed a Black man coming in the front door of the hotel.

He burst out, "Hey look, guys. That's B.B. King."

"Wow," Jeff said. "You're right. Wonder what he's doing here."

Just then, the lady at the concierge desk motioned for me to come over.

Pointing to the man, she said, "Mr. Burrill, this is your driver."

"How do you do?" the man said with a charming English accent. "The car is just out front."

"Thank you," I said, a bit puzzled. "There will be four of us and we will be with you in a minute."

He nodded and walked back out the door to the car. I went back and told the boys that he was not B.B. King, but rather our driver. They couldn't believe it.

"He has to be," Jigger said.

That is how much the guy resembled B.B. King. I swear, he was a dead ringer.

Still in disbelief, we all got into the Mercedes and headed for Stonehenge. Our driver was seated on the right side of the car and I was in the passenger seat to his left. It was a stick shift, with the gear shift on the floor between us, and he shifted with his left hand. It wasn't long after we were underway that I noticed he was wearing a pinky ring on his left hand with the initials, are you ready, BB. I do not lie. I turned to Jigger in the back seat and discreetly made motions for him to check out the ring. When he saw it, he was astounded.

"So," I said to the driver, loud enough for all to hear. "I am sorry, but I didn't catch your name."

"My name's Brian Brown," he said.

I had to ask.

"Do you play the guitar?"

I heard muffled laughter from the back seat.

"No, I just drive this car," he said.

More muffled laughter.

It wasn't long afterward that it became obvious that Brian Brown was not only not B.B. King, but he had also never driven anyone to Stonehenge before. And, I guessed, he had probably never ventured outside of greater London before. I say this because he got lost twice, having to stop to get directions, once at a petrol station, and another time at a pharmacy.

Eventually, however, after we were hours and miles and miles out of London, and we had just begun to crest over the top of a hill, we saw it, in a random field, in the distance, in the middle of nowhere. There it was, Stonehenge.

Keith, the photographer in the group, cried out, "There it is," as he leaned out of one of the rear windows of the Mercedes with his video camera.

We were all gawking and pointing and saying, "Look at that!"

Perplexed, Brian Brown shook his head and exclaimed, "You mean you came all the way out here to see those fucking rocks?"

I will never forget the look of incredulousness on his face.

We spent a lot of time at Stonehenge, marveling particularly at the massiveness of it and trying to imagine how it could ever have been constructed. Then after we had read all of the history of the place on the plaques and shared our thoughts, we realized it was time to get back into BB's car and continue on our journey to Bournemouth, with hopes that BB would be able to get us there. We arrived without further incident, however, and interestingly, without any further comment from Brian.

Tammy opened that evening at the Bournemouth venue; when she was about to close her set, I was standing in the wings next to Buck Owens, who was going to perform next. Buck wore a cowhide coat that hung from his shoulders to his boots and a ten gallon hat. His outfit made him look like a brown and white Guernsey with a hat. At Harvard, my roommate, Nick, was a big Buck Owens fan. Flashing back, I could still hear Nick's Buck Owens albums playing in our dorm room.

I turned to Buck and said, "Mr. Owens."

"Call me, Buck, please," he said.

"Buck, I have a favorite song of yours."

He turned toward me, interested. "Tiger by the Tail?" he asked.

"Nope."

"Act Naturally?"

"Nope."

"Together Again?"

"Nope, it's A-11," I said.

"You know that song?"

"Yes sir, that's my favorite."

"Well I'll be," he said.

Tammy closed out to thunderous applause to her second encore, "Stand By Your Man," and left the stage. After Buck took the stage, and, after his band was organized, he stepped up to the microphone and said:

"I want to start off this evening with an old favorite of mine that I hope you all will remember and I am going to send it out to a friend of mine. It goes like this."

He sang:

"I don't know you from Adam
but if you're gonna play the jukebox
please don't play A-11"

The tour continued on from Bournemouth to Ireland and, starting in a venue way out in northwestern County Mayo, ironically called Off the Beaten Path and continuing on to venues beyond, I was treated, as you will learn, to more unforgettable tour adventures.

You're goin' along, Hoss
Waylon Jenning

MY FAVORITE KIND OF VIEW

Shortly after having taken Marcia Withers deposition in the Michael lawsuit, attorney Jones was in his office, and he was agitated. He very much wanted to take Bill's deposition, which had been set for a specific day and time. As he had said at Marcia's deposition, he was one of Bill's biggest fans. But he had a personal date conflict and would not be able to take Bill's deposition on the day that he had scheduled.

He called and requested that we change the date. I refused, again giving him no quarter. Remember, this was a legal battle and this third opposing lawyer was fighting a fight that we and he knew he could not win. He was running up the fees and playing a game, so he had run out of the right to receive any more courtesies.

"You set the date, Mr. Jones," I said. "Mr. Withers is a very busy man, and he put this date aside for you to take his deposition. Let's go forward."

He was hoisted on his own petard. He could not conduct the deposition that he so desperately wanted to conduct himself. His associate would have to take his place.

On the appointed day, I drove along Pacific Coast Highway, through Malibu and into downtown Santa Monica to Jones' office on Wilshire Blvd.

The building in which Jones' office was located rose up ten floors on the east side of Wilshire. Bill met me in the garage of the building. He was wearing designer jeans and a Billboard sweatshirt. His short silver-gray hair was accented by his gray, manicured facial hair. He looked far younger than his years and he was clearly ready for what lay ahead.

The deposition was set to take place on the penthouse floor in the firm's conference room. Floor to ceiling windows offered a view of the Pacific. Bill and I sat next to each other on one side of the table facing the wall of glass.

The court reporter entered the room and set up his computer and other equipment.

Soon after, a young woman entered the room. She introduced herself as Mr. Jones' associate. I will call her Natasha; she would be conducting the deposition.

Looking at the court reporter, Natasha announced that we were "going on the record" and began asking Bill typical introductory questions: name, address, date of birth, education, and so on.

Bill was a terrific witness. He was slow, methodical, and polite in his responses. He answered her succinctly, embellishing only in areas and ways that I considered appropriate. He was anything but nervous and, I would say, very much in command of the situation. I was enjoying sitting next to him and had little or nothing to say by way of objections or otherwise, only an occasional request for a clarification.

A high point came in the following exchange.

Natasha began, "Mr. Withers. We took the deposition of your wife, Marcia, several weeks ago."

"Yes."

"And she testified that she runs the publishing company."

"Right."

"And she runs the production company, she's the office manager, and she handles the royalties receivable and royalties payable."

"That is correct."

"Well then, what do you do?"

The court reporter's hands stopped moving, as if he was in shock. He looked up in disbelief. I looked at Bill. He was staring right at Natasha. He did not wince. He did not blink. He held her gaze and said, "I think up stuff."

As best I could, I held back any reaction. I wanted to laugh but knew how terribly inappropriate that would be. The court reporter smiled at me. I was not sure whether or not Natasha understood her gaffe. I tried not to look at her.

Through a wall of glass behind Natasha, I could see a jet plane with a contrail streaking across the sky above the buildings on the other side of Wilshire. I tried to focus on it. Then I was shaken back to reality when Natasha went on.

"And just what kind of stuff do you think up?"

Unbelievably, she did it again. I turned away to hide my grin.

Sail boats bounced to and fro out on the ocean.

Again Bill did not wince or blink and, still staring directly into her eyes, he said, "You know, I'm thinking up stuff right now."

The court reporter looked at Natasha to catch her reaction. I faked a cough to conceal my laughter.

The boats were still bobbing in the background.

Natasha finally got it. She looked away and a slight blush came over her face. Then she immediately changed the subject.

Later, the court reporter requested that we take a break. The reporter left the room. We were "off the record."

Natasha stood up, looked at the two of us, and said, "Mr. Withers, I know that you are a very busy man, so I want you to know that I'll have just a few more questions for you after the break. But you have to admit, we gave you a great view."

She turned and gestured out the wall of glass behind her toward the Pacific Ocean.

Calmly, Bill said, "You know, I live in the Hollywood Hills, and when I get up in the morning and I go out into my backyard,

I look to the left and I see mountains. Then I look straight ahead and I see downtown L.A. Then I look to my right and I see the Pacific Ocean. So my favorite kind of view is when it's cloudy."

She did not respond. She looked confused.

Pausing for a beat and then looking at Bill, I said, "You know, Bill, that's my favorite kind of view also."

"Really?"

"Yup, and you know why?"

"No, why?"

"Ain't No Sunshine."

Bill smiled, gave me a little laugh and said, "Are you sure you're a lawyer?"

The reporter returned and the deposition was soon concluded. Natasha stood, thanked Bill for his attendance and cooperation, and gathered up her files. Bill and I thanked Natasha and the court reporter, said our goodbyes, followed Natasha out of the room, and found our way to the elevator.

The elevator arrived at the garage level and Bill exited, turning to go to his car. I exited and turned toward Bill and asked, "Hey Bill, are you going back to your office?"

"Yeah, why?"

"I figured you might be going back there, you know, to think up stuff."

Bill stopped, laughed, and turned and walked toward me. I knew that Bill had served in the U.S. Navy and he knew that I had also. He said with a grin on his face, "You know, counselor, you and I are going to have, I mean we must have, an 'Old Sailor's Lunch'." And we did.

Ain't No Sunshine
Bill Withers

BOBBY ZIMMERMAN

Gerry Margolis told me about David Braun, a successful music business lawyer in New York. Among other things, David had a New York license plate on his car that read "Lex Rex," Latin for "The Law is King," a reversal from what monarchs had used as a maxim, "Rex Lex," that is, "The King is the Law."

Early in David's career, an artist manager named Albert Grossman suggested to David that he should get himself to a cabaret in Greenwich Village, where an unknown young songster was performing. Years later, David told me that on a Saturday night sometime in the early 1960s, he walked into a seedy joint called Gerde's Folk City on West 4th Street, one block west of Broadway, and entered an environment he did not know existed. He was treated to an evening of what he called "very special" entertainment.

As he found a seat on one side of the crowded, smoke-filled room, a twentyish girl, with thick, blond, frizzy hair corralled around her head with an orange rope headpiece, carried a stool onto the foot-high makeshift stage and placed it in the center. Shortly thereafter, a few hoots of recognition went up as a young man with curly, dark hair bunched up on top of his head, with a guitar strapped to his body and a harmonica perched in front of his mouth, planted himself on the stool. He nodded and quietly, very gently, strummed a G-chord on his guitar. The atmosphere in the place seemed to change, the din of the crowd softened and then reduced to an awed silence as everyone turned and listened.

David said he sat and stared in wonderment. He was determined to meet this young man. He knew in his bones he was in the presence of someone very special. The songs poured out of him like natural poetry.

"If you'll gather 'round me, children – A story I will tell –
'Bout Pretty Boy Floyd, an outlaw – Oklahoma knew
him well"

I don't have to tell you that David stayed for the entire performance and met the young man and, fast forward, eventually began representing Bob Dylan, né Bobby Zimmerman from Hibbing, Minnesota.

David also told me that his representation of Bob led to his attracting other music clients, including Peter, Paul and Mary; Neil Diamond; and the Jackson Five, to name a few.

Fast forward again, David became a partner in our law firm, renamed Braun, Margolis, Burrill, and Besser. I saw this as my chance to meet a true idol of mine.

My first exposure to Bob Dylan came when my roommate at Harvard, Pete Haff, purchased the album *The Freewheelin' Bob Dylan*. Like me, Pete tinkered around on the guitar, and the two of us learned to play a few of Bob's songs from the album.

"How many roads – must a man walk down –
before you call him a man?
Yes – and – how many seas must a white dove sail –
before she sleeps in the sand?"

And on a later album, I will never forget:

"Johnny's in the basement – mixin' up the medicine –
I'm on the pavement – thinkin' about the government –

the man in a trench coat – badge out – laid off –
says he's got a bad cough – wants to get it paid off"

Soon after David Braun became my law partner, I shared my admiration of Bob Dylan with him and told him that over the years I had learned to play many of Bob's powerful songs.

David told me Bob was quiet and shy. On the rare times when he came to the office to meet with David, virtually no one knew he was coming, and no one other than David saw him while he was there. Although I had done some legal work for Bob, which I always presented to David, my magic moment to meet him did not come until one afternoon in 1987.

I was at my desk, preoccupied with some legal task, when my intercom buzzed. It was David. He asked me to come into his office, saying there was someone he'd like me to meet.

I walked down the hall, knocked on David's office door, and walked in. Bob Dylan rose from his seat. I was in shock. David introduced us. We shook hands.

Bob was taller than I thought he would be. He was neatly dressed in jeans, boots, and a horizontal-striped T-shirt under a leather jacket. His long narrow face was topped with lots of curly dark hair and framed by sideburns down to just below mid-ear.

David said, "As I mentioned, Bob, Clair did some work for you, on that Memphis gig."

"Thank you for that," Bob said.

I nodded, "You are welcome, of course."

"Clair also plays guitar and sings–he has been in several bands," David added.

I was totally embarrassed. I couldn't carry Bob Dylan's guitar case, much less play or sing like him. I felt like a complete unknown.

I said, "It is a pleasure to meet you, Mr. Dylan" and started thinking how weird that sounded, but what was I supposed to do? Call him Bob?

"I really like your music," I said. Was that tacky?

"The pleasure is mine," Bob said and sat down.

I stood frozen. I looked at David and he gave me a head nod toward the door.

"Well, I have to get back to work," I said, lying. I could have stayed there all day. "I hope to see you perform sometime." It was all I could muster to convey my regret at having to leave.

I closed the door and floated back to my office, on top of the world. I had just met and shook hands with Bob Dylan, one of my musical idols, a magisterial artistic presence.

David later told me that Bob had come in to see him to discuss Bob's having been awarded a Silver Anniversary Award, a 25-year songwriting achievement award presented by ASCAP, the American Society of Composers, Authors, and Publishers. I was aware that Bob shunned awards and award ceremonies. David said that like many artists, Bob simply did not believe in awards. He wrote and performed and hoped to please listeners and audiences and if he did so, that was good enough, that was award enough.

Bob told David in the meeting that he did not want to go to the ASCAP ceremony and did not want to accept the award.

Meanwhile, ASCAP had already planned the evening and reserved Chasen's Restaurant, a famous West Hollywood eatery, for the event.

David pleaded with Bob to attend.

"Come on, Bob," David said. "You don't have to perform. You don't have to make a speech. You just get up and accept the award. This is an award for songwriting, man, your passion."

Bob eventually acquiesced and the ceremonial night arrived. Denise and I attended, along with everyone else from our law firm.

The place was crawling with a huge crowd of celebrities. We soon found our table, seated with David, his wife, Merna, and others. The wine was poured, and welcoming speeches were made, but there was no sign of Bob.

David was getting nervous. He left the table to see if he could locate Bob. When he returned, it was obvious from his expression that he was unsuccessful.

"No one knows where he is," David remarked, shaking his head.

"Relax, he will be here," Merna said.

Another speech, the salad was served, and still no Bob.

The head of ASCAP, the MC, came over to David, who just shrugged his shoulders. The MC went back onto the small ceremonial stage and announced that the main course would be served.

We enjoyed steak and lobster, more wine, then dessert, but still no Bob.

A man at the table to our right accidentally dropped a fork on the floor, and the lady sitting next to him said, "Company's coming."

Then, as if on cue, Bob suddenly appeared, slowly making his way into the room. He had brought a date. On his arm was Elizabeth Taylor.

All eyes turned to Elizabeth. She literally lit up the room. No one seemed to notice Bob, no one except perhaps David. I couldn't tell you for sure because, like everyone else, I was looking at Elizabeth. And yes, her eyes were a captivating violet hue.

Bob made a beeline to a small table for two in a corner. He helped Elizabeth with her chair and sat down at the far side of the table, nearly out of sight. He must have arranged for that table in advance.

The MC took the stage again and this time launched into a litany of Bob's songwriting achievements. There was a round of applause at the mention of the title of each of the many songs Bob had written over the past 25 years. "Blowin' in the Wind," "Positively Fourth Street," "The Times They are a'Changin'," "Mr. Tambourine Man," "Just Like a Woman," etc., etc., and, of course, "Like a Rolling Stone."

"And now," the MC said, "I am both proud and honored to

award the ASCAP Silver Anniversary Award, for an incredible 25 years of songwriting achievement, to the one and only, Bob Dylan."

Elizabeth rose from her chair and everyone stood up. Was she leaving?

She smiled at everyone, then bent over and kissed Bob on the cheek. She headed directly to the stage, accepted the beautiful Silver Anniversary Award from a rather stunned MC, leaned into the microphone, and said, "Bob asked me to accept this award on his behalf. He thanks everyone at ASCAP and all of you very much."

And that was that.

Elizabeth returned to her seat at the table with Bob. There was a short round of applause, the MC made a gesture toward a guy sitting behind a wall of equipment, the music came up, and people got up to dance.

All I could think was, what a coup.

David said, "I'll have to remember this. Next time I want to avoid drawing attention to myself, I'll bring Elizabeth Taylor with me."

The music was still playing as I was returning to our table from the men's room. I saw Bob and Elizabeth making their way to the door, pausing briefly to say their farewells to David and Merna, then turning and coming toward me. I said "good night" as they passed me by, which they politely echoed. Bob looked relieved to be leaving, Elizabeth's scent lingered for a moment, and then they were gone.

Just bring Elizabeth Taylor
Bob Dylan

JOHN

I was commissioned into the U.S. Navy as an ensign in 1966 and owed Uncle Sam four years of service for the four years he paid for my Harvard education. The Navy gave me many choices. I opted for the Line Navy and requested any ship home ported in Japan. As a result, I was ordered to the USS Epping Forest, home ported in Sasebo, Japan. But first I had to attend Communications Officers School at the U.S. Naval Training Center in San Diego, California ("NTCSD").

All of the instructors at the NTCSD, regardless of their rank or rating, wore blue smocks, partially to distinguish them from everyone else and partially to protect their uniforms from chalk dust.

Each smock bore the instructor's name and rank or rating emblazoned just above the left breast pocket. The smock worn by the short, prematurely balding man who entered the classroom indicated that he was Butterfield, RM1, that is, Radioman First Class. It was through Butterfield, and, I am a bit ashamed to say, somewhat at Butterfield's expense, that I met John Mitchell, one of those once-in-a-lifetime characters you never forget.

The room was filled with fifteen or so newly commissioned ensigns, all destined to become Communications Officers in some billet or another.

It was the Wednesday of the first week of classes and I was

bored. I had met only a few of my classmates so far. Nice guys, but no one particularly interesting.

Classroom boredom was inescapable. Having just survived four grueling years at an Ivy League institution, the naval curriculum was far from challenging. It was next to impossible to stay alert or even give a semblance of paying attention.

It was not the fault of Butterfield or any of the other instructors. They were all competent, knew their stuff, and were more than tolerant of a room full of "college boy" officers. They were all career military and had spent many years achieving their respective ranks and ratings through hard work.

Rather, it was the subject matter, and though important, it was tedious. I felt I could take the book home, read it in an hour or so, and be done with it. But that was not the Navy way. And, in deference to Navy training, and I would guess military training in general, the course had to be developed and adapted to fit every person on the spectrum of those who would take it.

At any rate, this was Butterfield's first day with us and he was center stage describing various ways to communicate in the Navy. Today he was addressing communicating by light, sometimes called LiFi or light fidelity, which consisted of a large spotlight with a shutter that could be opened and closed to send Morse Code by flashing light, day or night. Butterfield called it a directional light as opposed to a non-directional light.

I raised my hand.

"What is a non-directional light?" I queried. "Doesn't every light shine in some direction? Even possibly in all directions?"

"Well," Butterfield said. "Our light can be pointed in a direction, making it a directional light. All other lights are non-directional."

"I would think to make a light non-directional, you would turn it off."

Laughter came from some guy in the back of the room. I did not turn around.

Butterfield dismissed my comments and soon moved on to the sending of numbers in naval communications.

"The most important thing to remember in sending numbers, whether by code, semaphore, flag hoist, or voice," he was saying, "is to send the number digit by digit."

"For example," he continued. "Let's take the number five hundred and forty-five." He wrote the number on the chalkboard. "This would not be sent as five hundred and forty-five, but rather would be sent digit by digit. That is, the first digit, five, then the second digit, four, then the third digit, five again."

I thought I heard a snicker that sounded like it came from the same guy in the back of the room. I turned and unobtrusively glanced in that direction. I spotted him for the first time. He was seated in the last row, next to the window, with his chair tilted back on its two hind legs. He was a ruggedly handsome, lanky, early twenties ensign, with a bit of a tan and a smile as big as Texas. His hand was raised. Butterfield recognized his raised hand and called on him. He spoke.

"Let me see if I get this straight, Butterfield," he said, with a bit of what I sensed to be a sarcastic tone. "If I want to send a number, no matter what number it is, I don't really send the actual number, but instead I send it digit by digit. Is that correct?"

"Correct," Butterfield responded, either not catching what I perceived as the barb or politely ignoring it.

I looked around for a reaction from any of the other ensign zombies but saw only a bunch of blank faces. I turned slowly again back in his direction. He was beaming.

"So," he said. "How then would you send eight thousand nine hundred and sixty-seven?"

"Well, let's just take a look at that," Butterfield said. "The first digit is eight, then nine, then six, and then seven." Butterfield wrote each digit on the board as he pronounced it.

I looked back at the guy in the back of the room. His eyes were searching the room. I wondered if he was looking to see if anyone was catching on. I thought of the "put-ons" in class over the past four years of college. All those, "I'm hip and I wonder who else is" send-ups; those "Is there anyone else out there who will do something other than blindly soaking this stuff up without some sort of rebellious attack" type challenges.

In college, yes; but here? I thought to myself. In the military? I decided to send up a trial balloon, to check out my theory.

"Butterfield," I called out as I raised my hand. Butterfield recognized me. "Yes, sir," he said.

"How about seventeen billion eighty-four million four hundred six thousand five hundred and one?" I asked.

From behind me, I could hear the guy trying to stop a loud burst of laughter, but it snorted out. I deliberately did not turn toward him.

Dutifully, Butterfield turned to the chalkboard. "Give that to me again, sir," he said.

"Seventeen billion eighty-four million four hundred six thousand five hundred and one," I repeated.

"Well, let's just see," Butterfield said as he wrote the complete number on the board and stepped back to examine it.

"Ah, ha!" he exclaimed. "You put some 'zeros' in there." Now the laughter from behind me was becoming uncontrollable. It reminded me of the time my brother passed gas in church and my other brother and I could not stop laughing.

"And with the seventeen, you put a one at the front," Butterfield continued. "That's very good! Does everybody see that?"

Butterfield turned half toward me while continuing to read from the board. "You would send one, seven, zero, eight, four, four, six, zero, five, zero, one." I was sure the lanky ensign was going to bust a gut.

"Does everybody see that?" Butterfield asked in total seriousness.

I again deliberately did not turn toward the guy in the back but kept my eyes straight ahead, locked on Butterfield. But I could tell nonetheless that the guy was struggling desperately now. I paused. Then, when I sensed that he was just about, but not quite, under control, I moved in for the clincher. I raised my hand again.

"Butterfield," I said. "Where did all the zeros come from?"

To his credit, no doubt in deference to my rank, Butterfield did not take offense. No matter, however, because the guffaw which exploded from the lanky ensign in the back of the room sent him lurching backward with such force that the hind legs of his chair slid out from under him and he crashed to the floor. Everyone turned to look at him; everyone except me. Some were laughing; some, concerned.

Through all the commotion, he never stopped laughing. Butterfield asked if he had hurt himself. He assured everyone that he was okay. Satisfied, Butterfield announced that it was time for the morning break.

I rose from my chair and made my way slowly out into the corridor. "Hey," said a voice behind me. "Hey. Wait up. Who the hell are you, anyway?"

He told me his name was John Mitchell and we hit it off immediately. I learned that he was a Yalie, originally from Connecticut, and that he had spent some time in the Navy's nuclear power program but had decided it was not for him. He had been to Alaska and had met a girl there named Muriel of whom he was very fond. He drove a pickup truck with a gun rack and an actual gun. He had the most infectious laugh.

I told him I was staying at the BOQ and asked if he was. He told me that he was not because he had come in late on Sunday evening, on purpose, when he knew the BOQ would be full. The steward mate would have to stamp his orders so he could find his own accommodations "on the beach."

"So I am ensconced in the Winston Motel," he said.

"Why would you do that?" I asked.

"So I could get TDY allowance," he said.

"What the hell is that?" I asked.

It was clear that I had been in the Navy for a very short time and had much to learn. On the other hand, he, with his nuclear power school stint, had a Navy leg up on me.

He explained TDY, a Navy acronym for Temporary Duty. If you are traveling to and from a military location (here the training center) on your way to your assigned duty location, you can collect travel and accommodation expenses en route. He suggested that I move out of the BOQ on Saturday; stay at the Winston one night, go back to the BOQ late on Sunday, when it would most assuredly be full, get my orders stamped, and go on TDY.

It worked, and to save on the cost of two motel rooms, we moved together into what we came to call the "pie-shaped" room; a triangular two twin-bed separate unit in a corner at the very back of the Winston Motel property which the proprietor let us share for $30 a week.

We chased around together for the next five weeks, going to Mission Bay or North Point on the weekends, trying our damnedest to hustle some chicks. He was much more adept at it than I was.

There was the time, for example, upon returning to the Winston one evening, that we were approached by a young lady who said she thought we were Marines. She told us that she had just dumped her boyfriend and that she was afraid he might get drunk and come over to her place and cause trouble. She asked John if he would stay with her for a while. I didn't believe the story and started to walk toward the pie-shaped room.

"Hold on there, partner," he said to me, acting and sounding more Alaskan than Yalie. Then, turning to her said, "No problem, ma'am." And without missing a beat went over to his truck and retrieved his 30-30 from the gun rack. "If he shows up, I'll blow him away," he said upon returning, sounding, I thought, a lot like Yosemite Sam.

"Lead the way," he said to her and motioned for me to join him.

I remember as we sat in the girl's apartment, he with his rifle across his lap and me wondering what I was doing there, that we must have looked like Matt Dillon and Chester, holed up in the Dodge City Marshal's office, with some heinous criminal in the cell behind us, waiting for the lynch mob, which we knew would inevitably be forming and making its way down the street towards us.

As midnight approached, she came out of the back bedroom and stood behind his chair.

"I guess maybe he knew better," she said and rubbed the back of his neck.

He stood up, threw the rifle at me, and pulled her close. He kissed her and scooped her legs up off the floor into his right arm.

"If the varmint shows up," he said to me. "Shoot the rotten scoundrel right between the eyes. I'll be back momentarily."

On the way back to the pie-shaped room, I asked him, "Why the rifle bit?"

"What if she was telling the truth?" he said with a grin as wide as Gibraltar.

On one of our trips out to Mission Bay, I spotted a music shop on the far side of the street. The sign read "The Blue Guitar." I had a flash of inspiration. I asked him to turn around and go back.

I had played in a rock band in high school and again during my last three years in college. My Fender Stratocaster and amp were in storage, and I always wanted an acoustic. I bought a Gibson B-25 for $125, every last cent I had until payday.

He thought I was crazy for spending all my money but when I played the guitar on the beach and the girls started to gather around, he congratulated me on the wise investment I had made.

In fact, the guitar introduced him to Angie, a sturdily built surfer girl, a veritable spark plug, who turned out to be nearly as crazy as he was.

She was an Admiral's daughter and I think, like most, she fell for that smile and incredible laugh. She and one of her friends invited us to some highfalutin dance thing at the Officers' Club on the base where her father was the Commanding Officer. We were in dress whites and the girls were in formals. I can still see him and Angie, three-quarters wasted, jumping off the diving board, fully clothed, into the Officers' Club Pool, well after hours.

He got formally reprimanded and she got grounded, but he told me later that it was all worth it because they made love that night. I asked him if he took any precautions, and he told me "Hell no." I questioned his wisdom, her being an Admiral's daughter and all, but he just laughed all the way through the telling of it.

Three days later we finished our classes and, after checking out, we loaded our stuff into his truck. We were going to drive up north together. He would drop me off at the home of my sister, Nancy, in Westminster and then proceed to report to the USS Topeka in Long Beach.

He swung by Angie's place for one last goodbye. I waited in the truck. She was standing in the driveway, waving and shouting "Write to me" as we drove away. I remember wondering who would miss him more.

I wrote to him several times while he was serving on the Topeka and heard back from him once or twice. But all things must pass, and, after a time, we lost track of one another.

I thought of him briefly from time to time and wondered if he ever hooked up with Muriel and if his and my paths would ever cross again.

So, what exactly is a non-directional light?
John Mitchell

KEN AND MITZIE WELCH
AND BARRY MANILOW

While representing Waylon Jennings, I became acquainted with Waylon's Hollywood agent, Bill Robinson. Bill told me he was referring a husband and wife writing team to me for legal representation. He said he thought I would enjoy working with them and that our personalities were a good fit. Bill was very good at that, putting people together, and it worked well for me in this instance.

The husband and wife team was Ken and Mitzie Welch. Extraordinary folks indeed. They wrote for the Garry Moore television show in the late 1950s, and it was on that show that a young female comedian named Carol Burnett made her first television appearance as part of a comedy team with Ken. She became a regular on that show and Ken and Mitzie continued to work with and write for Carol long after the Garry Moore Show faded into television history.

In addition to having a great comedic sense for television variety shows, Ken and Mitzie were both well-schooled in writing, arranging, and performing music. My job was negotiating contracts for their services.

Ken had an engaging chuckle that punctuated the end of his sentences. Sweaters and tweeds were his usual attire. He was unobtrusive and casual, yet with a proper and dignified English gentleman manner. Always gracious, he could also be a scamp with a charming wit. And all of this would flash through my head each time he answered the phone.

"Welch speaking."

Mitzie was full of life, with a kind-looking face and a gentle smile. She appeared mild mannered at first, but hold the phone, this lady could belt out a song, and you did not want to cross her. Her maiden name was Cottle, a name derived from the makers of chainmail. Do I have to say more? But I learned firsthand that underneath her gruff façade there was a softie, in the end never really wanting to engage in controversy and more often willing to compromise.

The Welches were a dynamic duo with an uncanny ability to deliver just what the doctor ordered for the shows they created.

In addition to Carol Burnett, they wrote for Barry Manilow, Barbara Streisand, Bob Hope, Lorna Luft, Hal Linden, Linda Lavin, and the Carpenters, to name a few, and they created one-woman shows for Suzanne Somers and Sally Kellerman.

I could recite many memorable happenings that grew out of my relationship with these two especially talented people, but let me mention just two in particular.

When Ken and Mitzie wrote shows for Barry Manilow, I negotiated the contracts with Barry's manager and partner, Garry Kief.

Often, after a finished show had been performed, Barry would suggest to Ken and Mitzie that they tweak the show a bit here and there. The contract did not call for any tweaking, so an amendment would be necessary.

Before calling Garry Kief to address the situation, I called Ken and Mitzie and asked them what they wanted in compensation. Every time this happened, we would have the same conversation that went like this:

I said, "OK, I understand Barry asked you to tweak the show and, of course, that will require an amendment to your contract, so I will give Garry a call. How much do you guys want for the additional work?"

"Kenny, let's just do it for nothing," Mitzie said. "I mean, after all, it's Barry."

Ken said nothing.

I said, "You know, Mitzie, I have to say, I think that's not right. You do the work, you should get paid."

Ken said nothing.

Mitzie said, "But we are not really going to do that much work."

"Look," I said. "You do the work, you are entitled to be paid. Garry knows that and Barry knows that."

Then Ken said, "And Clair knows that and I know that."

We all laughed and a price was agreed upon. Let's just say it was $10,000.

I placed the call to Garry.

"Garry, hi. It's Clair. I understand Barry wants Ken and Mitzie to tweak the show a bit."

"Right you are. What do you want?"

"We were thinking $10,000."

Garry paused, then said.

"Barry and I were thinking more like $15,000."

Remarkable? Yes, but true—a shining example of the tremendous respect and admiration Garry and Barry had for Ken and Mitzie.

I placed the call to the Welch residence.

"Welch speaking."

"Ken, I spoke to Garry."

"Wait, Clair, let me put Mitz on the line."

She joined us.

"Mitz, I was just telling Kenny that I spoke to Garry and he offered $15,000."

"What," Mitzie blurted out. "That's ridiculous. We can't accept that."

There was a long silence, then Ken spoke up.

"Well then, perhaps we should take the $10,000 you agreed to and give rest to Clair."

Ken chuckled.

Mitzie said, "We're not going that far off the farm, Kenny."

The $15,000 amendment was drafted and signed, the tweaking took place, the show was improved to Barry's liking, Barry was happy, and the show went on.

KEN AND MITZIE were excited that they were called upon to create a one-woman show for Suzanne Somers. I began negotiating the contract with Suzanne's husband and manager, Alan Hamel. This was a totally different set of circumstances, however. With all due respect to Alan, he was not Garry Kief. To his credit, he was a straight-up businessman and was looking out for Suzanne; hence, he drove a hard bargain.

The negotiations for Suzanne's show dragged on and on between Alan and me. Neither of us was willing to give in too much as we each strove for compromise. Meanwhile, the creative people, Ken, Mitzie, and Suzanne, could not be bothered with this "boys-will-be-boys" carrying on. They had a show to do.

Then the negotiations reached an impasse. This triggered Suzanne to bring up the negotiations to Ken and Mitzie. She wrote an email to them, which Ken shared with me. She wrote:

"You know this contract could have been concluded a long time ago if it wasn't for that incendiary lawyer of yours."

To break the ice, I suggested a concession on Ken and Mitzie's part, they agreed, the contract was concluded, and the show went on to great acclaim.

BACK TO BARRY MANILOW. Ken and Mitzie called me, and yes, they always called together. They told me they were going to be working with Barry on a special one-night performance at the Mandalay Bay Hotel in Las Vegas.

Again, my contract negotiations with Garry went smoothly. His and Barry's respect for Ken and Mitzie became reflected in the mutual respect Garry and I developed for each other.

The Mandalay Bay was packed, and Barry brought the house down. Denise and I were there, having been invited by Ken and Mitzie, and we sat with them. During the intermission, Ken leaned over and said that Denise and I were invited to the after-the-show party.

Mitzie added, "And more importantly, the party after the party." She winked.

Barry finished in a flourish with "I Write the Songs'" as a second encore. There was a standing ovation, Barry bowed and waved, and left the stage. Ken and Mitzie guided us backstage.

There were about eighty or so people at the after-the-show party with hor d'oeuvres and wine and a lot of chatter. Barry did not attend this party. An hour passed and the party attendees drifted out of the room and into the Las Vegas night.

Ken grabbed my arm and led me, Mitzie, and Denise down a long dark backstage passageway to a door with an attendant standing outside. We walked into a much smaller room with just a few people, but better hor d'oeuvres and better wine.

People drifted in until the room was filled with about thirty guests. Mitzie and Denise mingled and Ken and I stood off to one side, chatting. Ken pointed to a table across the room.

"Did you notice who is sitting over there?" he asked me.

I scanned the room and saw the table of guests he was referring to. Robert Goulet was talking to Suzanne Somers and Alan Hamel.

Suzanne noticed Ken and got up and came over towards us.

"Ken," she said as she arrived. "What a wonderful show. Barry was absolutely terrific. You and Mitzie have to be so proud."

"Thank you, Suzanne," Ken said. "That's very kind."

"And I can't thank you and Mitzie enough for the fabulous show you created for me," she went on.

Alan Hamel got up from his seat and joined us.

"Good evening, Alan," Ken said. "And thank you again, Suzanne."

"Oh, and by the way," Ken added, pointing at me. "I would like you to meet Clair Burrill, my incendiary lawyer."

Suzanne started to extend her hand toward me and then pulled it back. Alan looked away, took Suzanne's arm, and led her back to their table.

Ken was beaming with a smile as wide as the sky. We both broke out laughing.

"Wait 'til I tell Mitz about this," he said.

Ken and I wandered over to meet up with Mitzie and Denise. A murmur circulated. Barry is coming; he is on his way.

A crowd of young women gathered near the door in anticipation. The door opened and Garry Kief walked in followed closely by Barry. The women tittered and giggled and approached Barry with all kinds of accolades. Slowly but surely, Garry guided Barry through the throng and deeper into the room.

Denise and I were standing with Ken and Mitzie. Ken got my attention and discretely motioned over to our right to where Suzanne and Alan were standing. Ken was still smiling. Garry spotted Ken and Mitzie and started toward us. Arriving, he poured thanks and congratulations on Ken and Mitzie. Denise and I stepped forward and introduced ourselves to Garry.

"Clair Burrill," Garry said. "We finally meet." We shook hands.

Directly behind Garry, Barry heard the introduction and said, loud enough for all to hear, "Clair Burrill? Is Clair here? I have to meet him."

I was exhilarated, Denise smiled, and Ken and Mitzie were beaming.

I shook Barry's hand and told him it was a pleasure to meet him and that we very much enjoyed the show.

At the same moment, I noticed Ken out of the corner of my eye. He was smiling like the Cheshire Cat and again motioning with his head toward Suzanne and Alan as they were making their way out the door.

When we returned to L.A., I called Bill Robinson to share what had occurred. Bill got a big kick out of it and remarked that it was so like Kenny.

I'd like you to meet my incendiary lawyer
Ken and Mitzi Welch with Suzanne Somers

DO YOU HAVE A CAR?

Our New York office was located on the Avenue of the Americas in downtown Manhattan. One of the lawyers in the New York office, I will call him Larry, was the partner in charge of the accounts of several important clients of the firm, notably Bette Midler and Neil Sedaka.

As I drove to my office on Sunset Blvd. in Los Angeles, I thought the overcast sky might actually bring rain. I thought, no, this is Southern California. I started singing "It Never Rains In California" an Albert Hammond tune. I wondered who represented him.

Pulling into the garage in my new 1974 white two-door Honda Civic, of which I was very proud, I parked and took the elevator up to the office. Pam, my secretary, smiled and said hello.

Throwing my jacket and briefcase into a chair, I walked over to the floor-length window and looked out across Sunset. The overcast sky had turned to a mist. Rex's Fish Market was barely visible. Maybe it *will* rain. Nah.

I sat down at my desk and was looking through my inbox when Pam buzzed me on the intercom.

"Clair, Larry is on line three."

I punched up line three. He asked how things are in sunny Southern California. I told him it ain't so sunny here today. It might even rain, but you know what Albert Hammond said. He said yeah, I wonder who represents him.

Getting to the reason for the call, he asked if anyone in our California office was a Notary Public.

"Yeah, in fact, I'm a Notary."

"Great. I will be sending you some papers to be signed by Neil and Leba Sedaka and notarized. The Sedakas are in California for a while and won't be back in New York for a couple of weeks, so I want it taken care of while they are on the Coast. Give me a call when you get the papers, and we will take it from there."

The next morning a package with the papers arrived via FedEx. I looked through them and gave Larry a call. He told me Neil and Leba were staying in a suite in a condo-like place that Neil told him was behind Spago.

I recognized that as being the Shoreham Suites, and he told me to get up there right away. He would call Neil and tell him I was on my way

Putting the papers and my notary stuff into my briefcase, I went to the garage and got into my 1974 white two-door Honda Civic and headed up the Sunset Strip. For the first time in many months, I had to turn on my windshield wipers.

Passing Spago, the Shoreham Suites was visible through the mist—a long, low, three-story beige stucco building with a large green awning extending out from double doors in the center. Two large letters, SS, were stenciled on the awning in white.

Parking in the visitor area, I grabbed my briefcase and made my way to the front door. A heavier sprinkle started falling. The doorman greeted me saying, "Good morning, sir. Whom might you be coming to visit?"

"The Sedakas, in 311."

I found the elevator and pushed the button for the third floor. The car came to a rest and the doors opened. I exited, found 311, and rang the doorbell.

The door opened and a short man in his mid-thirties stood in front of me in a well-tailored navy blue bathrobe with the initials NS emblazoned in gold on the left breast pocket. He wore a welcoming smile. Dark hair slicked back, bright brown eyes, well groomed. He looked as I remembered seeing him on TV, even though he was in a bathrobe. There was a scent of an interesting masculine cologne about him.

"Good morning, I am Clair Burrill," I said. "I am the Notary Public sent by Larry, and you, of course, are Neil Sedaka."

"I am." He grinned, clearly pleased.

"How did you recognize me?"

He was looking for praise. Larry had told me it would be necessary to be nice, polite—a fan. Neil would require it, and I could see he was expecting it.

"'Stupid Cupid'," "'Calendar Girl'," "'Oh Carol'." Who wouldn't recognize you?" I said.

He gloated.

"As a matter of fact, I first saw you on American Bandstand several years ago. You look exactly the same. You performed "Happy Birthday Sweet Sixteen" with Dick Clark looking on," I added.

"Well, I *love* to hear that. And you apparently know all my songs."

I decided to service his ego.

"I play the guitar myself, but I have never been able to write songs, and I have always marveled at people like you who can write such wonderful music."

"It *is* a special talent, you know."

Now *there* was some ego.

"Would you like to hear one of my songs?"

He was getting excited now.

"It is one of my favorites. I wrote it with Howard Greenfield."

I was thinking to myself, is he going to play a record for me?

He stepped inside and beckoned me to follow.

I walked into a large living room. I caught the smell of coffee and bacon. The room was dimly lit by a ceiling fixture and a small lamp to my right sitting on a mahogany secretary, an antique writing desk. The desk was strewn with music scores with musical notes and words, no doubt potential lyrics, scribbled on them.

To my left was a large baby grand piano that filled the rest of the room. Sheet music was open on the music stand above the keyboard, but there was no candelabra.

The walls were a cheerful powder blue and behind me, a dark blue door opened to a long, narrow hallway leading to what would be the bedroom and bathroom. I could hear the shower running and a woman's voice singing some soft melody that I couldn't make out, her voice muffled by the spray of the shower.

Neil walked to the hallway door and pulled it closed.

"Leba is in the shower," he said. "Please have a seat."

He pointed to the chair in front of the desk. I sat down and realized he wasn't going to play a record, he was going to play the piano, and he was dying to perform.

As he sat down on the piano bench, his whole being said, "This is what I do and I am very good at it."

He struck a wonderfully harmonic chord on the piano with both hands and the beautiful sound filled the room. He looked right at me. I was dumbstruck. It must have shown on my face. He grinned and began to sing.

"Do do do, Down Dooby Down Down Down,
Comma Comma
Down Dooby Down Down Down, Comma Comma
Down Dooby Down Down Down,
Breaking up is hard to-o-o do"

Oh my God, I thought. I am having a private audience with Neil Sedaka playing and singing "Breaking Up Is Hard To Do," in *his* suite.

I sat in wonderment. My heart was pounding in rhythm to the song. Neil was enjoying himself immensely. There was flair in his hands and his arms as they flew effortlessly over the keyboard. Then he came to a dramatic pause. His hands stopped in place on the keys, holding a chord. He turned and leaned toward me and sang a capella.

"Instead of breaking up, I wish that
we were making up again
….. I beg of you…"

He was back in full motion on the keyboard and finished, pouncing on the final chord. A pregnant pause…and then he dramatically threw his hands up in the air, over his head, like Liberace.

He turned to me with a confident look.

"Did you like it?"

Reflexively, I stood up and started to applaud. He stood up and graciously bowed. We both laughed.

All I could think was, what a talent. Denise will not believe this. No one will.

He pointed to my briefcase.

"Now about those papers Larry sent to you," he said, motioning with his right hand as if he had a pen in it and pretending to write on his left palm.

"Let's get at it."

Pulling the papers out of my briefcase, I handed them to him and he asked me where to sign. I showed him as he spread the papers out on the top of his baby grand. Finishing, he said, "I will take these into the bathroom and have Leba sign them."

And before I could say that I have to see her sign, he was gone. Some time passed. Rain droplets were forming on the window.

Neil came back and handed the papers to me.

"Leba signed them, right there." He pointed to her signature.

That was good enough for me. I stuck the papers into my

briefcase, deciding to do my notary thing when I got back to the office.

"Is it raining?" Neil asked, walking over to the window and peering out.

"Yes, it started as I arrived."

Turning back from the window, he asked.

"Do you have a car?"

"Yes, I do."

"Great, you can drop me, if you don't mind."

"Not a problem."

"I will just jump into some clothes and be right with you," he said. He turned back toward me.

"Sorry, I don't have a guitar," he added. "I don't suppose you play the piano."

Did he really think I was going to follow his performance? And although I played the piano, and the church pipe organ as a matter of fact, when I was younger, I was not about to even touch *his* piano.

"Correct. I do not," I answered. "I leave that to the artists."

He soaked it up with pleasure.

"Right, I'll just be a minute."

He disappeared down the hallway. The music was echoing in my head. The rain was coming down harder now.

Neil reappeared, dressed in jeans, a light windbreaker, and an Irish pinch-brim hat. He gestured with his hands.

"Let's go."

Standing together under the awning, with the rain coming down much harder now, Neil was anxiously looking to his left and right with a somewhat puzzled look on his face. He pulled back his sleeve and looked at his watch.

"Where is your car?"

"I'll get it and be right back," I said as I sprinted toward the visitor parking area to retrieve my 1974 Civic.

Nearly drenched, I started up the car and swung around right in front of the awning

The doorman opened the passenger door for a somewhat startled Neil Sedaka and, since he had no other choice, he got in. He looked nervous and uncomfortable. He fussed with his jacket, glanced over at me, and sort of faked a smile. I could see he felt cramped and confined.

Wet and nervous now, I drove fifty yards down Shoreham and turned left past Spago toward Sunset Boulevard, wondering if I should turn right or left onto Sunset.

"Where shall I drop you?" I asked.

At that moment, the Old World Restaurant, catty-corner from Tower Records, came into view.

"There it is," pointing and nearly stubbing his fingers on the small windshield, a few inches from his nose.

"That restaurant. Right there."

I turned left onto Sunset and pulled over to the curb in front of the Old World.

Neil opened the passenger door and wasted no time dashing for the restaurant. I thought I saw him pull down on his hat as if to hide his face.

I started to say goodbye, but it was too late. He had shut the door and was gone.

We had spent three minutes in the car together, at the most. He didn't bring Leba with him. It was 9:30 in the morning. They had their breakfast, so he wasn't going to lunch.

Then, it suddenly dawned on me. When I said I had a car, Neil thought I had a car alright, yeah, a *car and driver*. Of course, that is what he would have. That is why he was looking to his left and right under the awning and was so uncomfortable in my 1974 white two-door Honda Civic.

I got back to the office and pondered whether or not to tell

Larry. I had to report about their signing and notarizing the papers. Besides, Larry would no doubt get a report from Neil.

So I called Larry and told him the whole story. My private concert, the signing, and Neil's trip to the Old World Restaurant in my Honda Civic.

There was a long pause.

Finally, Larry said, "We will have to get you a different car, a new car, a much better car. I will talk to Allen, but, of course, you will have to pay for it. We'll take it out of your salary."

I did get a different car, a new car, a much better car, and I did pay for it, but it was after I parted my ways with Larry and Allen and the rest of the boys in New York, and started my own law firm with Gerry Margolis and Bob Besser.

I'll bring the car around
Neil Sedaka

MICK JAGGER AND
THE PRINCE

It was the 1978 Rolling Stones Tour, and by this time, I was much more seasoned as an attorney and was soon to become much more familiar with the Rolling Stones' business affairs.

The tour kicked off in Lakeland, Florida, on June 10, and consisted of twenty-five performances in twenty-four cities, with two performance dates, July 23 and 24, at the Anaheim Stadium in Southern California.

As the Anaheim dates were approaching, Gerry came into my office and explained the various workings of the Rolling Stones as a business.

"As it turned out," Gerry began, "when the Stones were at odds with their then-manager, Allen Klein, back around 1968, leading up to the lawsuits against Klein, Mick Jagger believed that Klein was not paying the Stones everything to which they were entitled."

"Big surprise," I said.

"Yeah, so Mick was introduced to this banker in London, a guy named Prince Rupert Loewenstein, and he became the Stones' financial advisor. The guy is super smart and really turned things around for the group financially. Among other things, he set up a network of corporations and anstalts and foundations and..."

"What stalts?" I asked.

"Anstalts, they are like German or Belgian corporations, as I understand it. Anyway, good Prince Loewenstein is presently ensconced in a bungalow at the Beverly Hills Hotel and has an immediate need to talk to one of the Stones' lawyers in person, and I am on my way to Anaheim, so you are the guy."

"How do I address this guy? Like Your Highness?"

"No. I met him in New York once; I waited until someone else addressed him, and they called him Prince Rupert."

"So, do we know anything about why he wants to meet with us?"

"No, again, he said he preferred that it be in person."

"And when is this to take place?"

"Three o'clock this afternoon. He will be waiting for you. Bungalow 22, and for God's sake, don't be late. And give me a complete report after your meeting, OK?"

"Right on. This is going to be very interesting."

Before leaving, I went to the library and did some research on Prince Rupert and discovered he was a Bavarian Prince, born in Palma de Mallorca, Spain, whose full name was Rupert Louis Ferdinand Frederick Constantine Lofredo Leopold Herbert Maximilian Hubert John Henry zu Löwenstein-Wertheim-Freudenberg. I decided to call him Prince Rupert.

I got to the Beverly Hills Hotel early and found Bungalow 22. I waited outside until precisely 15 seconds before 3 o'clock by my watch and rang the bell.

A portly, exquisitely dressed distinguished-looking gentleman opened the door. I couldn't help thinking he looked like Robert Morley, the British actor.

"Good afternoon, Prince Rupert. I am Clair Burrill from ...."

"Yes, yes, do come in. Right on time. I like that. Do sit down."

The furnishings were as exquisite as Prince Rupert's attire.

The place was immaculate. I sat on a settee that looked like it had been brought in from Buckingham Palace.

"Would you like some tea?"

"No, but thank you."

He poured some for himself out of an exquisite Chinese clay teapot.

"We have some business to attend to regarding Mick Jagger," the Prince said as he took a seat on a Queen Anne chair, with a mahogany table between us, upon which he placed his saucer and cup.

He took some papers from a side table and handed them across to me.

"Please take a look," he said.

I read through the papers and noticed a few disturbing items. The crux of the matter centered around a disgruntled woman in Orange County, California, claiming that her child had been fathered by Mick Jagger. She had filed a petition for paternity in family court but also, in a separate proceeding, had sought, ex parte, and obtained, a prejudgment writ of attachment. When I had finished reading everything, I looked up at the Prince.

"What do you make of that?" he asked.

"My first question is, how did you come into possession of these papers?"

He said someone came to his door early that morning, woke him up actually, and claimed to be housekeeping. He opened the door and was about to give someone what for when this fellow handed him the papers.

I asked him if he had called Peter Rudge. He said he had not; he did not want to discuss anything on the phone. That's why he called our office and asked for someone to come over.

I asked if he knew if anyone else had been served with papers, particularly Mick. He said he had no idea.

I walked over to his phone and said I was going to call Peter.

I dialed the number and Peter answered. I told him I was with

Prince Rupert, that I had read some papers that had been served on the Prince, and that I was handling the situation. In response to my questions, he assured me that to his knowledge no one had been served with any papers, and further, that Mick was in a secure location with security personnel all over the place.

Remembering what had happened in the past, I flashed back to the time I defended an action for the Stones in federal court in San Francisco, opening up a default judgment that had been taken by a guy claiming copyright infringement. In that matter, there was an issue of proper service of process, and I was thinking maybe we would have the same issue in the present circumstances.

For lay people, in order to drag someone into court in circumstances such as this, you must serve them personally with a copy of your complaint and a summons issued by the court.

In the San Francisco matter, the Stones were walking across the tarmac toward the stairs to their private jet. A man wearing an airport maintenance person's uniform approached Keith Richards and handing him some papers, said "You are served." Keith simply threw the papers onto the tarmac, proceeded to board the plane, and told no one what had happened.

Getting back to Mick and the present matter, I said to Peter, "Please tell the security people to be particularly aware of anyone coming anywhere near Mick and to be particularly suspicious of anyone, no matter what they appear to be or what they claim to be because they will do anything to disguise themselves to make it appear that they belong."

He said, "I got it."

"Peter," I added. "As long as Mick is not personally served with these papers, we can quash any of these attempts to have him appear in court in Orange County."

I did not want to cloud the issues, so I did not go into all of the legal details. I knew that failure to serve Mick personally with the petition for paternity would forestall any action to proceed in the family court and soon, Mick would be out of California and the United States. The last performance of the tour, after the Anaheim performances, was in Oakland just four days hence.

Regarding the second matter, the prejudgment writ of attachment, that could be handled and dismissed, I reasoned, in that the writ was addressed to Mick personally and was obtained under circumstances that made it fairly easy to get it thrown out.

And here is where Prince Rupert and his financial acumen and maneuvering came into play.

The next day, while I was preparing papers to file with the court that had issued the writ, I received a call from Peter Rudge telling me that someone was attempting to serve papers on the box office at Anaheim Stadium, where the Stones were scheduled to appear.

"I am on my way there, Peter. Do whatever you can to stall them, and tell them your lawyer is on his way."

The traffic was not too bad. It was midday and I got to Anaheim in record time.

To make this story short without any more legal lingo, the bottom line is that the lawyers for the disgruntled woman were attempting to tie up the Rolling Stones' box office proceeds, specifically any monies destined for Mick Jagger, but the fact of the matter was, none of the box office proceeds were destined for Mick Jagger or any of the Rolling Stones.

The proceeds were one hundred percent payable to Sunday Promotions, Inc., a New York corporation, which in turn was owned by an offshore Bahamian company that was owned by a Belgian anstalt that was owned by a Lithuanian foundation that was owned by .... etc., etc..... Thank you, Prince Rupert.

I convinced the box office proprietors that they were not holding and would not be holding any proceeds belonging or payable to Mick Jagger. I turned away the lions at the gate and I stuck around to enjoy another Rolling Stones concert.

Nobody's children
Mick Jagger

WHO WOULD COME? NO ONE.

Hurricane, cyclone, typhoon, monsoon, do you know the difference? No matter. The fact is, you do not want anything to do with any of them and certainly do not want to get caught in one at sea.

So much for my luck. I was to be subjected to one of these monsters of Mother Nature in the Northwestern Pacific Ocean, off the coast of Kyushu, Japan's southernmost island, in October 1967. Her name was Dinah.

What was I doing off the coast of Kyushu in the Fall of 1967? I was tending to my duties as the Communications Officer aboard the U.S. Naval Ship, U.S.S. *Epping Forest*, MCS-7, homeported at the U.S. Naval Base at Sasebo, Kyushu, Japan.

Sasebo, with its natural deep-water harbor, was used as a base by the various Japanese navies dating back to 1886. In the 1930s and 40s, the Imperial Japanese Navy used the facilities at Sasebo to design and outfit destroyers and torpedo boats and to convert two battleships, *Akagi* and *Kaga*, into aircraft carriers that would participate in the Date of Infamy.

After the Japanese were defeated in WWII, Sasebo became a U.S. Naval Base. I came to Sasebo in the fall of 1966 and reported to the *Epping Forest*, named for the home of George Washington's mother, an estate in Virginia. The ship was a mother, alright, being home to 17 officers, and as the most junior officer, I was dubbed "George," the name traditionally assigned to the lowliest in rank.

The ship was converted to an MCS (mine countermeasures ship) from an LSD (landing ship dock), the significance of which for this story is that she had a flat bottom and only 8 feet of draft, meaning, she was top-heavy. She was 437 feet long, 72 feet wide at the beam, nearly 8000 tons loaded, with 50 feet of freeboard, that is, 50 feet of her stood above the waterline and only 8 feet of her was below the waterline. Very top-heavy.

She carried various mine countermeasures equipment, twelve MSLs (mine sweeping launches) for river mine sweeping in Viet Nam, practice mines, and several other small boats, all stowed in her well deck. She was also the Flag Ship for the Commander of Mine Flotilla One, Commodore John J. Stevenson, USN, complete with his staff of four additional officers.

In mid-October 1967, I was enjoying lunch in the wardroom with Lt. William Lounsberry, the ship's navigator. We were discussing the fact that our ship had been designated as "Dress Ship" at the U.S. Naval Base in Yokosuka, on Japan's main island of Honshu. The Commodore considered it to be quite a feather in his cap that his ship had been given this distinction by CincPacFleet, the Commander of the entire U.S. Pacific Fleet.

Bill informed me that he and the Commodore's navigation officer, Lt. Kolb, were concerned about the upcoming trip to Yokosuka because of severe weather warnings coming out of the Naval Weather Station (NWS) on Guam. It was well known that many of the typhoons in the Northwestern Pacific originate around Guam, travel westward, and usually blow out over mainland China. On occasion, however, being unpredictable, a storm might turn northward and blow out over our island, Kyushu, or continue northward up along the eastern coasts of Kyushu and Honshu. Bill said that he and Kolb were concerned because our deployment to Yokosuka would take us right up the eastern coasts of these two islands.

As an aside, I want to mention that U. S. Navy officers are permitted to wear baseball caps as part of their shipboard uniform while their ship is underway, or in layman's terms, at sea. They are navy blue, of course, and prominently display the name of the ship across the front, and most officers had something embroidered on the back. The back of my cap read: "Talk to Me," reflecting my role as Communications Officer.

The Captain of the Epping Forest was Commander William Clark, USN, and the back of his cap read: "Follow Me." The Commodore's read: "Not to Worry."

When presented with the weather concern by Lt. Lounsberry and Lt. Kolb, the Captain and the Commodore powwowed with them before the Commodore made his decision, which was final.

He said, "If I understand you gentlemen correctly, ninety-plus percent of these storms blow out over China, right?"

Yes sir, was the joint reply.

"Well then," the Commodore continued. "We are going to Yokosuka for the pleasure of CincPacFleet. And as for the storm? Not to worry."

That being that, on Thursday, October 26, 1967, we set the sea and anchor detail, cast off all lines, departed Sasebo, and headed for Yokosuka, a voyage of roughly 1250 nautical miles, which would take us about four days.

Meanwhile, "Dinah won't you blow" was doing exactly that, picking up steam, twirling faster and faster, and steadily gaining speed over the water as time rolled on.

In radio central, my regular duty station, I kept an eye on the weather reports coming to us over the teletype from NWS Guam, as well as NWS Philippines and NWS Japan. As each one arrived, I read it quickly, clipped it to a message board, and gave it to my messenger to circulate to Bill Lounsberry, the Captain, and the OOD (officer of the deck) on the bridge. Another copy was clipped to another message board and sent to the Commodore and his staff in staff quarters.

> *2205 hrs. 10/26/67 — NWS Guam – Tropical storm Dinah moving westerly at 12 knots over the water – winds gusting 40 - 50 knots.............*

> *0125 hrs. 10/27/67 ---- NWS Philippines – Tropical storm Dinah – winds increasing – upgraded to category 1 typhoon – winds 60 - 70 knots – speed over the water 13 knots – approaching Okinawa..........*

With some foreboding, I went down to my stateroom to turn in for the night.

I awoke the next morning at 6:30 am, showered, got into my work uniform with my baseball cap, and made my way to the wardroom to grab a cup of coffee and a roll and made my way to radio central. Chief Radioman Stoddinger met me with the latest weather teletypes from NWS Guam and Japan.

> *0510 hrs. 10/27/67 ---- NWS Guam – Typhoon Dinah stationary over Okinawa – winds steady at 65 knots*

> *0555 hrs. 10/27/67 ----- NWS Japan – Typhoon Dinah moving northeasterly – speed over water increasing – winds 70 - 75 knots*

I called the bridge on the JX internal telephone system. I asked for Bill Lounsberry.

"Bill," I said. "Did you see the latest WethReps (weather reports) I sent up?"

"Yeah, and like I said to you before we left, I don't like this. I don't care if the odds are 99 to 1. We should have stayed home."

"Roger that," I said. "How is the Captain?"

"He went down to his cabin a few hours ago to catch some sleep, but I know he is very concerned."

1041 hrs. 10/27/67 ---- NWS Japan – Typhoon Dinah upgraded to category 2 typhoon – winds 70 - 80 knots – speed over the water increasing to 20 knots

I rang Bill Lounsberry again.

"Bill, did you see the latest?" I asked.

"Clair, this fucking storm is coming right up our tailpipe. We are doing 16 knots, flat out, and the goddamn storm is coming up behind us at 20 knots."

At 30 minutes after noon, coming over the 1MC (the internal public address system) I heard the Bosun Mate's pipe, followed by the clanging of the ship's bell and:

"Now hear this – Now here this – General Quarters – I say again – General Quarters — all hands man your battle stations – this is not a drill – I say again – this is not a drill – General Quarters"

I froze. I stood silent for a moment or two. I looked at my men, the men in my charge in radio central, and then, somehow automatically, I sprang into action.

"OK, guys," I said. "Everybody put on your life jackets and helmets, tuck your pant legs into your socks, and remain at your stations."

I went into the crypto room portion of radio central and did the same.

1250 hrs. 10/27/67 – NWS Japan – Typhoon Dinah now category 3 – winds 80 - 100 knots – speed over the water 25 knots

I sat down at my crypto desk, pulled out my wallet, and stared at a picture of my girlfriend back home, Denise, in her American Airlines uniform.

So this is it, I thought.

The teletypes were rattling and my men were at their stations dutifully doing their jobs .

The ship's bulkheads were creaking. This flat-bottomed tub with very little draft and way too much freeboard was bobbing and pitching in the ocean like a heavy cork. Those who had been on the verge of, or were experiencing, seasickness were suddenly over it. Dr. Fear and Nurse Adrenaline had cured them all.

Three decks down from the main deck, I was suddenly thrown off my chair onto the deck.

I stood up a bit dazed. The JX rang. It was Bill from the bridge.

"Clair, Doug wants to see you up here, pronto."

Doug Hyatt was the Operation Officer, my boss, and the OOD at General Quarters.

I wormed my way up through the internal hatch in CIC (combat information center) to the chartroom above, and then on up through the next internal hatch to the bridge.

Doug was standing directly behind the helmsman, Bill was to my left at the chart desk, and the Captain was in his chair. No one was saying anything.

It was nearly 1300 hours, that is, one o'clock in the afternoon, but the sky was pitch black. It looked more like 1 am than 1 pm. The bridge was lit by red night-vision lights.

As Doug turned to me to say something, I looked forward out the bridge windows into the darkness ahead as a massive black wave barreled toward us and crashed thunderously over the bridge. As we were standing nearly fifty feet above the waterline, the wave had to be at least a 60-footer.

The rumbling of the huge wave's effect upon the ship could be felt for several minutes. I learned later that the wave had flooded the well deck, and several of the boats there had broken free from their chains and were floating about, smashing into other boats and equipment and the internal wing walls. We were genuinely in peril of severe damage; even sinking was not an unthinkable prospect.

Doug's attention turned immediately to the helmsman and to keeping the ship's bow pointed into the oncoming waves, 40 to 50 footers, crashing over the ship and pounding it again and again.

I hurried back down to radio central.

I was scared to death but refused to show it. I sat in silence at my desk thinking I might never see any of my family or Denise or anyone else again. Then came the call that I will never forget. I held the phone up to my ear.

"Mr. Burrill, this is the Captain. I want you to send the following message by all methods available and with Flash Priority."

Flash Priority in Navy communications can only be used to send a message when either an enemy attack or loss of life is imminent, and for no other reason, period.

"Yes, Captain," I said. "I understand. What is the message?"

"Send this:

Mayday, Mayday, Mayday. U.S.S. Epping Forest. Caught in Dinah. Have lost all steering control. Mayday, Mayday, Mayday."

"Aye, aye, sir. I've got it," I said as I wrote the message on the pad in front of me.

Flooding through my veins and into my brain were all the things I learned in Communications Officer School.

I heard my instructor, Lt. Madson's voice.

"All flash messages must be corroborated. All flash messages must be corroborated."

I pulled the JX from its cradle and called Bill Lounsberry on the bridge.

"Bill," I said. "I received an order from the Captain to send the following message by Flash Priority and I must have that order and message corroborated by another officer. Do you understand?"

He said yes, of course. I read him the Captain's message and he said, "Send it Clair, and God help us all."

I turned to Chief Stoddinger. He was the senior enlisted man in radio central and the best operator of the communications equipment.

"Chief, I have a message for you to send by all methods and with Flash Priority."

He looked grim. I followed him into the teletype room and stood behind him as he sat down in front of one of the machines. Every machine in the room was chattering and rattling as all sorts of messages were flying into and out of each one.

I placed the written message in front of him, and, looking over his shoulder, I watched the teletype arms, one after the other, spring up and plant a letter on the page of the outgoing message, as he typed.

"I have a FLASH. I have a FLASH."

Instantaneously, every machine in the room halted to a deathly silence. And I knew, in that same instant, every similar communications machine in the entire Pacific Fleet also came to an immediate halt and became silent as the Chief then typed out the Captain's message.

When he finished, the Chief turned to me and said, "It's gone, sir."

I said, "Thank you, Chief, and Chief — so who will come?"

He frowned and said, "I suspect no one, sir." And no one did.

My men and I spent the next forty-plus hours at General Quarters in radio central. We took turns sleeping on the deck in the crypto room, removing only our helmets, which lay next to us within easy reach.

The ship had been completely battened down upon the

setting of General Quarters and strict watertight integrity was being maintained; of course, no one was allowed outside the skin of the ship. Dry rations, sandwiches, and water were ferried in from the mess decks through internal passageways and a head was also reachable internally. The non-stop tossing and turning became so commonplace that only the most violent ones, throwing people and chairs and cups and files in all directions, gave pause to our attempts to maintain some semblance of order.

I came to learn later that, while I was in isolation in radio central, many heroic measures were being taken by fellow officers and shipmates elsewhere.

When the two LCMs (landing craft mechanized) broke free from the chains holding them in place in the well deck, they became an extreme hazard. They floated free and crashed into the MSLs, setting thousands of gallons of diesel fuel free to float on top of the churning seawater in the well deck. Any small spark would have set off an uncontrollable conflagration.

The LCMs were also battering the internal wing walls of the well deck, endangering the boiler rooms just inside those walls. Any puncture to either wall would have set off a devastating explosion.

Our First Lieutenant, Dallas Williams, grabbed three deckhands and, armed with fire axes, the four men jumped into the LCMs and chopped holes into their bottoms so that they sank, became stationary, and ceased to be a serious problem.

In sickbay, Lt. Michaels, M.D., set and wired the broken jaw of one seaman and strapped another seaman suffering from appendicitis to a gurney and attached the gurney to the bulkhead to keep both as motionless as possible under the circumstances.

But most incredible of all were the efforts of Lt. Bob Estep, the Electrical and Damage Control Officer.

Those were directly related to the Captain's Mayday message I was ordered to send.

As I learned later, what caused the Captain to order sending the Mayday message was twofold.

First, steering was lost on the bridge. Such a loss is uncommon but when it happens, steering is shifted to the after-steering compartment located four decks down in the stern of the ship, which was done in this case.

Second, and most catastrophic, however, was a report the Captain received that there was flooding in the after-steering compartment and that the electric telemotors located there that moved the rudders to steer the ship had shorted out.

Enter Bob Estep, who established a bucket brigade up four decks through hatches and up ladders to remove the water from the after-steering compartment and to restore the ship's steering control.

Eventually, as Dinah continued to pass over us, steering was restored to the bridge and Doug Hyatt was able to guide the ship to the northwest into the protection of the Bungo Channel between Kyushu and its neighboring island to the north, Shikoku.

After 50 hours, the call finally came out over the 1MC: "Now secure from General Quarters."

When I came to grips with everything that had happened and ventured out onto the main deck that Sunday afternoon, the sun shone in a clear blue sky dotted with fluffy white clouds. I paused for a moment to enjoy the fact that I was very much alive, but then reality set in as I observed the total devastation that had been visited upon the *Epping Forest* by Dinah.

There was literally nothing left other than the outer structural frame of the ship. Every railing, davit, antenna, lifeboat, the Captain's Gig, the Commodore's Gig, all were gone.

I proceeded down the main deck on the starboard side toward the stern and came to an area where I could look down into the well deck.

There was nothing left to be salvaged. Everything was a

twisted mass of junk. The largest piece of anything was a 3- by-8-foot chunk of what had been the hull of an MSL.

The ship pressed on through the Shimonoseki Straits, and we made our way back home to Sasebo, arriving at 0900 on Monday, October 30, 1967.

The *Epping Forest* was put into dry dock for much-needed repairs; rumors circulated that a court martial was going to be impaneled to conduct an investigation. All ship communications were shifted to the communications center on shore, and therefore, not having much to do, I put in for thirty days' leave stateside. I planned to contact Denise and make arrangements to meet her in San Francisco.

AN OLD SAILORS' LUNCH AND FOR YOUR AGE

You may recall that since Bill Withers knew I, like he, had served in the US Navy, he insisted we have an "Old Sailors' Lunch."

We arranged to meet at Delmonico's Steak and Lobster House in Encino one Tuesday at 12:30. I was early and found a booth near the rear in a quiet corner. Bill arrived and joined me.

A perky young waitress came over and asked, "Can I get you gentlemen something to drink?"

She had what I took to be an Eastern European accent. I don't know where it came from, but out of my mouth came the query, "How are things in Budapest?"

She blushed and her mouth dropped open.

I asked, "What's your name?"

"Dorika, but how did you know?"

Bill answered, "He's like that. Now here is what is more important. We are having an Old Sailors' Lunch, so please bring us two double vodka martinis each, with olives."

Bill then broke into marvelous stories of his growing up in Slab Fork and nearby Beckley, West Virginia, where he said when he was a kid he thought everyone was Black but later learned only his family was Black, and everyone else worked in the coal mines.

His yarns of being an airplane mechanic in the Navy in Florida also kept me in stitches.

Dorika returned and we ordered another round. When she returned with the drinks, she brought along some of Delmonico's house specialty cheese-garlic rolls.

Bill thanked her and returned to his Navy days. He said he was the only Black guy on his crew and was particularly targeted for odd and sometimes ridiculous work projects.

There was a dilapidated relic of a WWII Navy aircraft rusting away at the far end of an unused runway. One day his CO (Commanding Officer) called him into his office and, pointing out the window at the relic, said, "Withers, I want you to see if you can get that plane up and running."

From that moment on, everywhere Bill went, from the chow line to the latrine, he could hear the snickering.

A week or so later, the CO was sitting in his office looking out the same window when to his amazement he saw the plane taxiing down the runway. Bill said he was advanced in rate and treated differently from that day through the remainder of his time in the Navy.

My cell phone buzzed and I glanced at my watch. It was 4:30. It was Denise.

"How was lunch?" I told her we hadn't ordered yet.

Dorika returned and told us she was off her shift and would be replaced by Howard, a tall gawky-looking blond kid. Bill slipped Dorika some cash, and Howard replaced our long-ignored luncheon menus with dinner menus.

Bill ordered a seafood salad and I ordered shrimp fettuccine puttanesca.

By the time the entrees arrived, Bill's stories found him out of the Navy and recording his first album for Sussex Records, with his first hit single, "Ain't No Sunshine."

He said he was young, single, and popular. He was thinking

about hiring an agent. He met a potential agent for lunch at Hernando's Hideaway in Beverly Hills. Seated at a corner table by herself, he saw Lena Horne. He said he couldn't believe his eyes; he thought she was the most beautiful Black woman he'd ever seen. He told his wanna-be agent he was going to go over and talk to her. The wanna-be said don't be stupid, she obviously wants to be alone. Celebrities hate to be bothered.

Nevertheless, he couldn't help himself. He went over and asked her if he might join her. He was stunned when she said please sit down. They chatted for a while, mostly about music, and then quite casually, she placed her hand on his leg. He said he turned, touched her face ever so gently with his hand, and said, "You are the most beautiful woman in the world .... for your age."

In a flash, he could not believe what he had said. He froze. He said he wanted to reach out into space and pull those last few words back into his mouth.

Lena got up and walked out of the restaurant. He said it was the dumbest thing he'd ever done, then or since, and, at that moment, he suddenly had a brand-new appreciation for words.

At 7:45 we split the tab and went out to the valet to retrieve our cars. The Old Sailors' Lunch was over; a grand Old Sailors' Lunch it was. We vowed to do it again.

For your age
Lena Horne

THE GREAT ONE

I played a lot of golf in those days and got John Candy interested in the sport. John was big and strong and could hit the ball a mile, but we were never sure in which direction it would soar. Nevertheless, we had great fun together.

This particular morning I was staying at John and Rose's house in New Market, just north of Toronto. John knocked on my bedroom door and said we had to leave in about half an hour.

After dressing, I quietly made my way down the hallway toward the dining area, being careful not to wake Jennifer, John and Rose's infant daughter. John was seated at the table, sporting a bright green golf shirt and khaki pants. Rose was in the kitchen, and I could smell the familiar aroma of frying peameal bacon and potatoes. I sat down next to John, and Rose deposited a healthy plate full of breakfast before each of us.

"We're gonna play Pheasant Run this morning, Rosie" John announced.

We finished eating, John kissed Rose goodbye, we piled into John's 4x4, and headed for the golf course. A guy in the pro shop looking at some golf shirts noticed John and said, "Hey, Johnny LaRue." John smiled and waved at the guy who came over and asked John if he would autograph his hat. John asked the guy his name, personalized the autograph, and clearly made his day.

We were on the par four fifth hole and practically had the golf course to ourselves. I hit a decent drive, maybe two hundred and twenty yards just right of center, and John blasted one at least two hundred and eighty yards, straight down the middle. He turned to me with his boyish grin, we exchanged a high five, and off we went in the cart.

I hit my second shot toward the green, but short. John stood over his ball, and I asked what club he was using. He said a six iron. I thought to myself that I would probably hit a five wood.

John again blasted the ball, straight at the green and the flag, and it rolled up and dropped into the hole, an eagle two. He couldn't believe it. I couldn't believe it. We stood facing each other, stunned. Then John jumped up and down like a little kid and threw his six iron into the air. He gave me a hug that I thought would suffocate me.

Walking up onto the green after I had hit my third shot, John retrieved his ball from the cup, kissed it, and put it in his pocket. We finished the round and our scores really didn't matter, the highlight being John's eagle. We drank to his golf prowess and on the way home stopped at Mary Brown's Chicken & Taters and brought dinner back to the house.

A few days later, when I was back in L.A., I went to a trophy shop near my office in Century City and purchased a custom trophy for John. I had surreptitiously purloined, with Rose's help, the very ball that John had hit to score his eagle. I had it mounted on the trophy with the scorecard, which showed the course, the hole, and the score. John loved it and proudly displayed it at his home.

As time passed, John became far more successful and recognizable, and he and his family eventually moved to Los Angeles. This gave John and me much more time to play golf together. When one of John's agents at APA, Paul Flaherty, learned of John's interest in golf, he invited John and me to join him for a round at his course, Bel-Air, an upscale private country club.

John eventually became a regular at Bel-Air, and fortunately,

I got to play there with him a lot. John had his favorite forecaddie, Bill, and Bill liked John for many reasons, not the least of which was that John was an extremely generous person. I don't know exactly how much John tipped Bill at the end of each round, but I am sure it was many times over what anyone else tipped, even at that club.

Bill was a quiet Black man. He unobtrusively gave golf advice to John and me, and I came to think he knew every blade of grass on the golf course. He wore a genuine smile except when he was giving advice when he became all business. He wore a small tuft of facial hair just below his lower lip, in the middle, a soul patch.

One day, John called me to say he was going to play a round at Bel-Air with Bruce McNall and Wayne Gretzky. Bruce owned the Los Angeles Kings and had recently concluded a deal with the Edmonton Oilers that brought Wayne Gretzky to play for the Kings. John said they needed a fourth and would I be interested. Of course, I jumped at the chance.

I arrived at the course, dropped my clubs at the bag drop, went into the men's locker room, and changed into my golf gear. I made my way to the practice green where John, Bruce, and Wayne were practicing putting.

John and Bruce were a matched set, both portly and quite jovial, always laughing and chiding one another. When they rode in a golf cart together, the clearance of the cart above the ground was no more than a few inches.

Wayne's well-tuned athlete's body was decked out in Nike gear from top to bottom. He had a long, narrow, youthful face, with a pointy nose, and nicely groomed dark hair under an L.A. Kings ball cap. I imagined he was good at any sport he put his mind to.

Bill, standing to the one side of the practice green, nodded to me and smiled. I went over and said hello and asked if he was our forecaddie. He said yes and that we could head over to the first tee at any time.

I returned to putting and overheard Bruce suggesting to John that they should have a bet.

"I was thinking about a hundred-dollar Nassau," Bruce said.

"You're on," John responded.

John and Bruce played at about the same level with about the same handicap, so their bet would appropriately be even up.

Hearing their exchange, Wayne meandered over toward me and said, "Hey, Clair. You and I should have a bet. What's your handicap?"

I said, "I am an eighteen."

Wayne said, "Great. How about a fifty-dollar Nassau, even up?"

Bill stepped into my line of sight, behind Wayne and shook his head, no.

I asked Wayne, "What's your handicap?"

He said, "We're about the same."

Bill again shook his head, no.

I paused and said, "I'll think about it. I am going to hit the head before we tee off," and I walked back into the clubhouse.

On my return, I took a circuitous route through the pro shop specifically to look at the posted handicap sheet. Wayne Gretzky was listed as a nine handicap. I went back to the practice green.

I said, "I tell you what, Wayne. Let's do a twenty-five dollar Nassau and you give four strokes a side."

"No way. I don't give strokes to sandbaggers," he chuckled. "But I will do a twenty-five dollar Nassau even up."

Again, Bill shook his head, no.

"Can't do it," I said.

The topic was dropped and the four of us made our way to the first tee.

The first hole at Bel-Air is a straightaway par five. Wayne

parred it. So did I. John and Bruce each carded a seven. We went on to the second hole and, on the way, Wayne said to me, "See, we play even."

Bill frowned.

The second hole is a straightaway par four. Wayne bogeyed it with a five. So did I and I heard it again: "See, we play even."

The third hole is a par three downhill over water about a hundred and seventy yards. As we stepped out of the carts, Wayne hit me up again.

"Look," he said. "It's obvious we play even so let's play out the rest of the round even up, twenty-five dollar Nassau. Whatta ya say?"

He was getting on my nerves, and Bill could sense it.

John hit his drive into the houses to the right. Bruce hit his drive into the houses on the left. They stared at each other and simultaneously said, "Do over."

A large white crane flew in from nowhere and landed in the pond in front of the green.

John teed up another ball and hit it into the pond. The crane took off.

"Nearly a birdie," John grinned.

Bruce hit his second drive into the pond. "Do over."

Their third drives were both in play.

Maybe out of spite or whatever, I walked onto the tee and turned to Wayne, and said, "Okay, a twenty-five dollar Nassau, even up, no automatic presses."

Bill rolled his eyes, shook his head, and gave me a look like he thought I was the biggest sucker on the planet. But I had decided that, even if I lost, I could say I lost to a natural athlete, a professional hockey Hall of Famer.

I teed up my ball and hit my drive with a five iron. The ball cleared the water, hit on the green, and rolled onto the right side collar about thirty-five feet from the hole.

Wayne stepped up and drilled a seven iron, nice and high, and dead straight at the flag. His ball landed about ten feet short of and directly below the hole and checked up at about eight feet. He smiled and swaggered over to our cart.

Bill whispered to me, "You are in trouble," and took off down the hill to the green.

Bruce and John both got onto the green, the flag was removed from the hole, and I was away. I stood behind my ball as it sat perched on the collar, and plumbed the line to the hole with my putter. Bill was standing to my immediate right.

He whispered, "Mr. Burrill, you think your putt is downhill and will be fast."

I nodded yes.

"It is not. It is against the grain. Play it flat."

I nodded.

"And you think it is going to break a foot to the left."

I nodded yes again.

"It will not. Play it flat and six inches outside the right edge."

I did exactly as he had instructed. The ball cruised down toward the hole. I could tell the speed was right. The ball was on line and broke almost exactly six inches to the left and dropped into the center of the cup, a birdie two.

John hooted, Wayne grimaced, and Bill grinned from ear to ear. I walked up to the hole and withdrew my ball, careful not to step in anyone's line. John and Bruce putted out and Wayne stood behind his ball. He plumbed his line and approached his putt. He stroked his ball up toward the hole and left it just on the left edge. He tapped it in for a par three and clearly was not a happy camper.

I couldn't help myself. As I walked off the back of the green, I announced, "One up!"

Wayne was silent as he drove our cart to the fourth tee. I stared straight ahead.

Wayne lost the front nine to me by two holes, so, at that point he was down twenty-five dollars. As we proceeded to the tenth tee, he asked if I would accept a press. This means he proposed to double the bet for the back nine and total and, since Bill was my coach, I agreed.

Bill gave me accurate and invaluable advice throughout the entire round. I sensed he wanted me to win my bet. I won't bore you with a hole-by-hole replay, but I will share just these two tidbits.

The first was on the thirteenth hole. I was nearly two hundred yards from the green on a par four addressing my approach shot when Bill asked me, "What club do you have there?"

I said, "It's a four iron."

He said, "Put it back in your bag and hit your five wood."

I did, and the ball sailed to the green and stopped about ten feet from the flag near the back of the green. I looked at Bill, smiled, and said, "You are the best." He just grinned and walked off.

The second tidbit was on the eighteenth, the final hole. Wayne, as I said, had lost the front nine to me by two holes and was down one hole to me on the back nine. He stood to lose three ways, which he could not bear. He proposed an Aloha press; that is, he proposed double or nothing. If I agreed, I would be playing the last hole for everything.

That meant, if I won the last hole, he would owe me three hundred dollars. If we tied the last hole, he would owe me one hundred and fifty dollars. However, if *he* won the last hole, he would owe me nothing. So it all came down to the last hole with everything on the line. I would win $300 if I won the last hole, or I would win nothing if he won the last hole, or I could win $150 if we tied the last hole.

I looked at Bill who threw his arms up into the air as if to say, "Why not."

I said to Wayne, "You're on."

Wayne hit a very good drive to the center of the fairway. I hit my drive too far left and into a bunker. My bunker shot landed short of the green. Wayne hit a perfect second shot to the front part of the green below and about thirty feet from the cup. I put my third shot on the green, but a good twenty-five feet to the right of the cup, with a side hill lie.

Wayne was away and just missed his birdie putt, which, had he made it, would have ended the bet right then, with his owing me nothing, but he missed. He tapped in his par.

I plumbed my putt. It was impossible. It had to go up the hill slightly, not too little, not too much. And it had to be hit just right, not too hard, not too soft. Bill stepped in behind me.

"Mr. Burrill," he said. "Do you see that little light green leaf about ten feet in front of us in the middle of the hill?"

I said, "Yes," and started to walk toward the leaf thinking he was telling me to brush it out of the way, out of my line.

"No, no," he said. "Come back."

I backed up.

He said, "Roll your ball over that little leaf with just enough to get the ball to the hole." He stepped back.

Once again, I did exactly as he instructed. The ball rolled up the hill, approaching the leaf. It rolled over the leaf and began breaking to the left and picking up speed. It bent toward the hole and I knew that at that speed it would have to hit the cup dead center.

Bill whispered, "You got it," and, at that same instant, the ball plunked straight down into the center of the cup. It was a par, a par four, and not only that, it meant we tied the hole, and Wayne Gretzky owed me $150. Holy shit!

I turned around and hugged Bill. Wayne shook his head in disbelief and headed for the elevator to take him up to the clubhouse. Bruce joined him. John retrieved my ball from the hole and throwing it to me said, "If I hadn't seen that, I would not have believed it. I think you should have that ball mounted on a trophy."

The three of us laughed, John gave Bill a handful of cash, and John and I got into the elevator.

After freshening up in the locker room, John and I joined Bruce and Wayne in the Men's Grill. We ordered drinks and talked and, when it came time to pay, John, generous to a fault, insisted on buying.

Wayne got up, said his goodbyes, and left. After John settled the bill, he and I followed shortly behind. Bruce stayed to talk to some people at another table and bid us goodbye.

As John and I were walking out toward the parking valet, John stopped me and asked, "Why the long face?"

I said, "Wayne didn't pay me."

"What?"

"Wayne lost the bet. I accepted his Aloha press, we tied the last hole, so he owes me $150, and he didn't pay me."

John spotted Wayne talking to the valet and, pointing at me, shouted, "Hey Great One. Pay the man."

Wayne turned around with a stunned look.

People were making their way in and out of the club. Everyone heard John's bellowing and stopped to look around.

John repeated, just as loudly, "I said, pay the man."

Then walking up to Wayne he added with a sarcastic snicker.

"I believe you lost your bet, O Great One, and owe my friend here a hundred and fifty bucks."

Sheepishly, Wayne opened his wallet and counted out one hundred and fifty dollars. He handed the bills to me, said nothing, grabbed his keys from the valet, got into his car, and drove away.

John said, "That guy just signed a million-dollar deal with Anheuser-Busch and tried to stiff you for a buck and a half, go figure. Let's go to Spago and celebrate. You can buy with Gretzky's money," he grinned.

Shooting pool with John years later, he brought up the events of that day. We laughed and spent several hours remembering other experiences we had shared over the years.

Pay the man
Wayne Gretzky

MEET ME IN SAN FRANCISCO

As mentioned, I grew up in the small town of Plymouth located in the ridges and lowlands of Eastern Wisconsin, in the kettles and moraines dug out and piled up by a glacier thousands of years before I arrived on the scene. I was fortunate to have two older brothers and an older sister, my role models, mentors, and educators, who, with my parents, spoiled me rotten – and I loved it.

Growing up, Plymouth was all I knew. It was my world and everything else was someplace else, way off, perhaps to be explored later. It was a simple life. My mom was a great cook, a religious lady who lived for her husband and four kids. My dad worked hard, provided for his family, ruled the roost, and was mostly serious but enjoyed throwing out puns every now and then.

My best friend, Pat, lived across three backyards, up the hill on Collins Street, in a white house so big his family took in boarders. We rode our bikes, pedaled our newspapers, and at night rang people's doorbells, then ran and hid in the bushes and giggled when we saw them come to the door to find no one there.

The winters were special, cold, yes, but so much fun. Skiing, tobogganing, and best of all, ice skating.

The early settlers founded Plymouth on the Mullett River and dammed it up in the center of town to form a millrace to drive the water wheel at the grain mill. The dam created a mill pond that froze over each November, creating a 36-acre skating rink.

Right after Thanksgiving, Pat and I would bundle up, grab our skates, and head down to the mill pond every chance we could get. We put on our skates in Harry's ice shack, a small structure with a pot-bellied wood-burning stove in the center of a wood floor surrounded by benches against the walls. There was room for about twenty-five kids to sit on the benches in a warm room and put on and lace up skates.

The place smelled of wet leather gloves and woolen mittens warming near the stove.

On a chair in one corner, behind a counter, sat the proprietor, Harry Otterman, a gruff old guy in bib overalls, with unruly hair, who happened to love kids. A big door led out onto a wooden porch and five wooden steps that led right down onto the ice. The floor, porch, and steps were made of wood so as not to damage the blades of the skates.

We had each brought a dime with us, and after working up a good sweat in a rousing game of pom pom pull away, we'd go back into the shack and buy a grape pop and a Milky Way bar from Harry for a nickel each.

The mill pond was not only an ice skater's heaven; it was also a place to meet girls. The older boys would brag about taking their girlfriends "up to the island." Being much younger, Pat and I never understood what that meant until we began to bloom into our teens.

Pat was Catholic and attended St. John the Baptist elementary school and I attended the public elementary school, both through eighth grade. There was also a Lutheran elementary school in town but only one Plymouth High School. PHS was attended by Catholics, Lutherans, and publics alike, all mixed up into one diverse mass.

By the time Pat and I were PHS juniors, we were old enough

to drive and the coolest thing was to cruise around in a car after school.

The year was 1961 and on this day we were cruisin' in Pat's Ford. As we turned onto Grove Street, I saw a girl walking in front of the City Park. She was hot.

As we approached her, I asked, "Who is that?"

I craned my neck around to keep looking at her as we drove past.

"That's Denise Foy," Pat said. "She's a freshman. She went to St. John's. I'm thinking about asking her out."

Pat was not only my closest friend; he was also the drummer in our rock band, The Ravens. He did date Denise, and I saw her with him from time to time before and after dances when The Ravens performed. She had short dark hair and the prettiest face with a smile to melt the coldest heart. I would have liked to date her, but she was my best friend's girl and off limits.

Years passed; Pat and I graduated and went off to college, and after my first year at Harvard, I returned home to Plymouth for a few weeks before reporting to Norfolk, Virginia, for my NROTC third-class midshipman cruise. I was being badgered by my friend, Paul, another member of The Ravens, to get a date so we could double.

My former high school steady, Haley, and I had drifted apart since graduating. When Paul suggested Denise, I thought, why not. Paul said she no longer dated Pat and she worked part time at the Rexall drug store.

We dropped by the Rexall, I asked her out, and she said yes. When I picked her up at her house, she was even prettier than I remembered and had all the captivating features of a blossoming young woman. She was pert and smart, and her scent stayed with me long after I kissed her good night.

I saw her one more time that summer, on the Saturday night before I had to leave for Norfolk. It was a night marked with highs and lows. We were together, in the dark, on the couch at Paul's house, listening to Johnny Mathis singing "Chances Are." I wanted to spend the rest of my life there.

The doorbell rang and Paul told me Haley was at the door and wanted to talk to me. I went to the door. Haley demanded her ring back. I told her I didn't have it; it was at my house. She insisted, and I went to get my jacket.

Denise was no longer on the couch. I found her sitting by herself in the kitchen. I told her I had to leave for a little while, but I'd be back. She said she knew who was at the door, that she felt awful and didn't want to cause any trouble. I begged her to wait until I got back.

The trip to my house was painful as Haley berated me without so much as pausing for a breath.

It was late and my parents were asleep. I crept quietly to my room, rummaged through some stuff, and found the ring.

An owl hooted in the darkness as I returned to Haley's car.

"Here's your ring," I said. "Please take me back to Paul's."

My heart was pounding in my chest. Please let her still be there.

We pulled up in front of Paul's.

Haley said, "Can we talk?"

I got out of the car and walked around to her side. Her window was open.

I said, "I don't understand it, either."

I was inside Paul's house in a flash and went directly to the kitchen. Thank God! She was still there.

I held her hand. It quivered. We spoke softly. She had to go home. I walked her home. I kissed her good night and told her I wanted to see her again. She looked up at me in the faint porch light and the image of her face burned into my brain. We kissed again and she went inside. I was completely taken by her.

A few days later, I was relaxing in one of the lower bunks in the

Deck Division berthing quarters of the USS *John W. Weeks* when over someone's radio I heard Johnny Mathis singing "Chances Are." I closed my eyes and saw Denise's face.

After my cruise, I went directly from Norfolk to Cambridge to start my sophomore year and didn't have a chance to return home to see her. We wrote some and spoke on the phone once in a while, but she had her life and I was a thousand miles away. The little contact we had made her all the more enticing.

Everyone remembers where they were that November day when the bullets flew in Dallas and JFK was pronounced dead. Classes were canceled as was the Harvard-Yale football game. I flew home, driven by the chance of seeing her. The long weekend was somber; everyone's mood was dark, but we did get to spend a few hours together. Not wanting to, but having to leave again, I returned to Cambridge.

My attempts to get together with her over the next several years were met with scattered results. I was in one place; she in another. She was dating guys here and there; I dated too, but it wasn't the same.

She went on to American Airlines "Stewardess College" in Dallas-Fort Worth. Having been commissioned an officer into the US Navy, I shipped out to join the USS *Epping Forest* in Sasebo, Japan. I heard from her now and again but I couldn't help thinking it was only a matter of time before she would be out of reach; married, gone.

I had a year left on my hitch in Japan when my ship was severely damaged in a typhoon in the Sea of Japan and had to be put into dry dock for extensive repairs.

I took a chance. I put in for a stateside thirty-day leave, and the Captain approved it. I wrote to her that I was coming stateside and wanted to see her. She was based in Chicago. She wrote back and suggested we meet in San Francisco. I of course agreed; the most romantic city in the world.

Making connections on military flights, I got lucky and arrived in San Francisco a day early. I called her place in Des Plaines; no one answered.

I've got time, I told myself. I'll surprise her in Chicago, and we'll fly to San Francisco together. I caught a cab to SFO and flew military stand-by to O'Hare.

Five hours later, the cab from O'Hare dropped me at 262 Dover Lane. My adrenaline was soaring as I rang the bell. No answer. I went next door to 260, the other half of the duplex and rang that bell. No one was there either. I was trying to think of what to do next when a United Airlines crew shuttle pulled up to the curb and a stewardess got out and walked up the sidewalk toward me and said, "I'll bet you're Clair."

I was taken aback.

She said Denise told her about me. She had a key to 262 and let me in.

Once inside I felt somewhat uneasy. I found the liquor cabinet and poured myself a drink. The phone rang. I answered it and a guy asked for Linda. I told him Linda wasn't in and hung up.

His was one of many calls asking for one or the other of the four airline stewardesses who lived there. When one guy asked for Denise, I wanted to say she had moved away without a trace but didn't. When I ran out of excuses for my being there, I said I was the landlord. That worked until the landlord called. Shortly thereafter, the landlord appeared at the front door and demanded an explanation. When I finished, he bought it and left wishing me luck.

The phone rang again.

"This is the San Francisco overseas operator. I have a party who would like to place an overseas call to Sasebo, Japan, and charge it to this number. Will you accept the charge?"

I stood motionless; my mind was racing.

"Operator," I yelled into the phone. "I know who wants to

place the call. Please don't hang up. You are my only link to her. She is calling *me* in Japan and I'm not there. I'm here, at her place. Please, please don't lose her. Is she on the other line?"

"Yes, she is."

"Operator, please. Tell her not to call Japan. Tell her to call her place. Tell her the guy who she thinks is in Japan is in Chicago."

"Oh, my God. Are you kidding?"

"No, really."

"Okay, I'll tell her. This is crazy."

The next three minutes passed in super slow motion and finally, the phone rang but it was the landlord. He wanted to know how I was doing. I said, please call me back in twenty minutes and hung up. Had she gotten a busy signal? Would she try again? Would anyone believe this?

The phone rang. It was her voice. I think she said something like, "What on earth are you doing in Chicago?" and "Why didn't you tell me?" but it didn't matter what she said. Her voice, that wonderful, low, throaty, sexy, terrific voice.

"I'm here. I'm sorry. I was so early. Oh, God, when can I see you? I'll fly out tonight. Don't move. I'll be right there."

"Look," she said. "It makes no sense for you to fly here when I can fly there for nothing. I'll deadhead back tomorrow. I'll call you and let you know what flight I'm on. I can't believe this."

I told her again I was sorry.

The next day I caught a cab to O'Hare and waited at her gate. She walked off the plane.

If she was beautiful before, she could only be described as whatever is beyond that.

I walked up to her. I pulled her close. I kissed her and gazed into her beautiful eyes. And I have been looking into those beautiful eyes ever since, for the past fifty-plus years.

Don't ever change a bit
Denise

DOGGIE

Henry Robert Merrill Levan, better known as Bob Merrill, was, as I mentioned, referred to me by Billy Meshel of All Nations Music, Bob's music publisher.

Bob was a prolific songwriter. He wrote hundreds of popular songs, including "Honeycomb," "Mambo Italiano," "My Truly, Truly Fair," "Pittsburgh Pennsylvania," "Walkin' to Missouri," "How Much Is That Doggie In The Window," and many more.

Bob also wrote for the Broadway stage, including the entire score to *Carnival,* think "Love Makes The World Go 'Round," and all of the lyrics to the score of *Funny Girl,* now think "Don't Rain On My Parade," "I Am Woman," and of course, the all-time most incredible song, "People."

Bob was so talented and so well known for his live stage work that he became known as the "Doctor of Broadway." For example, Bob told me that when the producers couldn't come up with an ending for *Hello Dolly,* he got the call and wrote the finale. He also told me that I would not see his name on the work because he didn't think he deserved any credit, and he wasn't sure the play was all that good; he didn't think it was going anywhere.

In truth, I think the real reason he didn't put his name on it was because of his modesty: "I really didn't do that much. So many people did so much more."

Bob had a get-away flat, the upstairs half of a duplex he rented as a place to ponder, write, and smoke by himself. I was one of very few visitors to that flat, and I only went a few times. Over a cup of coffee in his flat one day, Bob told me he started writing songs for amusement when he was very young. Someone had given him a gift of a toy xylophone with eight metal strips that played the eight-note scale in the key of C when struck with a wooden striker.

He said, "Don't tell anybody, but I wrote "Honeycomb" in the key of C and then just modulated right up the scale as I had done so many times on that xylophone."

He was a tall, handsome man with a deep, resonant voice and a great sense of humor. Sometimes, in the middle of a business meeting, when we would be discussing some important legal matter, he would abruptly change the subject and say to me, "Cla-air." He would drag my name out like that, mainly when he wanted to get my attention.

"Cla-air, that reminds me of a joke I heard the other day. Stop me if you've heard it."

"OK, let's hear it, Bob."

"So these two guys walk into this bar and one of them is carrying an alligator…….."

When he finished, I would break into laughter, partly because of Bob's slow methodical, intentionally dramatic delivery; partly because of the circumstances, a business meeting; and partly because the joke was actually funny.

And more often than not, the situation would trigger a joke in my mind, and I would say that reminds me, and please stop me if you've heard this one. So this Lufthansa flight was taking off from Kennedy heading for Hamburg and……."

We had great fun. Humor was key to our relationship, both personal and professional.

Bob's favorite deli was the Roll and Rye in Culver City. He liked to have lunch there, especially on Fridays. Once we became good friends, Bob suggested that I meet him for lunch nearly every Friday.

"And you have to bring a joke. And here's the deal. If I laugh, I'll buy lunch. If I don't laugh, you'll buy lunch."

"It's a deal," I said, and this went on for many wonderful Fridays.

I must say that Bob always laughed, but I don't think that it was necessarily because my jokes were always funny, but rather that he had a genuine streak of generosity.

Then one day, I received a call from John Massa at All Nations Music, Bob's music publishing administrator, telling me that he received a call from someone at Warner/Chappell Music saying that one of Bob's songs, "How Much Is That Doggie In The Window," aka "Doggie," was used without a license in an animated film available only on video cassette. The film was the first-ever video featuring the claymation duo, Wallace and Gromit, entitled *The Wrong Trousers*.

To understand the situation better, you must know a little bit about the music publishing business. First, Bob had his own music publishing company called Golden Bell Songs. Golden Bell owned all of the copyrights to all of Bob's non-Broadway songs, which included "Doggie." Golden Bell had an agreement with All Nations, giving All Nations the right to exploit the Golden Bell songs in North America; Golden Bell also had an agreement with Warner/Chappell Music, allowing Warner/Chappell to exploit the Golden Bell songs throughout the rest of the world. And most importantly, any use of music in any audio-visual production, such as *The Wrong Trousers,* was required to be licensed, and under the law, the license *must* be in writing.

The Wallace and Gromit video was produced by a company in the U.K. When Warner/Chappell first learned of the video and the use of "Doggie" in it, Warner/Chappell knew that *it* had not issued a license for the use of the song. So Warner/Chappell contacted

All Nations to see if *it* had possibly issued a worldwide license. It had not. This is why I got the call. The use was not licensed by anyone. The use was therefore unauthorized and actionable as copyright infringement.

I purchased a video cassette of *The Wrong Trousers* and watched it. "Doggie" was used in the film twice. The total elapsed time of the two times the song played was not very much, but any amount of time would require a written license.

When All Nations told Warner/Chappell that it had not issued a license either, Warner/Chappell sent a demand letter to the U.K. company that produced *The Wrong Trousers,* Aardman Animations, claiming copyright infringement.

By the time I got involved, Aardman had responded to Warner/Chappell and offered to settle the claim for a certain amount in exchange for a complete worldwide perpetual license. Warner/Chappell could not agree to a worldwide license unless All Nations agreed to it as well and All Nations could only agree to it if Bob Merrill agreed to it.

I called Bob and mentioned the situation to him. He said, "Let's discuss it at lunch this Friday. And don't forget to bring a joke."

We were enjoying our lunch at the Roll and Rye and, after the laughter had subsided, I started explaining the whole situation in detail to Bob.

When I got to the point in my explanation about the settlement amount that Aardman had offered to Warner/Chappell for the worldwide license, Bob asked, "So how much of the settlement would I get?"

I did a quick calculation in my head and said, "You would wind up with about ten grand."

Bob paused and took a bite out of his corn beef sandwich.

"What do you think?"

"I think you can get a lot more if we sue. It just so happens that *The Wrong Trousers* won an Oscar for Best Animated Short Film."

"I see, sure, and then you will get a lot more too."

"Yes, of course."

"You know how much I hate to pay attorneys," he said with a grin.

"Uh, yeah."

"Well here's the deal," he went on. "You say I could get about ten grand now if I go along with what has been offered to Warner/Chappell."

"Right."

"So you go ahead and sue and I'll take the first ten grand off the top. If you can get more than ten grand for me, I'll split the rest with you, 50/50 — and you pay all the expenses."

"You drive a hard bargain, Bob."

"Do we have a deal?"

The waitress came over to our table and poured us more coffee and replaced the empty pickle plate with more Kosher dills.

I said, "OK, Bob, we have a deal. I'll draw up a piece of paper for the two of us to sign."

"OK, that's good." He took a bite out of one of the newly arrived pickles. Then he said, "So, there was this guy who had a cat, and it was his prized possession, and one day, while he was away, the cat got up on the roof of his neighbor's house, and ..."

We laughed, finished our lunch, and walked outside together.

I rushed back to my office and started right in to file a copyright infringement lawsuit against Wallace and Gromit, or I should say, Aardman Animations.

As a first step, I placed a call to my good friend, Don, the head of Warner/Chappell Music in Los Angeles.

"I knew you'd be calling," Don said. Then he sang, "How Much is that Doggie in the Window" and asked, "Am I right?"

"Yes sir, you are right on, and I know you guys received a settlement offer from Aardman, but I just had lunch with Bob Merrill and he's not crazy about their offer."

"Do you plan on countering?"

"As a matter of fact, no. Bob does not want to settle, he wants to sue. So I am asking you to have your people in the U.K. tell Aardman there will be no settlement. Then I am going to file an infringement suit and shake the trees."

"But Aardman is in the U.K. Do you plan to sue in the U.K., under their law?"

"No, and here's the beauty of it. The video cassette is distributed in the U.S. by CBS/Fox Video with offices right here in Los Angeles and CBS/Fox is in the chain of infringement. So I'll sue CBS/Fox in the U.S. District Court in downtown L.A. and it will be CBS/Fox's problem to pursue Aardman, or anyone else, for indemnity, or what have you."

"Brilliant," Don said. "Can we go along for the ride?"

"Of course."

"Go get 'em, tiger. Just keep me informed, please."

"Will do."

It was not long after the case was filed and served and discovery began that far more serious settlement discussions began between me and the attorneys for CBS/Fox. As I mentioned, there was no issue of liability. A license in writing signed by the licensor was required under the law, and none existed. Therefore, the only bone of contention was how much the alleged "infringers" would be willing to pay.

Now of course, Aardman derived profits from its exploitation of *The Wrong Trousers*, but how much of those profits could arguably be attributed to the 15 seconds or so of the unauthorized use of our song "Doggie"? That would be next to impossible to determine and therefore it becomes a matter of negotiation.

The infringers started with a lowball offer, we rejected it, and we countered with a highball offer. Eventually, we met in the middle someplace, and happy to say, it was more than ten grand.

Bob was thrilled and invited me to lunch at the Roll and Rye and said, "And this time you don't have to bring a joke, just the check."

Bob wrote another song that I mentioned, "Mambo Italiano," and there came a time when Lady Gaga allegedly decided to "borrow" a piece of it without a license.

If I laugh, I'll buy lunch
Bob Merrill

DO UNTO OTHERS AS YOU WOULD THEY SHOULD DO UNTO YOU

Perhaps one of the most spectacular sights from the air is to look down and see the sprawling beaches of Copacabana and Ipanema, with Pao de Acucar in between, and all guarded from above by Cristo Corcovado.

We arrived in Rio, Myron, Ronnie, and I, and landed again on a military airstrip outside of the city, but unlike Asunción, there were taxis available. Myron, of course, did the talking to the cabbie and, between Myron's fluent South American Spanish and the cabbie's native Portuguese, we found our way to the Miramar Hotel that was recommended to us by Colonel Samuels when we left Asunción.

The Miramar was a high-rise structure overlooking Copacabana Beach. The Seventh floor was reserved by the U.S. Air Force for visiting U.S. military personnel. We checked in and once again played the one-room game. Ronnie won the flip, of course, and claimed the bed, but this time I got the mattress on the floor.

After we had settled in, Myron and I went down to the lobby to exchange our U.S. dollars for Brazilian cruzeiros. The exchange rate was an incredible 1825 cruzeiros to the dollar. No wonder the cabbie accepted five U.S. dollars for the short ride to the hotel.

I exchanged $20 and received 36,500 cruzeiros in various

denominations including seven bright red 5000 cruzeiro notes, each bearing a portrait of a man underneath of which was printed the name "Tiradentes." I asked the concierge, Andressa, a beautiful young Brazilian girl who spoke perfect English, about the portrait. She informed me that Jose Joaquim de Silva Xavier, whose nickname was Tiradentes, was a Brazilian hero who led an unsuccessful revolutionary attempt to overthrow the Portuguese colonial authority in 1789.

Xavier espoused the formation of a republic with a constitution similar to the recently formed United States. He was arrested by the Portuguese Crown and tried along with many of his followers. The trial lasted three years. Xavier admitted he was the leader of the movement and was convicted, hanged, and quartered on April 21, 1792, in Rio de Janeiro. When the Republic of Brazil was established in 1889, April 21 was designated a national holiday, Tiradentes Day, in his honor.

"Very interesting, but why the nickname 'Tiradentes'?" I asked.

"Among other things," Andressa said, "he was a dentist and Tiradentes in Portuguese means "tooth-puller."

We laughed, and I thanked her for the history lesson.

Later that afternoon, we reported to General Waters, the U.S. Army Attaché, who welcomed us and said he had received cables from both Colonel Samuels in Asunción and Colonel Hutchinson in Montevideo announcing our pending arrival. He gave us some tips on places to see, things to do, and where to dine, as well as warnings about what parts of the city to avoid.

The next day, following his suggestions, we hired a taxi to take us up to the top of Corcovado Mountain, the highest peak in the area, which overlooks all of Rio. By this time, my multilingual friend Myron was conversing fluently in Portuguese. The cabbie informed us that the mountain was named for its shape, corcovado in Portuguese translating to "hunchback."

The view was absolutely breathtaking, and at the very top stood the magnificent statue of Christ the Redeemer, Cristo Corcovado. From the base, we looked directly up at Christ rising 125 feet above us. His head was tilted slightly downward, looking at us, with his outstretched arms spanning 92 feet in width; he seemed to be saying "welcome."

Later, on our last day in Rio, before taking the supply flight back to Montevideo the next morning, we rode the funicular to the top of Pao de Acucar (Sugar Loaf) which presented a lower and different perspective of our surroundings with a particular focus out to the Atlantic and to Sao Joao beach below. Myron and I vowed to hit a beach upon our return to the hotel. Ronnie mentioned that he spotted several ham radio antennas, which made his day.

Back at the hotel, Andressa told us that the hotel gift shop provided plenty of choices for beach attire as well as beach blankets, suntan lotion, and other accessories. She said the hotel also had a beach elevator which descended to a level marked "praia" (beach) on the floor selector. The doors opened, she explained, to a tunnel which extended under Avenida Atlantica, the main thoroughfare running parallel to Copacabana Beach, and opened onto the beach itself.

So while Ronnie was scouting ham radio antennas, Myron and I donned our beach gear and sandals and headed for the Atlantic Ocean.

Their names were Padrina and Yara. We spotted them at about the same time as they spotted us. They were wearing typical Brazilian bikinis which showed off ninety-five percent of their twenty-something bodies and left very little to the imagination. Thank God Myron could speak some Portuguese.

They walked toward us. Padrina was a bit taller with deep brown eyes and jet black hair pulled back in a ponytail. Yara's dark brown hair was wet and hung down to her shoulders. Yara had dimples on either side of her smile. Padrina's gaze and smile were mysterious and suggestive. They both had alluring breasts, just the right size and shape for their young bodies. Myron said hello in Portuguese. I looked straight at Yara and said hello in English. She laughed and repeated hello in English. They both giggled.

We flirted, they flirted. They said something in Portuguese and Myron interpreted for me. They wanted us to jump into the surf with them. They ran toward the ocean in front of us presenting a most enticing view of two barely covered derrieres. Yara had additional dimples.

We splashed each other with the salty water and laughed and flirted some more. We ran back up onto the sand and lay down on our beach towels, me next to Yara and Myron next to Padrina. I pulled Yara closer to me and she said something very sexy sounding in a smooth low register. I was getting turned on and asked Myron what she said.

"She wants you to buy her some sorvete, some ice cream," he said.

He then explained everything to the girls, including the fact that I thought Yara had said something sexy; that I thought she wanted something other than ice cream. All three of them were laughing at me but I didn't care. I pulled Yara closer and we kissed. A long wet wonderful kiss.

I looked at Myron.

"Tell Yara I'll buy her sorvete and anything else she wants," I said with a big grin on my face.

We bought sorvete from a beach vendor, the moment of truth arrived, and Myron invited them up to our room for a drink. They accepted.

Ronnie was still somewhere else, not in the room. While the girls showered and slipped into shorts and bra tops, Myron called down and ordered ice, a few bottles of Coke, and a bottle of Bacardi, their choice, from room service. I showered while Myron poured the drinks and explained to the girls how it was that we had come to Rio.

While Myron showered, I drank and gazed wantonly at these two young women especially Yara, and had to pinch myself to be certain it was all real. There is no language barrier when it comes to the sexual attraction of the female body.

When we were four again, it came time for a game, at the girls' suggestion. The game was called "da ou recebe", literally, you give or you receive. One person was randomly designated "it." The other three would secretly decide on something to be given to or received by "it." Then "it" would be asked: Do you want to give or receive?

Yara was "it" first. The three us powwowed and selected a kiss on the cheek to or from Myron. Yara opted to give and she was told to give Myron a kiss on the cheek. Sounds innocent enough, right? So now use your imagination as more rum and Cokes are consumed and before long, the kisses were on the lips, okay, and then elsewhere.

Then just as things began to get really interesting, there came a knock on the door. Myron looked at me and we shared the same thought. It can't be Ronnie. He has a key. Quickly, Myron told the girls in Portuguese to hide behind the drapes. They did.

Myron went to the door and opened it. It was a room steward. I learned later from Myron that the room service guy who brought the drinks saw the girls and reported his findings to the front desk. Our room was registered to two male guests on the U.S. military floor and there were strict rules about female guests being limited to wives and family members.

Myron denied the presence of any females. The room steward gazed around the room and spotted several feet protruding from under the drapes. He turned to Myron and pulled the lower eyelid of his right eye down with the little finger of his right hand, a gesture that Myron explained later as a Brazilian way of saying "fuck you." Then, according to Myron, he said he would be back with the manager."

We corralled the girls, shoved them and their stuff into the beach elevator and said we would meet them on the beach in an hour or so to take them to dinner at their favorite restaurant. We kissed them goodbye, pushed the "praia" button, and scurried back to our room just as Ronnie was inserting his key in the door. Myron pushed Ronnie inside and told him to hide in the bathroom and lock the bathroom door. Ronnie rebelled but Myron insisted, saying the manager was on his way up to the room, and only two of us registered for the room.

Myron and I sat on the couch and poured two more rum and Cokes. In a few minutes, once again there came a knock on the door. Myron opened the door and in burst the manager and the room steward. They demanded to see the girls. We gave them looks that said "What girls?" and shrugged our shoulders.

The manager went to the bathroom, tried the door, found it locked, and insisted that it be opened. From inside, Ronnie opened the door and sheepishly looked out at the manager.

Just then the room steward said something to the manager in Portuguese and pointed to the drapes. The manager went to the drapes and threw them open. He stood in disbelief. He turned and stared at Myron.

Myron stared back and then, with the little finger of his right hand, pulled down the lower eyelid of his right eye.

The manager stormed out of the room, pushed the room steward in front of him, and shouted something in Portuguese which I could not understand but took to be swearing.

Myron closed the door, and we clinked our glasses as we had done so many times before. Ronnie started with his castigation routine again, but we ignored him, bid him good night, and headed for the beach elevator.

Padrina and Yara were waiting for us and asked what had

happened. We hailed a taxi, the girls told the cabbie where to go, and on the way Myron recounted the episode with the room steward and manager. We were all still laughing when we arrived at Café Lamas. The filet mignon, the drinks, and the company were all spectacular.

We returned to Copacabana and, with the moon shining on the Atlantic, we topped off the evening by making love on the beach.

Returning to our room via the beach elevator, Myron and I were on top of the world. When we entered the room, we were boisterous and bragging of our sexual exploits when suddenly we were confronted with an extremely upset Midshipman Ronald Wesley. He paced about and went on and on about what wretched people we were; how we didn't belong in the Navy; that we would never be officers in *his* Navy; that we would rot in hell.

Myron told him to buzz off and I got into bed on the mattress on the floor. Myron headed for the box spring, while Ronnie continued to rant about what disgraceful unchristian good-for-nothings we were. He finally went to his bed and turned out the light. As I was drifting off to sleep, he was still mumbling.

The next I knew, the sun was beating in the window.

I woke up and sat up abruptly and for a moment didn't know where I was or what day it was or –Jesus – what time is it?

I focused on my watch and felt a sick feeling in my stomach. I had overslept. It was twenty minutes to eight and the supply flight was scheduled to leave at eight o'clock.

I stood up. Myron was sound asleep on the box spring, lightly snoring.

But Ronnie, Ronnie was gone. Ronnie, his Bible, his gear– gone. The son-of-a-bitch packed up and headed off to the plane and did not wake us up.

"Myron," I shouted. "Wake up."

Myron rolled over, groggy, eyes half open.

"What's up, man?"

"Myron. It's quarter to eight, the plane leaves at eight, and your fucking Annapolis buddy will be on it, but you and I will not. We are in deep shit, amigo."

It started to sink in and Myron came around. He cussed Ronnie out.

"You don't do this to shipmates," he said.

"What do we do now?" I asked.

"Let me think," he said.

We decided to shower, get dressed, pack up, and deal with it.

We went down to the lobby with our gear. Our biggest problem would be that Ronnie would show up in Montevideo, report to Colonel Hutchinson per our orders, and God knows what he would tell the Colonel about our not being with him. Whatever he might say, it would not be good.

We went over to Andressa and told her we needed to send a cable, a telegram to Montevideo. She agreed to help us. We sat down and started drafting an explanatory telegram to Colonel Hutchinson. We agonized over what to say, but decided, when in doubt, tell the truth. We overslept and we would catch the next flight.

But wait. The next supply flight wouldn't be for days. And Ronnie, that prick, knew it.

Okay, how much money do we have and how much does it cost to fly commercial from Rio to Montevideo, on an hour's notice, and when is the next commercial flight?

Help, Andressa!

She made a few calls and told us that the next commercial flight would leave on Panagra Air at 4 pm and a one way ticket would cost 456,250 cruzeiros each; that's $250 each.

I looked at Myron and said, "Man, I don't have that kinda cash."

He said, "Me either. That fucking Wesley."

Who can we touch? Who could wire us cash?

Then, when we thought all hope was lost, Myron said, "Well look who just walked in the front door."

I turned around and there, red faced nearly out of recognition, stood Ronnie Wesley, bag and all.

Myron walked over to him and, after cussing him out in what sounded like all five, no six, of his languages, he hit him hard in the gut. Ronnie doubled over, catching his breath.

I couldn't look. I couldn't talk. I wondered which scripture spoke to this situation. I wanted to walk outside and look up at Cristo Corcovado and thank him.

I heard Ronnie pleading with Myron. He was in tears. He said he should have woken us up, but he was mad at us and wanted to teach us a lesson. Then he got into a cab and went on the joy ride of his life with a cabbie who spoke no English and didn't understand Ronnie's fractured Spanish. The cabbie took him to three different airports, none of which were military, and eventually, when it was too late, brought him back to the hotel. It cost him 90,000 cruzeiros.

Myron took charge. We would now, all three of us, send a telegram to Colonel Hutchinson. We would explain we missed the flight, apologize, and tell him we would make immediate arrangements to catch the next supply flight to Montevideo.

Next, we would contact General Waters and arrange to have our orders modified accordingly.

We all agreed.

I called General Waters and explained our plight. He was great.

"Hey, people miss flights all the time," he said. "Besides, why do you want to go back to Montevideo? That flight won't be here for five days, but tomorrow's flight goes to Santiago, Chile. Ever been there?"

Now I was definitely going out into the street to look up and thank good old Cristo.

As the General went on about our new orders and his sending a cable to Colonel Hutchinson to explain our new destination, a thought ran through my mind. Could I leave Ronnie out of the new orders? Could I say just Myron and I would be going to Santiago? That Midshipman Wesley had to be back in Montevideo sooner for some reason?

Luke 6:31 Do to others as you would have them do to you

Matthew 7:12 Therefore all things whatsoever ye would that men should do to you: do ye even so to them

I talked it over with Myron, and we decided to give Ronnie a pass.

RECORD PLANT REVISITED AND THE WHISTLE BLOWER

After Gary Kellgren drowned in his swimming pool and the transaction for the sale of the Record Plant fell through, the Plant was owned by Chris Stone, Gary Kellgren's widow, Marta Kellgren, and Gary's estate, and each had their own attorney. I was the corporate attorney for the Plant and did not represent any of the owners individually.

Marta and Chris comprised the board of directors of the Plant, and the Plant could not carry on its business if Chris and Marta disagreed. As the corporate attorney, I had to have clear unequivocal instructions from both Chris and Marta, and if they disagreed, I could not act. To avoid stalemates, Chris and Marta selected a mutually acceptable third-party swing director, a trusted CPA who had handled the Plant's books and prepared its tax returns, to be the tie-breaking vote.

With the swing director in place, the search went out for a buyer for the Plant; there were a few nibbles but nothing serious developed until Chrysalis Records decided to venture into the recording studio business and made a formal bid to purchase the Plant. The sale went through, and it was during the negotiations leading up to the sale that I met the CFO of Chrysalis, Paul Hutchinson.

Years later, Paul left Chrysalis and went into business for himself as an auditor, specializing in auditing recording and music publishing companies for artists. He knew where to look in the companies' books and was very effective for his clients. Paul engaged my legal services from time to time for both personal and business affairs, and he and I became close.

Paul called one day, saying he needed my help. He had been hired by the rock band, Skyrocket, to conduct an audit of a record company and a music publishing company, and what he had uncovered disturbed him. During his review of various documents, he came across conduct by Skyrocket's attorney, Harold Ecleston, that he considered legal malpractice. He was in a quandary because he had been hired by Harold Ecleston to conduct the audit. He went to Harold and reported what he had uncovered and insisted that Harold report his findings to Skyrocket. Instead, Harold fired Paul, and that, he said, is why he needed my help.

I asked to see the contract for his auditing services, and we set up a meeting.

The contract was straightforward. Paul had been hired by Skyrocket and the contract was signed by two of its members. Harold was the conduit acting on behalf of the band, but Harold was not the contracting party.

I explained to Paul that, although Harold may have suggested to Skyrocket that they hire him and probably also had the authority to fire him, in fact, he was hired by Skyrocket, and his professional and ethical duties and responsibilities were to Skyrocket, not to Harold.

"So what do I do?" he asked.

"I think you definitely have an obligation to report the situation to Skyrocket."

"But I have never met them. I don't know how to contact them. My only contact with them was through Harold."

I looked at the names of the two members who had signed the contract.

"We can begin by trying to find one of these two guys," I said pointing to their names on the contract.

Shortly after Paul left, a friend, an attorney from down the hall, came into my office and said he couldn't help overhearing me mention the name Skyrocket. He said he was familiar with that band and, in fact, knew the father of one of the members.

"Are you kidding me," I said. "Do you know where this guy lives?"

"I see him from time to time at Starbucks. He owns a business not far from my house."

He gave me the names of the father and his business. I punched the business name into my computer and called the number on the website. The woman who answered said Mr. Hanson was not in, but would I like to leave a message. I asked her to ask Mr. Hanson to please call me; I wished to speak to him about his son and Skyrocket. I shared the news with Paul and he marveled at the coincidence. He took it as an omen.

Mr. Hanson called later that afternoon. I explained who I was, who Paul was, how Paul came to be hired by Skyrocket, and what subsequently transpired. He said he would contact his son.

The next day, Zach Hanson called and said he, his fellow Skyrocket member Kyle, and their attorney would like to meet with me and Paul. Zach, Kyle, and Frank Morris, their attorney, who specialized in professional malpractice litigation, showed up for the meeting. It was a Monday afternoon.

Paul told the whole story. He laid out what he had uncovered and why it led to his calling me. Zach and Kyle were fully attentive and told Paul they appreciated his coming forward. Frank asked Paul if he would provide a written report of the situation, Paul agreed to do so, and the meeting concluded.

Tuesday afternoon, Paul completed his report and provided a copy to Frank.

Wednesday afternoon, Frank called and told me Skyrocket would be rehiring Paul to complete the audits.

Thursday morning, Paul called and told me Skyrocket rehired him, AND they fired Harold.

Harold did not take too kindly to being fired by Skyrocket, a premier client. He also did not take it lying down. He found a way to get a copy of Paul's report and retaliated by filing a lawsuit against Paul for defamation. Harold claimed he had been fired by Skyrocket because of defamatory statements contained in Paul's report.

Harold's attorney was Charles J. D. Ramsey, Esq., well known but not well-liked by other attorneys, who said the J. D. stood for "junkyard dog." The litigation was ugly and raged on for months. Paul was grilled by Ramsey at multiple sessions of a deposition that extended over several days. I assured Paul we would have our day, and it came in a most unexpected way.

Ramsey scheduled the deposition of Zach Hanson. We all showed up at Ramsey's office and the deposition began. After the usual preliminaries, Ramsey got to the heart of the matter.

Staring at Zach, seated directly across from him, Ramsey growled, "So, then there came a time when you fired Harold Ecleston, isn't that a fact?"

"Yes," Zach said. He was calm and not intimidated.

"And this was after you had read Mr. Hutchinson's report, correct?"

"Correct."

"And isn't it a fact that you fired Harold Ecleston based on Hutchinson's report, on the statements Hutchinson made about Harold Ecleston in that report?"

Zach paused briefly. "No, that was not the basis. It was not the reason we fired Harold."

"Oh, really?" Ramsey replied in disbelief. "Then if it was not the report and the defamatory statements, what was the reason?"

Whoa. Charles J. D. Ramsey, Esq. Did you actually just step on your own dick?

"The reason we fired Harold was his lack of transparency," Zach said. "Harold should have come to us and explained himself. Instead, he fired our auditor and covered up his wrongdoing. That's why we fired him."

Yup, that is exactly what Ramsey did. He stepped on it, alright. You could see it on his face. He broke the cardinal rule of witness questioning. You never ask a question you do not know the answer to. He was cocksure there could be no other reason; the report was the reason.

Zach had dropped a bombshell.

Looking pale, Ramsey got up and announced, "We're taking a break. We'll reconvene in twenty minutes."

And he left the room.

Paul and I went out into the hallway where we could be alone.

I said, "God bless Zach Hanson."

Paul said, "Amen." Then he asked, "Is it over?"

I answered, "The deposition, no, the lawsuit, yes."

The deposition quickly wrapped up and the case settled the next day.

DOC NELSON AND THE
NOT-SO-RIGHTEOUS BROTHER

John Candy called to say he was going to play in a celebrity charity golf tournament in Santa Maria, California, run by Bill Murray's brother, Ed. The charity was the Tri-County YMCA, and a lot of the friends of John and Bill would be there, including Dan Aykroyd, Jim Belushi, Don Novello (of Father Guido Sarducci fame), and Bobby Hatfield, among others.

John said, "Get your swing ready, grab your clubs, and come along."

I agreed enthusiastically.

John drove his Rolls, I rode shotgun, and we arrived at the Santa Maria Country Club around 10 am. A valet helped us with our gear and we were escorted to an area in the men's locker room where Dan Aykroyd and Jim Belushi were donning their golf apparel. There were high fives and grins and laughter all around.

There was a 1 o'clock shotgun start for the tournament, and as we were milling about talking and practicing our putting on the practice green, John took me aside and told me he had been talking to Bill and Ed Murray. They were one celebrity short.

I'll pause here to explain to non-golfers. A celebrity charity golf event is customarily conducted as follows: Golfers sign up, usually in foursomes, and pay a fee per golfer, for example, $250 each, and they expect to play with a celebrity assigned to their foursome, making it a fivesome. The event sponsor, the Tri-County YMCA in this instance, also sells the holes to contributors like the local Merrill Lynch office, typically for $1000, which allows the contributor to put a sponsor sign on the tee for the hole they purchased. The net proceeds, after paying the country club whatever it charges, are donated to the charity.

Each fivesome is assigned to a starting hole from which they will tee off, and typically, two fivesomes are assigned to the same starting hole, so you have five times two times eighteen holes equals 180 golfers on the golf course and, at the sound of the shotgun being fired (in the old days, hence a "shotgun start", but nowadays usually a loud horn), the first fivesome on each hole tees off and we are underway. And if your fivesome starts on hole 15, for example, you play hole after hole until you have played your eighteenth hole, which would be hole 14, and everyone finishes at about the same time. The golfers clean up and congregate in the club's dining room for an awards ceremony and dinner, again seated together with two fivesomes at an assigned table for ten.

The celebrities are entertainers, sports figures, and other recognizable folks. This tournament included not only John Candy and Bill Murray and their friends from the entertainment world, but also pitchers, catchers, and fielders from the LA Dodgers, San Diego Padres, and San Francisco Giants, as well as some LA Lakers, Golden State Warriors, LA Kings, SF 49ers, and Oakland Raiders. Of course, the Raider Girls and Laker Girls were there in full regalia.

A very colorful and fun-filled event if you and your foursome just love to play and can't wait to play a round of golf with Bill Murray, Dwight Clark, or Orel Hershiser.

So now John has come to me and announced that the tournament is one celebrity short; he has suggested to Bill and Ed, and they have agreed, that I would be designated a celebrity and would play with the foursome assigned to the 13th hole. Thirteen, how fitting.

I said to John that he had to be kidding, but he gave me his little boy look and said if anybody can pull this off, you can. I shook my head but agreed to do it for him.

What could I do? I got my clubs and put them on a cart and drove out to the 13th hole where "my" foursome was waiting, eagerly anticipating the arrival of their celebrity. As I drove up, I couldn't help but see the looks on their faces, like, "Who the hell are you?"

I had no choice other than to explain the truth of the matter. Thankfully, they accepted it after a bit and even laughed at their "misfortune." Also thankfully, we played well together, had some fun, and won a few prizes. They were good sports, to a man.

The 13th hole at Santa Maria CC is a 118-yard, downhill, par three, and immediately to the right of the tee sat a Nissan 300ZX that was the prize for a hole-in-one, should anyone be so fortunate. We all hit our drives and two of us hit the green, but, of course, no one hit the ball into the hole. Not even close.

We finished on the 12th hole and found our way to the locker room and then to our assigned table. A little wine, maybe a cocktail, some hors d'oeuvres, some golf conversation, and then Ed Murray, the MC, took to the stage. He welcomed everyone and then presented some awards.

The salad was served, and Bobby Hatfield dropped by to say hi to Don Novello, the other celebrity at our table

Ed brought his brother up onto the stage and Bill said some funny things and brought Dan Aykroyd to the stage for some banter and mutual putdowns.

Ed reclaimed the stage and invited his next guest to step up, a long-time member of Santa Maria Country Club, Doc Nelson. He said it was Doc Nelson's 80th birthday, and he received a special birthday present because he hit a hole-in-one on the 13th hole and won the Nissan 300ZX.

A loud cheer and some hooting filled the room.

A very distinguished-looking, white-haired man gracefully mounted the stage and accepted the microphone from Ed. He said yes, it was his 80th birthday, and yes, he did hit a hole-in-one on the 13th hole.

The cheers and hoots grew louder.

Ed took the mic back and asked Doc to tell everybody the rest of the story.

Doc said, "Well, I went to Jim Walker, the Nissan dealer here in town. So anyway, I went to Jim and I told him I would give him the car back if he would give me $25,000, and he agreed."

Ed leaned into the mic and said, "Keep goin', Doc."

"So then I went to Ed here, and I told him I would donate the $25,000 to the Tri-County YMCA if he would arrange to give me two first-class roundtrip airline tickets to Hawaii for me and my wife for our wedding anniversary next month."

Wonderment filled the room.

Ed said, "And why would you do such a thing, Doc?"

"Well, because that is the seventh car I have won with a hole-in-one."

I could not believe what I had just heard and neither could anyone else. The guys at my table exchanged puzzled looks. Then everyone in the room stood up and gave Doc a standing ovation.

We sat down and while the entrees were served, each golfer at my table recounted whether or not he had ever hit a hole-in-one. Several had, and one guy had hit two, but no one had ever won a car. On the contrary, as golf custom has it, instead of winning anything, a car no less, when you hit a hole-in-one, you are required to buy a round of drinks for everyone playing on the course on that day at that time. So it is usually a losing, not a winning proposition.

We finished dessert, and I had to speak to Doc Nelson. I sought him out.

"So, I am truly amazed, to say the least, Doc. Tell me, if you have won seven cars with holes-in-one, how many total holes-in-one have you hit?"

"Eighteen."

"What? Eighteen?"

"Well, I am 80 years old," he explained, "and I have been playing golf for over 68 years so that's only about one every five years."

I took my leave of him with a look of amazement still on my face.

Ed Murray brought his brother back up to the stage, and he in turn brought John Candy up, and then Don Novello and Jim Belushi joined in, and the gags and jokes flowed.

Bill Murray grabbed the mic and called Bobby Hatfield up to the stage. John Candy coaxed Bill and Bobby to do a duet, explaining that Bill sang with his church choir, as a boy.

"Really, folks. Heh heh, heh. He's got a great voice. Of course, he ain't no Bill Medley, but...."

Laughter.

"Come on guys, give it to them," John said.

They shared the mic and Bill sang the opening lines to "You've Lost That Lovin' Feelin'."

But when it came to Bobby's piercing, unforgettable falsetto, he couldn't do it. Though he tried, the pipes were gone. It was embarrassing.

He should have stopped, but didn't. I felt so sad and sorry for him. I had to leave the room.

I slipped out a back door and as I walked into the parking lot, I saw John. He had left also.

John was as much, maybe even more, into music as I was.

John said, "I never should have done that. I never should have goaded him into singing. I feel like shit."

"Hey, man. He didn't have to…"

"Let's get outta here."

We got into the Rolls, drove away, and were quiet for twenty miles. Breaking the ice, finally John said, "Let's talk about what we can do with Frostbacks, you and me."

And we talked about plans and schemes and dreams to be shared.

Can't find that lovin' feelin'
Bobby Hatfield

DU-PAR'S RESTAURANT AND THE PEOPLE'S COURT

W e lived out in Thousand Oaks and I commuted to the Sunset Blvd. office each day. At first, in 1976, the drive was not too bad. I could get on the 101 freeway and make it all the way to the 405 without stopping or even slowing down. But, as the years passed, the backup on the 101 moved inexorably westward through the San Fernando Valley toward Thousand Oaks.

One day, on my commute, I had my radio tuned to the Lohman and Barkley Show on KFI, which periodically had a news and traffic break. Today the traffic report included an accident on the eastbound 101 about five miles ahead of me.

To avoid what would undoubtedly be a considerable delay, I decided to jump off the 101 at Topanga and proceed down Ventura Blvd., which ran parallel to the 101 through the Valley to the 405.

Over in Century City, my law partner, Bob Besser, had left his condo and proceeded to the Valley for a breakfast meeting with a client at Du-par's restaurant. He parked in the lot next to the restaurant off Libbit Avenue and found a seat in the front window where he could watch for the approach of his client.

Ventura Blvd. normally has two lanes of traffic in each direction, with a parking lane next to the curb on each side. But during the morning commuting hours from 6 to 9 am, parking is prohibited in the parking lane on the eastbound side to keep that lane open to traffic.

I proceeded eastward on Ventura Blvd. in the curb lane in my black Nissan 300ZX. The traffic was heavy. Obviously many other commuters had gotten off the 101 to avoid the accident backup. The cars ahead in my eastbound curb lane were moving a bit faster than the cars in the two eastbound lanes to my left as we approached the intersection at Libbit Avenue.

Although the traffic signal was green, the traffic in the two lanes to my left had come to a halt at the crosswalk, leaving the intersection open. My lane, however, was clear through the intersection and ahead for at least four or five car lengths.

Just as I began to enter the intersection, a westbound white Volkswagen Rabbit made a left hand turn in front of the two eastbound lanes to my left that had stopped at the crosswalk. The Rabbit continued left and appeared seemingly out of nowhere directly in front of me. I was going about 15 miles per hour. I had no time to react, and "BANG." My ZX slammed into the passenger side of the Rabbit.

The impact carried both vehicles out of the intersection onto Libbit. Dazed for a moment, I sat still and then slowly realized what had happened. I got out of my car. The driver of the Rabbit exited his car and I shouted to him, "Are you all right?" He nodded yes. I looked at the woman in the passenger seat of the Rabbit. She was screaming. She sounded hysterical. She scrambled to get out of the Rabbit from the driver's side.

"Are you all right, ma'am?" I asked.

She was yelling and screaming. "You smashed our car. You could have killed me. You should be arrested."

The driver tried to calm her down. He told her to get back in the car. She refused and remained standing on the sidewalk, glaring at me. The Rabbit was drivable. The driver jumped back in and pulled it over to the curb. Fluids were draining out from under the hood of my car onto the pavement. It was not drivable.

As I was pacing on the sidewalk contemplating what to do next, out of the restaurant walked Bob Besser. I could not believe my eyes. What in the world was he doing here?

The driver got out of the Rabbit and walked toward us.

Looking at me, Bob said, "Hey Clair, I saw the whole thing."

"Who the hell are you?" the woman demanded of Bob.

"Good morning, ma'am. My name is Bob Besser. I happened to be sitting in the window over there," he said pointing, "and I saw what happened. I saw your car turn left in front of Clair's car."

The driver said, "Do you two know each other?"

I introduced myself to the driver, told him I was a lawyer, and that Bob was my law partner.

"Oh my God, honey," the woman said to her husband. "This was a setup."

Bob said, "No ma'am. This was totally coincidental. I just happened to be sitting at the table in the window. I was waiting for someone."

"I don't believe you," she snorted. "Honey, call the cops."

The driver took his wife back to their car and made her get in. He returned, told us his name was Joe Blanda, and apologized for his wife. We exchanged information. He told me he was a television screenwriter.

The Writer's Guild, of which I figured he was a member, was on strike at the time.

Several looky-loos walked by surveying the two cars.

I said, "So you are a television writer; you must be out of work for the moment."

"Yes," he said. "It's a bummer. So where do you guys have your office?"

"The Luckman Building on Sunset," Bob said.

"That's handy," he said. "My business manager has his office in the same building. John Wellman, do you guys know him?"

I told him I knew him. He asked me to give John a call or drop by his office, and that John would take care of everything. He said John handled his business affairs, including his insurance.

I thanked him, we shook hands, and he and Bob and I pushed my car over to the curb. He got into his car and drove away.

Bob and I went into the restaurant. Bob's client had arrived and they sat down to order breakfast. I went to a pay phone and called my neighbor, Dan, who had a car repair shop in Sherman Oaks. I told Dan what happened, and he said he would send his tow truck to tow my car to his shop. I joined Bob and his client, had a cup of coffee, and when Bob and his client finished their meeting, Bob gave me a ride over to Dan's shop.

We arrived at Dan's shop, and Dan came out to meet us. He had a big smile on his face. He said, "Hey, Clair, your car is here. We'll fix her up, but check this out. You are not going to believe it. Shortly after you called me, a guy pulled into my lot driving a banged-up white Volkswagen Rabbit. He said he had been in an accident and was referred to me by his business manager."

"What?" I said.

"Yeah, and his business manager told him I ran the best repair shop in the Valley."

"Was his wife with him?" I asked.

Dan said, "No, but get this. I said to the guy, 'Your business manager is right. I am the best. Let me show you just how good I am.' I walked around his Rabbit. I rubbed my hand on the caved-in passenger side. I stepped back and scratched my chin. Then I looked at him and said, "You were hit by a black Nissan 300 ZX.'"

And the guy said, 'Holy shit, that's right.'

I continued on: 'It was probably in the Valley around Libbit.'

He was flabbergasted. I let it soak in. Then I took him over to the tow yard and showed him your car."

Bob was laughing.

Dan added, "When he saw your car, he flipped out and said, 'This fucking guy knows everybody.'"

Joe Blanda seemed like a decent guy, but when it came time to settle up the affairs of the accident, he became a different man, perhaps at the urging of his wife.

YOU'RE GONNA DIE, HOSS AND IT'S YOURS!

In the spring of 1989, as part of the lawsuit settlement with Mervyn Cohn, Waylon Jennings agreed to appear and perform in a replacement Wembley Tour with Buck Owens and Tammy Wynette. In addition, he agreed to several individual performances scheduled in between the Wembley Tour dates. He was not the happiest of campers about that latter part of the settlement and did not care for Mervyn Cohn one iota. He felt no compunction in referring to him as the "Slimy Limey."

One such solo performance took us to northwestern Ireland. Our DC-9 took off from Gatwick, and an hour or so later, the Irish Sea came into view below.

Waylon and Jessi were seated across the aisle from me and we talked a bit to kill time. Waylon spoke of the time he first met Willie Nelson and how he and Willie became close friends and friendly rivals. He said it was commonplace; he had the same relationship with Johnny Cash, or John Cash, as Waylon liked to call him. Waylon and Willie recorded and performed several duets and loved to throw musical darts at each other on stage as well as in the recording studio.

Jessi commented that they all acted like schoolboys, but she got used to it. It was obvious that like June Carter to Johnny Cash,

Jessi was to Waylon—that strong woman behind her man. Drop-dead beautiful, she was also the no-nonsense stalwart guardian of their home and reputation.

We landed at the Knock airport, a single runway built by the Vatican to accommodate tourists making a pilgrimage to the Knock Shrine.

We did not visit the Shrine, but rather loaded ourselves into two tour buses and headed to Castlebar in County Mayo. One of the buses was the personnel bus, with Waylon, Jessi, Waylon's band members, our Irish promoter, Ethan, and me on board. The other bus carried the roadies and all of the musical and related tour equipment.

Ethan was a congenial young Irishman, all business and details and somewhat uptight. He spoke rapidly with a charming Irish accent.

The bed and breakfast outside Castlebar was rustic, comfortable, and clean. The food was superb and the staff accommodating. The next day we made our way out to the performance venue – appropriately called Off the Beaten Path. But before Waylon and Jessi came out to board the bus, Ethan gathered the rest of us together for a special announcement.

"We will be closin' the show a wee bit late tonight, what with this being a one night stand and all, so when it comes time to make yur dooter to the coaches, just remember, Waylon'll be boardin' the coach as the very last, and when he does, the coach door will be latched. So don't be thinkin' you can get wired to the moon or nothing, cuz you'd be left behind."

There were nods of understanding all around.

We arrived at Off the Beaten Path, and as the roadies began setting up the stage, Waylon and Jessi found their way to their dressing rooms backstage.

I wandered about inside the establishment, which consisted

of two levels of semi-circular seating facing the stage; behind each level was a semi-circular bar.

Noticing the walls all around the interior were adorned just above eye level with Irish family crests, I scanned them up close from one to the other marveling at their details and unique patterns. Then, hello, I came upon the Jennings family crest. I stared at it. Smiling, I flashed on an idea.

I went backstage, found Waylon, and told him I had something I wanted to show him.

"This better be good, Hoss," he said, not really wanting to be bothered.

When he saw the crest, however, he was impressed and said he had never seen it before. He admired it carefully for some time. Then I said, "But here's what you have to know, Waylon. Tonight, after your performance is over, they peel off that Jennings banner on the bottom, and underneath it reads 'Nelson'."

He stared at me with his beady piercing eyes, under his signature black Stetson, and sneered, "You're gonna die, Hoss."

He paused, then laughed and slapped me on the back in good spirit as he turned and headed backstage.

The show was vintage Waylon. Jessi joined him for their teasing duet of "Suspicious Minds."

The place was packed with an especially appreciative crowd and the performance came to a close near midnight after the third encore, "Mamas Don't Let Your Babies Grow Up to be Cowboys," left everyone standing, cheering, and begging for more. Waylon always said that's the way you want to leave them.

The boys in the band had worked particularly hard without a break. I corralled Jerry "Jigger" Bridges, the lead guitar player, and Jeff Hale, the drummer, and led them to the nearest bar to buy them each a Guinness.

If you have never been to Ireland, you are missing out on

many things, one of them in particular being the art of pulling a draught of Guinness. I ordered three pints.

Smiling throughout, the flush-faced barman started the drawing process. Tilting the first pint glass at an angle under the tap, he gently pulled the tap handle toward himself, and the dark brown nearly black fluid began sliding into the glass; foaming as the glass began to fill. When the first pint was about one-third full, he set it aside and repeated the same process with the second pint, then the third. By the time he set the third aside, it was time to return to the first. This process continued on carefully and intricately, one pint after the other, without the slightest indication that he could be interrupted or hurried before completing his masterful task.

In the meantime, Jeff and Jigger, both handsome guys in their band gear, were engaged in conversation with two young Irish lasses, both obviously wanting to meet the boys in the band, and the boys loving every minute.

A good five or six minutes elapsed before the barman finished his artistry and set before us three pints of Dublin's special brew, each complete with a full inch of foamy cream-colored head on top.

I paid the barman, and the three of us clinked our glasses with a "great show" and a "thank you" and enjoyed that marvelous first sip.

Jeff smiled at the girls and toasted them, but suddenly his smiling face turned to concern. Ethan was approaching, waving frantically. He arrived nearly out of breath and blurted out, "Gentlemen, you best better toss those down in short order as Waylon is headed for the coach."

Before I could raise my glass, Ethan turned and hightailed it out the side door.

Now, this is not the way to enjoy a Guinness; rather it's an insult to the artistry.

Nonetheless, I chugged mine down, placed my glass on the bar, and made fast for the side door. I heard the sound of glasses being placed on the bar and then footsteps behind me.

It was pitch black in the parking lot with but a trace of illumination emitting from mood lights in the personnel bus. The roadie bus was gone.

The gravel crunched beneath my feet as I ran to the bus. The bus door was still open and I could make out Waylon's silhouette in the frontmost seat.

The footsteps behind me were getting louder and closer. I reached the open bus door. As I took my first step up into the bus, I could feel Waylon's eyes looking down at me.

Looking back up at him and pointing behind me, I said, "I found' em, Waylon."

A low chuckle emitted from somewhere in the darkness behind Waylon.

The bus driver's face shone pale yellow from the lights on the dash in front of him.

Waylon said, "You found 'em alright, Hoss, and you know what else?"

Before he could finish, I said, "Yeah, I know, I'm gonna die."

More laughter came from the darkness. Waylon said nothing more but I did catch a glimpse of a smile on his face. I continued on past him, down the aisle, followed by Jeff and Jigger. We found some empty seats, the door closed, and we were on our way to Dublin.

The three Waylon, Buck, and Tammy shows in Dublin brought the house down each night as usual. Irish men and women, thousands of them, young and old alike, were decked out in cowboy and cowgirl shirts, skirts, and hats, and some guys even wore chaps. You would have thought we were in Tennessee or Texas.

The third show closed in a flourish to a standing ovation with Waylon, Buck, and Tammy all taking the stage and singing together a medley comprised of "Tiger by the Tail," "A Good Hearted Woman," and "Stand by Your Man."

The next evening, Waylon was scheduled to do another Waylon-only gig, this time in the town of Omagh, in Ulster (Northern Ireland). Ethan explained that the trip to Omagh and back was going to require special attention from all of us.

It was 1989, and there was tension throughout Ireland. Bombs were going off here and there, especially in the north, for which the IRA (Irish Republican Army) claimed responsibility.

To get to Omagh, it was necessary to cross the border from the Republic of Ireland in the south into the English-controlled province of Ulster to the north. Of course, the reverse would also be necessary for returning to Dublin.

It was mid-afternoon when we arrived at the border. It was heavily patrolled. In order to cross from south to north, vehicles were required to traverse through a U-shaped high-walled labyrinth consisting of four consecutive 90-degree turns: left, right, right, left.

Atop the walls were British soldiers with Heckler & Koch MP5 automatic weapons and blackened faces wearing dark green, brown, and black camouflage uniforms and black berets. Several British soldiers inspected the undercarriages of our vehicles with large mirrors on the ends of long poles. Others guided leashed explosive-sniffing dogs.

No one uttered a sound as our buses were inspected and slowly navigated through the maze.

Clearing the walled obstacle, we exited into Ulster. Looking out the window to the left, we saw the burned-out hulk of what once was a small truck. There were what appeared to be two burned bodies in the remnants of the bed of the truck, and a sign that read: "Former IRA."

An eerie silence attended the rest of the journey deeper into Ulster.

The venue in Omagh was small, nowhere near the size of Off the Beaten Path. The ambiance was definitely different as well: somber, to say the least. It seemed to be reflective of the whole mood of Ulster, a province under siege. This was also apparent in the nearby shops we visited. There was an uneasiness about; the venue patrons were much subdued. Not a lot of happy faces; no joking or laughter.

No matter, Waylon was Waylon, the band was terrific, Waylon and Jessi performed their duet, and the Bass Ale was quite tasty. The show wrapped close to midnight.

Back on the bus, Ralph Mooney, affectionately "Mr. Moon" or "Moonie," Waylon's steel guitar player par excellence, straw cowboy hat turned up on both sides, white mustache, wire-rimmed glasses and all, was seated in the horseshoe-shaped lounge area in the rear of the bus. Next to him sat Jigger Bridges with his slicked-back black hair and good ol' Alabama boy smile on his face. On the floor in front of them was a washtub full of iced beers. As I approached in the dim mood light overhead, they each hoisted a cold one toward me with a gesture to sit down and join them. Moonie explained they were too wired to sleep. We enjoyed our beers and spoke quietly. Everyone else was sound asleep in their seats.

The bus motored along. The traffic was light.

It was near two o'clock in the morning when we arrived at the border, heading back south to Dublin. There were searchlights shining down from atop the walled labyrinth lighting the way for the soldiers with their mirrors and dogs.

Before our bus was allowed to enter the maze, we were boarded by an ominous-looking British soldier. He walked down the aisle toward us and, as he grew closer, we could see his blackened face and that he was carrying his Heckler & Koch MP5 at the ready.

As he made his way, he looked to his left and right observing the sleeping passengers. Mr. Moon's face lost its usual jovial glow.

Jigger shifted nervously in his seat. We each moved slowly to set our beer bottles down and I clumsily dropped mine. It was empty and clanked loudly on the floor. In reaction, the soldier's hand tightened on his weapon. Then he came to a halt directly in front of us.

He said nothing. We sat frozen. He slid his weapon on its strap down to his side and reached up into the overhead compartment above me with both hands, feeling around.

He brought down my tour jacket; a one-of-a-kind, black satin jacket with my name embroidered in red on the front and Waylon's Eagle Logo emblazoned on the back.

Turning it from side to side so that he could view the front and the back, he said, "Nice jacket."

I looked up at him; then directed my eyes down to the weapon hanging at his side and, slowly raising my open hands up toward him in an offering gesture, I said, "It's yours!"

He paused, folded my jacket neatly, and placed it back into the overhead compartment.

"I couldn't do that," he said, touching the brim of his black beret and tipping it gently in our direction. "It wouldn't be right, you know."

With that, he turned, made his way back down the aisle to the front, and got off the bus.

There was a lump in my throat. Mr. Moon, Jigger, and I stared at each other, absorbing what we had seen and heard. We sat without saying a word.

As our bus rolled southward out of the maze, assuring us that we were back in the Republic, we finally were able to smile. We polished off one last beer, said good night, and dozed off.

You're gonna die, Hoss
Waylon Jennings

SIX DEGREES OF SEPARATION

Sometime after I was born I came to realize that I had two brothers and a sister. Nancy was the oldest, followed by Jack, then Bill.

I was lucky to be the baby in the family, spoiled and pampered, yes, but the best part was that I was "sibling educated." I learned a lot from my older siblings, and I know they loved teaching me stuff. Nancy was smart and talented and would be my vicarious mom when my real mom wasn't around. Jack was an all-around athlete and sportsman. Bill played baseball and was the quintessential musician. I learned from each of them; different things from each; and I can't thank them enough to this day.

Jack played football in high school and college. He hunted and fished every season and was a handyman around the house. Bill was handy also and loved to fish. He caught a record-setting Muskie and was proud of it.

Somewhere along the line, many years after I had grown up and moved away, I learned that Jack and Bill went to a sports fishing exposition in Milwaukee one year and hooked up (pun intended) with a charter boat captain (Captain Dan) who chartered fishing parties on Lake Erie during walleye season. The walleye is a tasty, white-fleshed fish, sometimes called walleyed pike, ol' marble eyes, and perch pike. In fact, it is more in the perch family than the pike family.

Jack and Bill went walleye fishing with some friends on Captain Dan's boat, chartered out of Port Clinton, Ohio. They caught their limit, and the trip became an annual tradition for some 25-plus years, halting only when Bill passed away in 2011.

Then, a year or so later, Jack did a very generous thing in memory of Bill. He invited all of his male relatives to go on a three-day walleye fishing adventure on Lake Erie (requiring two charter boats) and said he would pick up the tab for the charters. I of course was invited and looked forward to this aquatic family sojourn.

We had a great time. Needless to say, there was competition between the two boats, and the family dinners were memorable. To quote one of my nephews in attendance, "Everyone had a blast."

And thereupon, the tradition was born anew; I told Jack we should do it again. And we did. In fact, before we left Port Clinton that June, Jack arranged with Captain Dan to reserve three days in June the following year. But that next year it was just Jack and Jack's grandson, one of Jack's friends, and me.

The following year, planning again to journey to Port Clinton for a third post-Bill charter, Jack suggested to me that I might want to invite a friend to join us.

I knew John Mitchell, my old Navy buddy, lived in Ohio, so I invited him, and he and his son, Todd, drove up to Port Clinton, and five of us, plus Captain Dan and his first mate, his son, also named Dan, set upon yet another walleye fishing excursion on Lake Erie.

You may recall I mentioned that I first met John Mitchell in San Diego, at the Navy Communications Officer School. What I didn't mention is that John's and my paths had crossed a few times over the years since then, and one time was when he came to our home in Thousand Oaks. We were sitting in the backyard, relaxing with a bottle of Jim Beam, John's favorite bourbon, just shootin' the breeze. One story led to another and the next thing we knew, we ran out of bourbon. We couldn't have that. The night was young. Off to the liquor store we went only to find, to John's chagrin, they were out of Jim Beam. We had to settle for Hiram Walker Imperial. From that evening on, we referred to each other as Jim and Hiram, with John as Jim, of course, and me as Hiram.

Back on the boat, a good ten miles out into the American half of Lake Erie, "Jim" and I exchanged memories and stories and jokes after not having seen each other in nearly 20 years. The conversations were as enjoyable as the fishing.

One particularly interesting memory of that trip with Jim is that Jack and everyone else on the boat all knew me as Clair, and John, of course, was introduced as John Mitchell. But from word one on the boat between John and me, we referred to each other as Jim and Hiram. So it didn't take long before Captain Dan said, "Hey, wait a minute here. Who is Jim and who is Hiram? I thought you were Clair and John."

Jim and I laughed and Jim then recounted the events leading up to and resulting in our renaming each other. From that moment on, everyone else referred to us as Jim and Hiram.

As amusing as that was, still something crazier came out of our conversations on the third and last day of the trip. I refer to it as six degrees of separation.

As I recall it, Jim was seated aft on the starboard side gunwale when he started the conversation.

"Hiram, I seem to remember you telling me about a boondoggle you went on to South America, Argentina or Uruguay, back in the 60s."

"Right, it was Uruguay."

"And you were there with two midshipmen from Annapolis, right?"

"Yeah, why?"

"And wasn't the one guy's name Myron something?"

"Yes, Myron Hura."

"And wasn't he a soccer player?"

"Yeah, he was an All-American soccer player at the Academy. Where are you going with this?"

"Well, I had this close friend in high school, in New Haven. His name is Bob Brooks. He went to the Academy and was a very good soccer player on the Academy team. He was class of 1965, and I'll bet he knew Myron."

"Well if he was on the soccer team, class of '65, and Myron was an All-American, class of '66, there is no doubt they knew each other, so?"

"So Bob, in his last year at Annapolis, like every other first-class midshipman in their last year, was entitled, for the first time while attending the Academy, to have a car.

"So Bob gets a car and, shortly thereafter, while driving down a road, completely sober and for no known reason, slams into a tree and winds up with major injuries."

"Jesus!"

"Yeah, and he never got commissioned but instead wound up on disability to this day. He lives in Maine. I have been in touch with him now and then over time, and I think it would be great if Myron could get in touch with him."

"Sure, great idea, but I haven't seen or heard from Myron Hura since we got off a Pan Am flight from Buenos Aires to New York in the late summer of 1965. That was over fifty years ago."

"Gotcha, but maybe you could Google him or something. Worth a try, right?"

"Hell yes. When I get back to LA, I'll give it a shot."

And I did. What first popped up was an article in the LA Times that reported something about a senior project manager at the Rand Corporation named Myron Hura. I thought, how many can there be? I found a Myron Hura on the Rand Corporation website, Naval Academy graduate, class of 1966, USN Retired, MS, Ph.D., etc., etc., with an email address.

I sent the following email:

"Myron: If you are the Myron Hura I think you are, you were in Montevideo, Uruguay, in the summer of 1965 with me and Doris and Graciella. Clair"

He responded by email.

"I am that Myron Hura. Where are you?"

I responded.

"I live in Thousand Oaks, California."

Within seconds, my phone rang. It was Myron.

"Hey, buddy. It's Myron. Check this out. I live in Westlake Village, on Devonshire Court."

"Holy shit," I said. "My office is on Bridgegate in Westlake, like four blocks from your house."

After 52 years, we were living within a stone's throw of each other. And but for Jack and Bill meeting Captain Dan, and their walleye fishing, and Jack's memorial family fishing event and the continued tradition, and my inviting Jim, and his bringing up Academy soccer player Bob Brooks, I would never have been reunited with Myron.

We met at B.J.'s the next afternoon and talked and talked. We drank beer and ate burgers and revisited practically every moment of our time in South America together.

"And what about Ronnie," I asked. "Do you know what happened to him? I'm wondering if he is still waiting to have a good time when you and I are in hell."

"Ronnie got an Admiral's star and retired, best I know."

"Hey, you musta got a star too, right?"

"Nope. Wasn't to be."

"Why not?"

"You ever been to Charleston, South Carolina?"

"Yeah, I was stationed there from 1968 to 1970."

"You know the weapons station?"

"Sure."

"Well, I'll swear to this day that those damn channel marker buoys are in the wrong place. I was CO of a tin can and, well, let's just say my sonar dome got a bit scratched up."

"OK, got it. No Admiral's star for Captain Hura."

"'Fraid not, but I'll drink to that."

We laughed and clinked our glasses, and there were more salty memories and war stories. We vowed to meet again with our significant others, and Myron did connect with Bob Brooks.

Myron Hura   John Mitchell

John meet Myron, Myron meet John

INHERITING SUZANNE AND
AN ENCOUNTER WITH LADY GAGA

Bob Merrill called and invited me to another lunch at the Roll and Rye. I met him there, brought a joke, and, as my luck would have it, he laughed. He wanted to talk to me about his estate plan. He told me he had a will and a trust and wondered if I could go over some things with him. I said of course, and he said he would bring some particulars the next time we had lunch.

Many years earlier, Bob married Suzanne Reynolds, and they lived together in a beautiful home in Beverly Hills. At our next lunch at the Roll and Rye several weeks later, Bob told me he changed his mind about his estate plan and that he was not going to make any changes at all.

"Suzanne will inherit everything. And you, my friend, you will inherit Suzanne."

"What a nice thing for you to say, Bob," I said. "So, meanwhile, did you hear the one about the Jewish scrap metal dealer from Brooklyn who passed away and ......"

The lunch ended in laughter, and I never heard Bob say another thing about estate planning.

Then on a cold February morning in 1998, I received a call from Suzanne.

"Clair, it's just terrible, unbelievable." She was crying.

"What is it, Suzanne?"

"Bob, oh Clair," she began. "Bob took his own life."

"What?"

"Yes, it's just terrible. Can you come over, right now?"

"I'll be there as soon as I can."

The news came out. Bob apparently suffered from many ailments that he kept concealed from nearly everyone, me included. It was the tragic end to a beautiful life.

Suzanne did, of course, inherit everything, and she and I became very close professionally and personally and, I am happy to say, our wonderful relationship remains to this day.

Time passed and the thoughts of Bob's death slipped into ancient memory but not his music. There were times when I would flash back not only to our lunches but also to the meetings we would have in his home away from home. It was his flat in the upper half of the duplex that I mentioned he rented and where he went to escape and create. I recall another time when I went there to talk to him about a project he had been asked to work on; someone thought it would be a grand idea to make a musical out of Mark Twain's *The Adventures of Tom Sawyer*.

I mounted the stairs to his hideaway, knocked three times as was our signal, and entered a smoke-filled room. Bob was an avid smoker. He had a keyboard and a cassette tape recorder in front of him, alongside a butt-filled ashtray. He turned to his right in a swivel chair and hastily wrote some notes on a pad next to a cup of coffee.

"Come in, counselor," he said. "Have a seat. You want some coffee?"

"I've had mine this morning, but thanks."

Looking up from his notes he said, "This is the craziest thing I have ever worked on." He held up a leather-bound copy of *Tom Sawyer*. "They think it can be a musical."

"*Tom Sawyer?*"

"Yeah, you know, it's a murder mystery, really. Twain spins a great yarn, but this ain't no musical."

Bob turned on the tape recorder and played a few bars of a rough melody he had recorded, then stopped the recording in midstream and said, "You see, this isn't going to work at all. I'm going to tell them I can't do this. I just can't get into it. And I think Sam Clemens, wherever he is, would agree. *Tom Sawyer* was never meant to be a musical."

He stubbed out his cigarette in the ashtray. I picked up the ashtray, went into the kitchenette, and dumped the contents into the trash. When I returned Bob said, "Let's talk about something else. Have you heard any good jokes lately?"

Bob eventually dropped the *Tom Sawyer* project and turned to other things.

Three years after Bob's death, in 2001, *The Adventures of Tom Sawyer,* the musical, written and composed by Ken Ludwig and Don Schlitz, opened on Broadway to mostly negative critical reviews and closed after 21 performances.

Fast forward to 2014. I received another one of those wonderful phone calls from John Massa suggesting that someone had used a portion of one of Bob's songs without the required permission, without a license. The song was "Mambo Italiano" and the alleged wrongdoer was Lady Gaga.

Over one of our lunches, Bob told me the story of his creation of "Mambo Italiano." He was working in New York City with Mitch Miller, who was producing a record album featuring the performances of Rosemary Clooney. The year was 1954 and the recording session was fast approaching a deadline. Mitch Miller stressed to Bob that they needed one more song to complete the album.

Bob went to lunch at his favorite Italian restaurant. The mambo craze was everywhere, in New York City and throughout the country. Bob was looking over the menu when lightning struck and his creativity took over. He scribbled lyrics on a napkin between the bruschetta and the zuppa, thought some more, and hummed and wrote while enjoying the tagliatelle al pomodoro.

He went to the wall payphone, called the recording studio, and asked to speak to the studio pianist. He dictated the melody, rhythm, and lyrics to the pianist, and "Mambo Italiano" was born.

If you don't know the song, you should give it a listen. It starts with an intriguing ballad-type intro:

> *"A girl went back to Napoli*
> *Because she missed the scenery*
> *The native dances and the charming songs"*

Then it shocks you with a warning of what is to come

> *"But wait a minute, something's wrong"*

It springs into a crazy mambo rhythm with clever, sometimes comical, lyrics incorporating English with Italian and Spanish, Siciliano, tarantella, mozzarella, enchilada, paisano, Giovanno. It was a huge hit for Rosemary Clooney and Dean Martin, and it was covered by other performers all over the world.

So in 2014, John Massa suggested I listen to a song recorded by Lady Gaga in 2011 entitled "Americano." It began with an intriguing ballad-type intro to the same tune as "Mambo Italiano."

> *"I met a girl in East L.A.*
> *In floral shorts as sweet as May*
> *She sang in eights and two-barrio chords*
> *We fell in love, but not in court"*

I am not a musicologist, and in listening, I was admittedly prejudiced in favor of my client, Suzanne Merrill, the owner of "Mambo Italiano," but I could hear the unmistakable similarity.

I called Suzanne, told her what had come up, and emailed her a YouTube version of each song. I told her that I thought she had a valid claim for the misappropriation of Bob's song.

After some time, she called and said she agreed and asked what we should do next.

"We should hire a musicologist to do a formal comparison of the two songs and render an expert's report," I said. "If the report comes back as I think it will, namely that there is an actionable misappropriation, we would then proceed to contact Lady Gaga and demand recompense."

"Will we have to sue?"

"We may have to, but maybe not. We will only be able to tell after we receive her response."

"This reminds me of "How Much is that Doggie in the Window."

"Precisely, it is basically the same thing; the same type of claim."

"And, as I recall, Bob didn't want to pay the cost of filing and pursuing a lawsuit."

"That's correct."

"So can we do the same deal that Bob made with you for 'Doggie?' Can we make the same arrangement?"

And we did. We got the expert report, which said what we thought it would say. Lady Gaga denied the claim; the whole thing was settled–a confidential settlement–and Lady Gaga went on with her career.

Who me?"
Lady Gaga

IT'S NOT OVER 'TIL IT'S OVER

Anyone who has ever played the wicked game fraught with self-examination and self-assessment called golf knows that some crazy and unforgettable things can take place on a golf course, especially in tournament play.

I have played the addictive game and competed in tournaments for many years. I have been fortunate to have known the thrill of victory and, less fortunately, the agony of defeat.

Not to dwell on the agony side, here is an account of one of my more enjoyable moments on the links.

THE PRESIDENT'S CUP TOURNAMENT—the President being the President of the Men's Club. An all male event.

The trophy for first place was an actual cup (more like a bowl) presented to the individual winner with an inscription including his name and the date of victory.

The tournament was a match play event to be distinguished from medal play and team play events.

In match play, one plays against a single opponent and the score is kept hole by hole.

For example, assume you won eight holes and your opponent won seven and three were tied. You would be victorious in the match and would move on to play against an opponent who was also victorious in his first round. One plays additional match rounds as long as one remains victorious. Lose, and you are eliminated. This continues until there is but one winner in the last match round.

What can be especially exciting is when the match round comes down to the very last hole. And even more exciting is when the match ends in a tie after 18 holes and the match carries over to a sudden death elimination.

In this particular tournament, I had survived to play in the very last match round for the trophy– the President's Cup. My opponent was considered by all, including me, to be the superior player, proven by the score up to that point: he won seven of the first 10 holes, there were three ties, and I won none. I was in dire straits as there were only eight holes to go.

We were playing the 11th hole, a par 5. My second shot flew way over to the right and appeared to have landed out of bounds, which portended disaster.

My opponent accompanied me to view my ball's location. Fortunately, it was in bounds if only by a mere six inches.

However, I still had a serious problem. Directly in the line of flight between my ball and the 11th green was a Rainbird irrigation box. It didn't interfere with my stance or my swing, so I had to play the ball where it lay.

I struck the ball; it hit the Rainbird box, came directly back toward me, hit my right knee, and caromed out of bounds.

Uh – oh – now what?

My opponent said, "I think there is a one-stroke penalty for the ball striking your body and an additional one-stroke penalty for the ball landing out of bounds, and therefore you will be hitting your sixth shot."

As luck would have it, riding up in his golf cart, totally by happenstance, was none other than the Club's Golf Professional. He got out of his cart and came over to us.

"What seems to be the problem, gentlemen?" he asked.

We explained the situation. He pondered awhile and then pronounced:

Upon striking my body, the ball became dead and out of play. Where it went after that was irrelevant. I was to drop a ball with a one-stroke penalty. I would be hitting my fifth, not sixth, shot.

My opponent scratched his head but accepted the ruling.

With everyone watching, I dropped a ball. I selected a club with more loft this time to assure the ball had a better chance of clearing the Rainbird box.

I took a deep breath and struck the ball. It cleared the Rainbird box, thank God, and bounced up onto the green. It began rolling toward the hole and, continuing on of its own momentum, dropped into the hole. I had parred the hole with a 5.

The Pro said, "Nice shot."

My opponent was devastated. He walked to his ball and hit his third shot. It landed in the green side bunker to the left of the hole.

He attacked his fourth shot with reckless abandon—a mistake. He took too much sand and his ball advanced a mere three feet. His fifth shot landed on the green but far from the hole.

He walked up onto the green and picked up his ball, conceding the hole.

In a truly sportsman-like gesture, as we walked off the green together, he put his arm around my shoulders and said matter-of-factly, "It's not over 'til it's over."

He was six holes up with seven holes to play.

By this time, word of our match had gotten out and a small gallery of fellow golfers gathered to watch the ensuing competition.

My adrenaline was running high. I won the 12th, 13th, and 14th holes. I could do no wrong. He struggled. The score was now his 7 to my 4 with four holes to go. I was still alive.

I played the best I had ever played and won the 15th, 16th, and

17th holes to even the match at 7 holes each. We were headed to the 18th and final hole, even up.

We both hit decent drives and our second shots landed on the green of the par 4 18th. We both two-putted. The match remained tied, and we moved on to the first hole to commence a sudden death playoff.

We both bogeyed the first playoff hole; the match remained even.

The par 4 second hole was the most difficult hole on the golf course. Again, we both hit good drives and this time, both of our second shots landed short of the green.

We could see the flagstick in the hole on the back upper tier of the green. My opponent was slightly farther from the hole, meaning he was "away" and would have to hit his third chip shot before I hit mine.

He chunked his chip shot; it did not reach the putting surface. He groaned, as did several onlookers.

My chip landed on the upper tier, and my ball came to rest about ten feet from the hole. My ball lay three as did his, only his was still not on the green.

He chipped again and his ball stopped on the lower tier. His ball lay four to my three and he was still away.

The air was as still as a sleeping baby. There was no breeze. The gallery was tense and politely silent, broken by muffled laughter as a squirrel scampered across the green.

My opponent struck his 30-foot uphill putt only to see his ball run out of gas. It did not reach the top of the slope and rolled back toward him, past the spot from which he had struck it in the first place.

His ball lay five and it may as well have been a mile from the hole.

He looked at me, smiled, and picked up his ball. He walked over, picked up my ball and handed it to me. He grabbed both my hands, shook them, and said, "Congratulations, it was a great match. And it just goes to show, it ain't never over, 'til it's over."

He was a true gentleman through it all, a bit different than the fellow I was soon to encounter in the North Ranch Rodeo Golf Tournament.

WHO YA GONNA CALL?

Hugh Anthony Gregg III, born July 5, 1950, in New York City, would go on to be much better known as Huey Lewis, of Huey Lewis and the News.

A great musician, harmonica player, singer, and songwriter of "The Power of Love," "The Heart of Rock & Roll," "If This Is It," and "I Want A New Drug," to name a few, Huey and the boys of the News came into our law firm's repertoire of clients along with their manager, Bob Brown.

Huey used to say to me, "Have you heard the news?"

A few things that are most memorable:

There was the confrontation between Bob Brown and record company attorney, Alan Grubman, in Grubman's New York office. Both men were large, with type-A personalities, and both had egos the size of Texas. Push came to shove over a disagreement between Huey Lewis and the News and a record company, and, according to someone in the room, Bob Brown simply grabbed one of the legs of Grubman's desk chair and tipped him over onto the floor behind his desk and left.

And then there were the cola wars. This was a real mind-blower. It was the MTV era, and product placement was rampant. Huey and the boys had a hit with "The Heart of Rock & Roll" and were set to shoot the music video for MTV. Pepsi offered a ton of money to place cans of Pepsi in various locations on the set, on the piano, on an amplifier, and so forth. The boys didn't have to drink the stuff, it could just look like they did.

When Coke found out, they doubled the offer, but my law partner Gerry and Bob Brown and the boys in the band sanctimoniously, I think, said they did not want any part of the cola wars, so they declined both offers and told both Pepsi and Coke not to bother to offer again. One of my other law partners at the time, David Braun, went berserk. He could not believe what happened. Sometime later he told me that, if he would have had any say in the matter, he would have pitted one cola company against the other and run the offers up, in exchange for a piece. That was one of the differences between David and Gerry.

And then there was the film, *Ghostbusters*, originally conceived by Dan Aykroyd for himself and John Belushi. Then, after Belushi's death, it was further developed by Aykroyd and Harold Ramis for Columbia Pictures. Ivan Reitman was tapped to direct *Ghostbusters*, starring Bill Murray along with Aykroyd and Ramis. John Candy was asked to portray the neighbor, Louis Tully, but turned it down, which is how Rick Moranis (think The Great White North and the McKenzie Brothers from *SCTV*) got the part.

When the film came out and the *Ghostbusters* theme song was heard across the land, we got a call from Bob Brown. He said that Huey believed that the theme was a rip off of Huey Lewis and the News' song, "I Want a New Drug." We listened, heard what seemed to our amateur ears to be something quite similar, and hired a musicologist. His report concluded—no question—copying and copyright infringement.

It was lawsuit time, but first, a chance was given to Columbia Pictures, Ivan Reitman, and Ray Parker, Jr., the author and composer of the *Ghostbusters* theme song, to make things right. They all denied any wrongdoing. So we filed a lawsuit in the U.S. District Court for the Central District of California in downtown Los Angeles, claiming copyright infringement, that is, claiming that the *Ghostbusters* theme song infringed upon the copyright in the Huey Lewis and the News song "I Want a New Drug."

You might want to stop reading here and go to your computer or phone and listen to "I Want a New Drug" by Huey Lewis and the News on YouTube and then listen to the *Ghostbusters* theme song by Ray Parker, Jr., also on YouTube, and decide for yourself. I think you will agree—it is a no-brainer.

In a copyright infringement lawsuit, everyone in the chain of infringement can be held equally responsible for the alleged wrongdoing. What lawyers call joint and several liability. This means we could file the lawsuit against Reitman and Parker and Columbia Pictures, so we did.

And here are some of the goodies that flowed from this lawsuit.

In every lawsuit, there is a discovery period when the lawyers use legal means to discover as much as they can about the other side. This period includes depositions under oath, requests for production of documents and other things, and other available discovery procedures.

In taking the depositions of Ivan Reitman and Ray Parker, Jr., for example, we discovered that Reitman told Parker that he really liked "I Want a New Drug" by Huey Lewis and the News and asked Parker if he could come up with something "like that" for the *Ghostbusters* theme. Yup. He actually asked him to do that.

Then to top it off, Reitman produced, because legally he had to, his director's cut of *Ghostbusters*. This is the version of the film created by and for the director before it is subjected to final enhancement and editing and is completed. It is the version that represents the scenes in the sequence that the director thinks should be in the film. The copy of Reitman's director's cut of *Ghostbusters* was produced before Parker had completed his theme song. So what do you think was laid on as the opening theme on the soundtrack of the director's cut? You guessed it. Huey Lewis and the News performing "I Want a New Drug."

Straw in the wind, cat out of the bag, smoking gun, call it what you will, but remember to turn out the lights because the party's over.

Ca-ching!! Fireman's Fund, get out your checkbook.

Now, if you don't remember anything else about *Ghostbusters*, surely you remember the film's logo.

Therefore, after we were victorious in our copyright infringement lawsuit against Reitman and Parker and Columbia Pictures, I came up with a new logo for our law firm.

Who you gonna call? Margolis, Burrill & Besser.

THE BELL HELICOPTER AND
THE BIRTHDAY PARTY

It turned out that after he managed to resurrect the old plane and was elevated in rate, Bill Withers was assigned to a brand-new project. The Navy had engaged Bell Helicopters out of Texas to come up with a drone helicopter to be flown off the fantail of a destroyer or other anti-submarine warship and deploy sonar gear into the ocean to hunt for submarines.

Bill and a technician from Bell were in a two-man mini helicopter doing a bunch of tests with a prototype. The Bell tech was the pilot, with Bill riding shotgun.

When control of the vehicle was to be shifted from human control aboard the craft to drone control on the ground, Bill recalled that, within seconds of the switchover, and without warning or any time for the pilot to react, the chopper went into a spin and crashed, fortunately from a low altitude.

Next thing Bill knew, the copter was in a ditch on its side preventing him from escaping through his door. He could smell leaking fuel, and seconds later, the craft burst into flames.

At the same instant, the pilot, standing over the open door on the other side of the copter, reached down and pulled Bill up and out of the burning machine. Bill said he kept in touch with his savior for the rest of the guy's life. And knowing Bill, I am sure the guy received lots of framed gold and platinum albums and attended many a Bill Withers concert.

As I have said before, Bill came to detest the record business, especially record company executives, and basically checked out, choosing to spend his time doing other things.

It was the late 1980s. Bill chose to withdraw, never to perform musically in public again. Rather, when invited, he agreed to make a few limited speaking engagements at various gatherings, some recognizing the achievements of his friends, like Elgin Baylor, Oprah Winfrey, and others. His doing so was always marked by his intelligence and humor. Witness his induction into the Rock 'n' Roll Hall of Fame. He was introduced by Stevie Wonder and Stevie and John Legend performed several of Bill's hit songs. Taking the stage to address the audience, Bill said how special it was to be introduced by a Wonder and a Legend.

Because he chose a private life, when I received a call from an agent in San Diego with a request for Bill to perform, as always, I simply turned him away saying Mr. Withers has chosen not to perform, but thank you.

But the guy wouldn't take no for an answer. He insisted that this would be something very special and very private.

He implored "Won't you please just ask?"

I told him he was wasting his time. He then hit me with the following:

He said his client was a woman whose husband was the biggest Bill Withers fan in the world, bar none. She was planning a special surprise 50th birthday party for her husband and would pay handsomely for Bill to appear and perform a few of his songs. She had rented a small airport hangar and invited only 300 guests, all well-behaved and respectable adults. She was suggesting no more than 45 minutes of songs followed by a short 10-minute Q and A session in a private room with Bill and just her and her husband and four other people.

I said forget it, and the guy said, "But don't you have an obligation to at least inquire?"

He was right.

I called Marcia Withers, explained everything, and she said she would talk it over with Bill.

Bill called me the next day and said he wanted me to graciously decline on his behalf.

I called the guy in San Diego and gave him the bad news. He was relentless.

"Listen, I have the authority to double the money. I am talking six figures. This woman is adamant. She is not used to being turned down."

I told him I would get back to him and called Bill, once again certain I had to, ethically.

Bill asked me what I thought "double the money" and "six figures" meant. I told him what they meant.

I can't tell you who the woman was, but there was a birthday party, and Bill was paid.

She'll pay how much?
Bill Withers

DID HE ACTUALLY BLOW
ON THE BALL?

The North Ranch Rodeo Golf Tournament was a two-man team event. Each team played an opposing two-man team, with special match play rules.

The event was "flighted," meaning the competition would first take place within designated flights of opposing teams followed by the flight winners playing off against each other to determine the overall winning team.

My teammate, Michael Silver, invited me to his home course. We were in the fifth of six flights. The event was played over three consecutive days, Friday through Sunday.

At the end of the first day, Michael and I were "in the hunt," advancing nicely within our flight. There were challenging ups and disappointing downs on the second day, but we survived to play in the flight finals on the last day.

Michael was steady as a rock that Sunday and I made one memorable long double-breaking putt to win a hole. We played on to victory.

Having won our flight, we advanced to the grueling playoff, a total of eight two-man teams.

All sixteen of us went to the first hole tee ground with the

Club's Golf Professional, Scott, and the Director of Golf, Brian, who would be marshaling the playoff.

"So here's the deal, guys," Scott said. "We will be playing alternate shot and the three worst team scores on this par 5 hole will be eliminated. The other five teams will move on."

Michael hit our drive; it was fine. The other seven drives were all basically in good shape as well.

I hit our second shot and placed it in a spot where Michael would have a decent shot at the green.

Michael and I finished with a par 5. Three teams were eliminated. We were told two teams would be eliminated on the next hole.

On that hole, Michael made a super putt to keep us in the running. Three teams left; we were in the money because Brian had announced that there was a $1000 purse for third place; $2000 for second place; and $3000 for the grand prize first place winning team, in addition to the Rodeo Trophy.

In the alternate shot format, since Michael made the putt, I was required to hit our drive on the next hole, a par 5. My drive was not terribly long, but it was straight. The other two teams did well with their drives.

Michael hit a crushing 3 wood shot down the right side of the fairway.

"Great shot," I trumpeted to Michael and offered him a high five.

"Not really all that great, amigo," Michael responded with a bit of reticence. "I am afraid I may have hit it too far and put you in the rough behind a tree."

After the last of the two opposing guys had hit his shot, Michael drove our golf cart to where he reckoned our ball would be.

We found it in eight-inch high grass, behind a weeping willow, 120 yards from the green.

"I'm sorry, man," Michael said, which I sloughed off.

Between our ball and the green, there was a "window" in the willow tree branches, about five feet high and five feet wide, that opened up to a clear shot at the green. However, there was also a green side bunker, on the line of flight, that would have to be cleared in order to land the ball on the putting surface.

I selected my seven iron, took a stance over the ball, but did not feel confident.

All of the golfers who had been eliminated gathered around, watching the last three teams.

Wives and friends and onlookers galore were everywhere. I had never played in front of so many people.

I spotted Michael's wife, Melissa, in the crowd. She looked deep in prayer. I looked at the ball—a speck of white in a forest of green.

I stepped away from the ball, returned to our golf cart, put my seven iron back in my bag, and drew out my eight iron. I thought of the Rainbird box and my shot in the President's Cup years ago. I wanted more loft, to get the ball through the window in the willow.

Michael came over and asked, "Why are you changing clubs?"

"It's just for effect."

He laughed.

I went back and took my stance over the ball thinking, there is no tomorrow.

I swung the eight iron. It turned out to be the right choice. The ball sailed through the willow window.

I caught a glimpse of Melissa jumping up into the air. She was watching the ball clear the bunker by a whisker and bounce onto the putting surface. It rolled toward and just missed the hole, stopping eight feet behind it.

Cheers came up from everyone, except our opponents. Scott walked over to me and said, "You couldn't do that again in a hundred years." Brian said, "He's the slasher."

Michael slapped me on the back, and I felt a surge of euphoria.

As we walked up to the green together, we strategized. Our ball lay three. One team would be eliminated and the other two teams would move on. If a score of par 5 would advance us, then Michael should not, we agreed, make the birdie 4 putt. Rather he should putt the ball as close to the hole as possible, but without making it. This would allow me to tap it in for 5 and then Michael, the better driver, could hit our drive on the next hole.

That is exactly what happened. One opposing team scored a 6 and the losing team made 7. Michael rolled our ball to within two inches of the hole and I tapped it in for a 5.

I retrieved our ball from the hole and flipped it to Michael. I looked around at the cheering crowd and doffed my cap. Melissa ran up to me and gave me a hug. I sauntered off the green with her toward where our golf cart had been parked on the cart path, but the cart was gone. Melissa told me that Michael, to avoid any possible distraction, had jumped into the cart and sped off to the next tee to hit our drive before the masses arrived.

By the time I jogged over to the ninth tee, Michael had already blasted our drive on a perfect beeline, long and deep, down the center of the fairway. He turned to me as I approached; there was triumph all over his face.

"I didn't put you in the rough or behind a tree this time, buddy," he said with a smirk of bravado.

Our opponent struck his drive on an excellent trajectory as well but short of Michael's. They would be hitting their second shot first, and we would know where their ball ended up before I would have to hit our second shot on this par 4 hole.

Michael explained that the green was tricky, consisting of three tiers. The third and highest and most distant tier was the smallest of the three and today the flagstick was positioned in the center of that top tier.

Our opponents' second shot landed on the green but on the

lowest tier, to the left side of the green and forty-five feet from the hole. They would have a difficult putt. It would have to traverse up two slopes to get to the hole on the uppermost tier.

The heat was on as I addressed our ball.

Michael told me the distance to the flag was about 135 yards, straight uphill. We agreed to add 10 yards to compensate for the hill. I chose my 6 iron.

The shot landed pin high to the right in what is called the "first cut of the rough."

Our ball, although not on the putting surface, was closer to the hole. Under the rules, our opponents were "away" and had to play the next shot: the long putt.

The putt was strong but, unfortunately for them, it came to rest on the second tier. Michael whispered, "That helps."

He decided to putt our ball, even though it was in the rough. It went through the rough and stopped on the collar, five feet from the hole.

We both lay three and they were away. Our opponent made a smooth stroke, the ball glided up the slope toward the hole and stopped 2 inches short.

Inexplicably, our opponent knelt down behind the ball and began to blow on it, as if to blow it into the hole.

In unison, an inhaled gasp went up from the gallery and the other opponent yelled "Stop!"

He was aware, as were we, that had his partner actually succeeded in blowing the ball into the hole, they would have been disqualified.

Then, again inexplicably, his partner stood up grinning, making a motion with his putter as if he were about to tap the ball into the hole. That also would have resulted in disqualification for his having hit the ball out of turn.

His partner grabbed his arm, preventing him from striking

the ball. He stepped in front of his partner and tapped the ball into the hole for a bogey 5.

The heat was on again — my turn.

I rolled our putt toward the hole. It caught the upper lip of the cup and did not drop in. Michael casually tapped the ball in, also for a bogey 5. The match was even.

Now what?

One thing was certain. We were either going to win this thing and walk off with $3k and a trophy and a ton of bragging rights–or––we would be runners up with $2k, no trophy, and semi-bragging rights. Either way, we were feeling pretty damn good.

Scott explained what was to happen next.

"Gents, we are going to have a sudden death playoff and it is going to be played on a hole that is not in regulation play."

He was greeted with puzzled looks from the four of us – the last surviving four – the four vying for the final victory.

He picked up the explanation.

"You will be teeing off from the tee ground of the first hole, BUT, you will be playing back to the green on the ninth hole."

This meant that our tee shot would be over the practice green and over a bunker onto a green that sloped away from us and was guarded to the left by a lake.

Scott said the distance to the flag was about 90 yards. Michael had tapped in the bogey 5. Again, it was my turn.

We flipped a coin to see which team would go first. We won the flip and chose to go first. More heat.

I selected my sand wedge. I lofted the ball over the practice green and over the bunker, favoring the right side of the green away from the lake. The ball rolled passed the flag stick and came to rest roughly 30 feet from the hole.

Our opponent using his sand wedge lofted their ball over the practice green but it landed in the bunker.

Once again Michael whispered, "That helps."

The gallery grew larger with people watching from around the green, on the cart paths, and up on the second-story balcony of the clubhouse. There had to be 300 onlookers.

Our opponents' bunker shot was a good one. The ball popped up into the air in a cloud of sand, then plopped down onto the putting surface, and rolled past the hole coming to rest 10 feet below the hole.

I spoke softly to Michael.

"It would be great if you made this putt to win the match, but whatever you do, please don't leave me anything over three feet."

He nodded confidently and made a smooth stroke on the ball, which came to rest three feet to the left of the hole.

I smiled and said, "Or you could have made it."

He laughed. I walked up to our ball, placed a dime behind it, and picked it up.

We stood in silence as our opponent lined up the uphill ten-footer for a score of 3. It was a good strong putt, but a shade to the right of the hole.

The other opponent strode forward and knocked it in to score a 4. More heat.

I plumb bobbed the three-footer. I figured it would not break if I hit it firmly to the hole.

Whoa — I happened to glance up and spotted Melissa standing up on the second-story balcony and standing next to her was my wife, Denise.

Extra heat.

Michael murmured into my right ear. "Do you need a line?"

I placed our ball in front of my dime, picked up my dime, put it in my pocket, grounded my putter firmly directly behind the ball, turned to Michael and said, "Nope."

And in the same motion, I turned back around and stroked the ball directly into the center of the cup.

For a split second, I went deaf to the outside world. I could not hear a thing other than my heart beating in my ears.

Suddenly a cacophony of cheers descended upon Michael and me. We hugged each other, high-fived and laughed until we cried.

"We won, man!" Michael exclaimed.

"We won, man," I repeated.

People were taking pictures with their phones and cameras, Scott and Brian, in true professional style, congratulated all four of us, and Michael and I kept saying thank you, thank you, thank you, to everyone and anyone, as we made our way to the clubhouse.

Melissa and Denise were there to greet us in the clubhouse dining area. Michael ordered a bottle of Dom Perignon.

As Scott asked for attention, standing with a large trophy on the table in front of him, I leaned over to Michael and suggested that perhaps we should team up again, for another tournament, somewhere, at another time.

WHAT EXACTLY ARE YOU DOING IN THIS NEIGHBORHOOD?

There is probably a significant amount of scamming that goes on in the entertainment industry, but this scam might just take the cake.

It was just another Friday in LA LA Land. My law partner, Gerry, was sitting in his office. His phone buzzed; it was Judy, his secretary, on the intercom.

"Gerry, there's a man on the phone asking for you. He says his name is Tyrone Washington and he would like to have an appointment with you sometime today, if possible."

Gerry punched the phone line button.

"This is Gerry Margolis."

"Mr. Margolis, my name is Tyrone Washington. I think I know you from New York. Could I swing by and talk to you about a legal situation I have? Sometime today, hopefully?"

Gerry recognized the name Tyrone Washington from back when he was in the New York office. He asked what the matter was about but Washington said he couldn't discuss it on the phone. Gerry agreed to see him at 4 o'clock.

Gerry and I went to lunch at the Cock 'n' Bull, and over lunch he told me about the Tyrone Washington call. He said he had never met the guy, but was pretty sure he was in the record business, so he agreed to meet with him.

Four o'clock rolled around and Mr. Washington and another man came into our office. Mr. Washington was a tall thin Black man sporting dreadlocks and a pair of mirrored sunglasses.

The other man was a short, fat White man in a tan business suit, with a buzz cut, maybe former military. There were beads of sweat on his forehead. Mr. Washington approached Debbie at the reception window.

"I am Tyrone Washington and I am here to see Mr. Margolis. I have an appointment."

"Yes, Mr. Washington. Please take a seat and I will tell Mr. Margolis you are here."

Washington sat down next to the other man and picked up a copy of *Billboard* magazine and started flipping through the pages. He told the other man that he didn't think he would be too long. The other man nodded. A couple minutes went by.

A few minutes later, Washington followed Debbie across the hallway into Gerry's office. The other man remained seated in the lobby.

Meanwhile, I was in my office, next door to Gerry's, drafting a music publishing contract for Billy Meshel over at Arista Music. Pausing, I got up to go to the men's room. Passing through the reception area, I smiled at the man sitting there, and he smiled back.

A half hour or so later, I was back in my office pouring over my draft when my intercom buzzed. It was Judy. She told me Gerry would like me to join him in his office. She said Tyrone Washington was with him, and Gerry wanted me in there to be a witness.

Thinking that was odd, I walked into Gerry's office.

"Mr. Washington, this is my associate, Clair Burrill," Gerry said. "I asked him to join us. If we take your case, he will be working on it with me."

"Fine," Washington said. He did not get up from his chair. I nodded to him, a "nice to meet you" nod, and took a seat in the other client chair, next to him.

Gerry explained that Mr. Washington told him that he was a freelance photographer and he had taken a lot of candid shots of celebrities, which he sold and did quite well. He also did commercial shoots and some photo sessions for album covers for record companies.

Washington smiled. He had three gold chains around his neck, a watch the size of a small clock on his wrist, and two rings on each hand.

The roar of the traffic in the street below was quite loud, and I moved my chair a bit closer to both Gerry and Washington, so that I could hear them both better.

Washington said he was telling Gerry about a shoot he did in upstate New York last month; Mohammed Ali was there and he didn't like the fact that his photograph was being taken, so he took a swing at Washington and hit him in the jaw. He pointed to the left side of his face.

And you're still alive, I thought.

Washington looked at me. He said, "So anyways, like I said to Mr. Margolis here, that don't seem right. Then a coupla guys I know says I should sue Ali."

Gerry gave me a "you wonder why I called you in here" look.

"And then, this lady friend of mine, Angela, said I should give Mr. Margolis a call, cuz that's what you guys do, right? You sue people, even important people."

"Were you hospitalized?" I asked.

"Oh, yeah. I mean, you get hit by Mohammed Ali, you goin' to the hospital." He laughed.

Gerry smiled.

"Were there any witnesses to Ali hitting you?" Gerry asked.

"You bet, and I got a bunch of sworn statements from 'em."

"Do you have any of those sworn witness statements with you?" I asked.

Washington was fumbling with his gold chains.

"Yeah, I got 'em down in my car. Do you want to see 'em? Should I go get 'em?"

Gerry said, "That would be very helpful."

Washington got up and headed for the door saying he would be right back.

After he was gone, Gerry looked at me and asked me what I thought. I told him I didn't think it passed the smell test. He agreed and said, "Let's see what these witnesses have to say."

When I went back to my office Debbie followed me. She looked concerned. She said the man in the waiting area, not Washington, the other guy, said he needed to talk to someone. She didn't want to bother Gerry, so could I come out there.

I stepped into the waiting area and the man in the tan suit stood up. He appeared agitated. He shifted his weight from side to side and stuck out his hand.

"I'm Bill Hooper. Where's your client?"

I told him Washington technically was not our client. I told him that Washington went to his car to retrieve some legal papers.

"And who are you?" I asked. "Are you a friend of Mr. Washington?"

The guy responded, "Wait a minute. He told me he was going to the men's room."

I was confused.

Suddenly Hooper slapped his forehead, rolled his eyes, and dropped down into the chair behind him.

"Are you alright?" I asked.

"Oh, fuck. He stole the car."

His face turned beet red. He lunged forward and sat with his elbows on his knees and his red face in his hands.

"What do you mean, he stole the car?"

"I am screwed. I am so screwed."

I sat down next to him.

"I am a car salesman at Beverly Hills Rolls Royce and I think this guy, Tyrone Washington, if that is his name, just stole a car. I gotta go down to the garage."

He got up and hurried out the door.

A few minutes later, Hooper came back through the door.

"The car is gone. I gotta call my boss. Can I use your phone?"

"Yes, of course, but what car is gone?"

"Look," he said. "This guy Washington said he really liked the Silver Shadow. He asked the price and I told him. Then he said he wanted to buy it and could he use our phone. I said, of course. He said he was going to call his lawyer to arrange for the money to buy the Silver Shadow."

I sat down again.

"Then he asked me if he could take the Shadow for a test drive and, as we always do with potential buyers, I said yes. I had our shop guy get the car out of the showroom and Washington and I took it out for a test drive."

He raised his eyes up to the ceiling, shook his head as if to clear it. Then he followed me into my office and called his boss.

Hearing all the ruckus, Gerry came into my office.

"What's going on?"

"Your client stole my car," Hooper said.

"He's not our client."

"The car is gone. It's not in the garage. And Washington's gone. Don't you get it?"

"Settle down, man. Take it easy."

Out the window, rain was starting to come down quite hard.

"My boss said I should call the police."

Gerry pointed to the phone.

"Go ahead."

He finished the call and hung up the phone. It was about

5 o'clock. Gerry and I sat there with this poor guy. Nobody said anything and Hooper just held his head in his hands and shook it from side to side. The police were on their way.

Then Hooper got up and said, "You see, and you guys know this, but you probably never think about it, because you rent your garage spaces by the month and have passes to get you in and out of your garage, right?"

"That's right," I said.

"But if you are a visitor, when you drive in, you take a ticket, and then you pay to get out when you exit, right?"

"Right."

"So Washington is driving the Shadow and he's coming to your office to get the money to buy the Shadow, and he drives into your garage and gets the ticket and puts it in his pocket."

Gerry turned and walked over to the window.

"And Washington tells you he is going to his car to get some papers, and he tells me he is going to the men's room. And instead, he goes down to the garage and drives away with a Rolls Royce Silver Shadow for seven dollars and fifty cents, the parking charge to get out of your garage."

There was a knock on the outer door. A West Hollywood sheriff's deputy walked in.

He was wearing rain gear over his uniform and was dripping wet.

"It's pouring out there, cats and dogs. Now what's all this about a stolen car?"

Hooper repeated the whole story to the deputy, who wrote things down on a small note pad.

"Can you put out an APB or something?" Hooper asked. "I can get you a complete description of the car. The VIN number, the tags."

The deputy took a deep breath.

"Well, I am sorry, sir. But the car has not been stolen."

"What?" Hooper was dumbstruck.

"You entrusted the vehicle to this guy, Washington, right?"

"Yeah."

"Well then, technically, what we have here is not theft, but embezzlement."

Hooper sat down on the couch in disbelief. Gerry was still looking out the window at the rain, which was coming down much harder and streaking down the window in sheets.

Remembering a little bit about embezzlement from law school, I looked at the deputy.

I said, "Wait a minute. Are you saying you have to wait to see if the guy brings the car back?"

"Either that or wait until thirty days have passed, after which time it will be presumed that he is not bringing it back. Then it will be grand theft auto."

Hooper slumped back into the couch and moaned.

"You gotta be fucking kidding me."

"That's the law and these lawyers will vouch for that," the deputy added.

There was a pause. Gerry spoke to the glass: "The deputy is right, technically." Then, turning back from the window, he continued: "But I think, with all respect, deputy, that we ought to call your supervisor.".

"Be my guest. His name is Sergeant Sampson."

Gerry called Sergeant Sampson.

"The sergeant is on his way over here. I am sorry, gentlemen, but I have to leave. You are welcome to stay here, and Clair will stay with you."

Gerry picked up his coat, an umbrella, and his briefcase, and headed for the door. The deputy followed him out. Hooper and I waited for the sergeant.

Hooper used my phone again to call his boss to report

everything that had happened thus far. He also got from him a complete description of the car.

Sergeant Sampson arrived. Hooper repeated his story again.

The rain had let up somewhat but was still running down my window.

The sergeant, looking a lot like Joe Friday from *Dragnet*, had digested everything.

Hooper looked at him with pleading eyes.

The sergeant said, "I'm going out on a limb here, Mr. Hooper. Give me the complete description of the car, please."

Hooper gave it to him.

"I am going to put out an APB on the car for you. This is not embezzlement. It's a con. You were swindled. I feel bad for you, Mr. Hooper. You can just hope this guy Washington hasn't crossed the border by now and that your car is otherwise still in one piece."

Hooper turned as pale as a ghost and looked like he was going to throw up.

The sergeant gave him a "hang in there" look and said, "Hey, we may get lucky and catch the bastard."

And with that, I showed the sergeant and Hooper out the door, packed up, and left.

Driving out of the garage, I showed my pass to the parking guard, and couldn't help but think about Tyrone Washington paying seven dollars and fifty cents to drive away in a Silver Shadow Rolls Royce.

Two days later, on Sunday afternoon, I was home when the phone rang.

"Mr. Burrill. It's Sergeant Sampson with the West Hollywood sheriff's office."

I had given the sergeant my home number and asked him to call me if there were any developments.

"Yes, Sergeant. Thanks for calling. Any news?"

"Yeah, I just thought you might want to know that Mr. Tyrone Washington was picked up in El Paso, Texas, about a half hour ago."

"No way."

"Yes, sir. It seems Mr. Washington was driving around in a Rolls Royce in a part of town where he looked out of place. Enough so that an officer on patrol there took down the car's tag number on a hunch, and ran it through the system and, lo and behold, our APB popped up."

"Have you told Hooper?" I asked.

"I'm calling him next. By the way, the officer kinda chuckled and told me that after he read the APB, and it matched the Rolls, he pulled Mr. Washington over. He then walked up to the open driver side window and inquired, "So, may I ask you, sir, what exactly are you doing in this neighborhood?

I laughed and thanked the sergeant for the call.

TUTTI FRUTTI

A small record label we represented out of our New York office had a claim to fame for having signed Emerson, Lake, and Palmer. The partner in charge of the label's account in New York called and said the head of the label was interested in signing Richard Penniman, better known as Little Richard.

It was the early 1990s, and it seemed that Richard was suffering from one of the downturns of his up-and-down career, but he insisted he was tuned up and primed for a comeback album.

Richard was living in Los Angeles, so I was tapped to handle the negotiations on behalf of the label. I was told that, notwithstanding Little Richard's fame and iconic reputation as an "originator" of rock 'n' roll, the label clearly would have the upper hand in the deal-making. I was instructed to offer the label's "A Form" contract to open the negotiations and to hold tight on all major deal points.

The "A" in the "A Form" contract stood for "Amateur." It was the contract offered to entry-level talent with little or no bargaining power. And although you would probably think that Little Richard would have significant bargaining power, such was not the case after his having admitted his addiction to drugs and alcohol followed by his intermittent conversion to fundamentalist Christianity

I prepared the first draft of the contract using the "A Form," inserting the best deal terms imaginable for the label and adjusting everything to adhere to California law. I sent the opening gambit to the agent I was told represented Richard.

A few days later I received a call from Lawrence Everson, identifying himself as representing Little Richard, not his agent, but his lawyer. He was less than cordial.

"I received this piece of shit you call a contract," he said to open the conversation. "You certainly have some nerve sending this crap to the Architect of Rock and Roll."

"I would be open to any comments you would like to make to the draft," I replied.

"My comment is, rip up this garbage and send me a draft with terms fit for an artist of Little Richard's status."

I was warned by the boys in New York that this might be the response. However, under no circumstances was I to yield. I was assured that, after blowing off steam and throwing a tantrum laced with insults, the fact remained that our client's offer was Richard's only deal in town. If he wanted a comeback shot, it was our client or nobody.

I said, "Larry. May I call you that?"

He did not reply. I continued.

"This is the draft we will be working from. I suggest you either give me your comments and requested changes verbally, have them typed up and sent to me, or mark them on the draft and send that to me. And we can take it from there."

He hung up.

I heard a door slam down the hall and two people shouting at each other.

I closed my door and called the partner in charge in New York and recited everything that happened. He laughed.

"It's all for show," he said. "Don't do anything. Believe me, he will get back to you and I expect he will have hundreds of comments and will demand hundreds of changes."

I said OK and went back to other business.

A book fell over in the bookcase across from my desk. Maybe it was caused by the door slamming.

Several days later, I received in the mail a copy of my draft "A Form" contract marked up with hundreds of comments and hundreds of demands for changes. I sent a copy to the partner in New York. He called me.

"OK," he said, laughing again. "I will send you a memo with the changes we will agree to make, and they will be the only allowable changes, period. Got it?"

"Got it."

The memo arrived a few days later. I called Larry. I politely explained the 16 modifications and changes we would make to the contract. He argued and screamed and swore and carried on and on, while I just listened.

After he cooled off a bit, he said,

"Well, this is total crap, but I will take it up with Richard. But rest assured, I will tell him that he can do far better than this and you people are assholes for treating him this way."

He hung up and I reported back to New York. The partner laughed.

It was the beginning of my real-life appreciation for the part of lawyering they do not teach in law school.

A messenger picked up my new draft of the contract to take to Larry. It included the 16 changes our client agreed to make. In my cover letter, I referred to it as the final draft and asked Larry to have Richard sign it and return it to me for counter signature on behalf of my client.

The next morning I received a call from Larry insisting that we have a face-to-face meeting to sort out the "open items." He demanded that I come to his office with full authority to finalize the agreement.

It was raining as I drove out of our office garage and headed to Century City.

On the side of a large city bus to my left was an ad for *The Jerk* with a picture of Steve Martin in a bathrobe and carrying a chair.

Larry's office was small and dark. Hearing my name, the receptionist pointed to a door to my left and said I was expected.

Larry was seated behind his desk. He was not smiling.

In a chair to Larry's left sat the one and only Little Richard. He was dressed in an outfit straight out of Sergeant Pepper's Lonely Hearts Club Band. Multiple choker rings of gold beads circled his neck, while his hair was a bouffant beehive rising eight to ten inches straight up. He stood and extended his hand. As I shook it, I caught his scent and could only describe it the way a buddy of mine in the Navy would have described it. He smelled like a French whorehouse.

Richard pointed to a man seated in a chair to my left and introduced him as his brother and manager, George Penniman.

Pleasantries concluded, Richard and I sat down. I placed four copies of the last draft of the contract on Larry's desk in front of him and said.

"There are four copies for signature. One for each of our clients and one for each of us."

Larry shoved the contracts to the side, put on his show hat, and launched into a tirade of outrage as to the totally unacceptable terms of the latest draft that I had the chutzpah to call the final execution copy.

When he had finished, I stood up, picked up the copies of the contract, and began putting them back into my briefcase.

Little Richard jumped up and looking directly at Larry said, "Oh, Larry. Let them have what they want."

Larry began, "But Richard..."

"Larry," Richard went on. "It's OK. I haven't felt this good ... since 'Tutti Frutti'."

Oh let them have it
Little Richard

CONSPICUOUS GERRY

A very sad thing happened to my good friend and former law partner Gerry Margolis in the summer of 2002. He was 58 years old and, as he told me when we got together for lunch at Charlie's in Malibu, he first started noticing the problem when he went to a court hearing in Portland, Oregon.

He checked himself into a hotel near the courthouse, and when he woke up in the morning he had trouble buttoning his shirt. It seemed his hands and arms were not functioning the way they should. He called the front desk and asked to have a valet come up to his room to help him get dressed.

This was strange, as I always thought of Gerry as physically strong. After all, he played quarterback on his high school football team and worked as a lifeguard at Jones Beach on Long Island.

I digress to earlier events.

GERRY AND I FIRST MET in the spring of 1963 as a result of several coincidences. A few weeks prior to our meeting, my Harvard roommate, Pete Haff, and I attended a mixer at Wellesley. In those days, Harvard was all men, and Wellesley was all women.

I recall a large common room with a four-piece band playing rock music like I played back home in Wisconsin with my band, The Ravens. When the band took a break, I asked the guy who appeared to be the leader how much the band was paid for the night. He said $500 and I started thinking. I knew I could play the same music as well as these guys.

I had left my Fender Stratocaster and amplifier back in Wisconsin. I figured I would be studying and wouldn't have time for rock 'n' roll, but $500 for four guys for four hours of "fun," who could pass that up? So when my brother Jack planned a trip east to visit, I asked him to throw my Strat and amp in his car.

I practiced in my room at Stoughton Hall. Pete would stick around from time to time to give a listen. It was Pete who spotted an ad in the Harvard Crimson and showed it to me. It read:

Money Money Money — If you can play guitar, drums, or keyboard, call Gerry Orlen at University 8-5723

I called the number and asked for Gerry Orlen. The guy who answered said that was a misprint. It should have read "Call Gerry or Len." His name was Lenny Merski and his roommate was Gerry Margolis. I told him my name and that I was a freshman in Stoughton Hall. I told him I played guitar; that I had a Fender Stratocaster and an amp, and could play rock and R&B. He suggested that I come over to their room in Kirkland House for an audition.

It was Cornell weekend, and I schlepped my Strat and amp over to Kirkland House and up four flights of stairs to Gerry and Lenny's room and set up my stuff. A friend of Gerry's, Steve Hirsch, was visiting from Cornell. Gerry said he played guitar and Lenny played bass.

After I was all set up, they asked me to play something. I played the most difficult guitar instrumental I knew at the time, called "Rik-A-Tik" by The Fireballs.

When I finished, I saw stunned looks on all their faces.

I held my Strat out to Gerry and said, "Here, why don't you play something."

He said he had really just started playing. Then he got up, went into another room, and came back with a three-quarter Martin acoustic guitar with a pick-up in the auditorium. He plugged the pick-up cord into my amp and strummed a few chords.

Steve said, "So I wonder who is auditioning whom," and everyone laughed.

Gerry, Lenny, and I eventually formed a band. We found a drummer named Pete Lang and Brad Thomas a blind piano player and practiced in the Harvard Union. A month or so later, we played our first gig. It was a "Battle of the Bands," which we won, but that's another story.

BACK TO 2002 AND LUNCH at Charlie's. Gerry had driven his car to the restaurant but he would not be driving much longer. We ordered wine. Gerry had with him a glass straw bent at about 60°. He asked me to place it in his glass and hold it up to his mouth. He said he had seen many doctors and the prognosis was not good. He had Lou Gehrig's disease, ALS, a neurodegenerative disease with no known cure.

My heart sank. Although our law firm had split up years earlier, Gerry and I remained friends and this was devastating news.

Months passed. My wife, Denise, and I were invited to a Christmas party at Gerry's home in Redondo Beach. Many of our former clients were there. Gerry was struggling physically from the disease, but his mind was sharp, and he still had his keen sense of humor. His 24/7 male nurse, Jesse, pushed him around in a run-of-the-mill medical supply store wheelchair with a brace to support his neck and head.

Denise and I stayed overnight in a nearby motel, and the next day we met Gerry for lunch with Steve Hirsch and Bill McGroarty. Steve and Bill and I took turns feeding Gerry, who could no longer use his arms.

Much later, on a Sunday in 2008, Bob Besser called me and said he was going down to see Gerry, and did I want to join him. He said Gerry's wife was in New Jersey visiting family so Gerry was home alone, except, of course, for Jesse.

I took my Martin HD-28 acoustic guitar with me. We reminisced, and I played some songs from the old days. We drank some wine, Gerry with the bent straw held up to his mouth by Jesse. I played some more songs, especially those Gerry requested. In jest, he called me Mr. Uni-Rhythm. We laughed. Gerry then turned to Bob and said: "He actually knows at least fifteen different rhythms. I know because he taught me all of them."

The day wore on and it was time for us to leave. Gerry was getting weary.

As we said our goodbyes, I noticed a very expensive-looking wheelchair in the corner of the dining room. I remember thinking it looked like Stephen Hawking's wheelchair with all kinds of technological bells and whistles. Sometime later, I asked Gerry's wife about it and she told me she had bought it for him, but he was too proud to use it, preferring to stick with his run-of-the-mill chair.

Time was running out for Gerry as he approached his 65th birthday in August, 2008. A birthday party was planned at his favorite Italian restaurant in Santa Monica. He liked the food and it was wheelchair friendly. There were about ten of us seated around the table in a private dining area enjoying cocktails and wine and awaiting Gerry's arrival.

Gerry came in through the doorway to the room with Jesse wheeling him from behind. He was in the Stephen Hawking chair I had seen in his dining room.

Jesse got Gerry situated at the head of the table. There were happy birthday greetings all around; people came over to him and presented gifts, which Jesse opened for him. After those festivities were concluded, Gerry, with his head stabilized by the chair's head brace, looked out at all of us, thanked us for coming and said, "I suppose you all noticed, I came in my new wheelchair. The other one was too conspicuous."

Tears came to my eyes. I looked over at Bob, crying also and trying to hide his emotions. Denise squeezed my hand. I couldn't help thinking, our good friend Gerry, near death and still mentally alert, and still sharing his wonderful sense of humor.

Sadly, it was shortly thereafter that Gerry succumbed to ALS.

It was too conspicuous
Me, Bob Besser, and Gerry Margolis

PISSING ON MY POETRY

What does one consider to be music? Perhaps it is a generational thing. I know what I consider to be music and what I consider not to be music, even though the latter may contain vocal and instrumental sounds.

I recognize centuries-old symphonies as music, being instrumental sounds without words conveying themes and emotions. And operas are music, basically symphonies with vocal storytelling. Big band music from my parents' generation is music. And of course, I recognize my music, whether it be R&B, rock 'n' roll, country western, or jazz.

But rap or hip hop, I am sorry, but to me, that is not music.

I have played my music professionally and still take out my Martin guitar and entertain myself, and sometimes others, with a tune or two now and then. And I have been blessed to know great songwriters and musicians in my lifetime. Several stand out, but this story is about one in particular. I have mentioned Bill Withers before and here goes again.

Sometime back in the 1970s, Bill wrote a song entitled "Don't You Want To Stay" together with Melvin Dunlap and Ray Jackson. It begins with a haunting melody written in E ♭ minor and has a sweet love ballad lyric but with the words tempered by the minor key.

"Busy hanging curtains Children in the way
Woh! That's what the future holds with me
Don't you want to stay?
Better talk to Billy
His doggie died today
Woh! That's what the future holds with me
Don't you want to stay?"
Sundays in the meadow
See the children play
Woh! That's what the future holds with me
Don't you want to stay?"

It is no secret that many of today's wanna-be and even established musical performers and songwriters often borrow from the past, and there are a few things of importance to be aware of in that regard.

First, the creation of music is protected by the U.S. Copyright Act as well as by related treaties and similar laws throughout the world.

Next, it is possible to use previously created music in creating new music, if, in the first case, the prior music has entered into what is called the public domain, which means the legal protection for the music has expired. Or, in the second case, if the previously existing music is still legally protected, you can approach the owner of the protected music and request a license, which must be in writing and signed by the owner.

So if you sat down to compose some music and you decided to include some existing music, you could research whether or not it had entered the public domain, and if it has, you can use it without liability. Or, if it has not as yet entered into the public domain, you could seek out the owner and request a license for the proposed use.

One of the problems, however, is that the owner of the

protected music does not have to grant you a license and, of course, you have alerted the owner to your proposed use.

So it should come as no surprise that there are those who use existing protected music in creating new music and do not bother to obtain the required license. This is dangerous, of course, and perhaps these folks naively think they won't get caught, or, if caught, they plan to claim ignorance if detected, forgetting, of course, that ignorance of the law is no excuse.

If the owner of existing protected music discovers that some of its protected music has been used without permission, that is, without a license, then the owner can pursue legal redress through an action which, under the U.S. Copyright Act, is called an action for copyright infringement.

There are two basic requirements for a viable action for copyright infringement: access and substantial similarity.

Now back to Bill Withers and "Don't You Want To Stay." It was, as I mentioned, written and composed by Bill Withers, Melvin Dunlap, and Ray Jackson. And a recorded performance of it featuring Bill Withers was released for sale in 1975. Needless to say, there would be no question concerning access, except possibly for someone living on Mars.

Therefore, the question becomes one of substantial similarity. This usually requires the assistance of an expert known as a musicologist. There are several of these folks, well known in the music industry, who provide their expert services in this regard. One of my favorites is Alexander Stewart, Ph.D., who is also a professor of music at the University of Vermont.

Now along comes a rapper, Kendrick Lamar, né Kendrick Lamar Duckworth. He comes out with a recording entitled "I Do This."

I am not a musicologist nor a professor of music, but even to my ear, there is no doubt that Mr. Duckworth infringed the copyright in "Don't You Want To Stay." At this point, you may want to pause and Google the YouTube versions of both "Don't You Want To Stay" and "I Do This." And in case you cannot hear or understand the words being rapped over the existing protected music, you won't be surprised that they contain references to his penis, his balls, and his girlfriends as bitches.

In anticipation of probably having to file a copyright infringement lawsuit against Mr. Duckworth and others, I recommended to my clients that the expert services of Alexander Stewart be engaged to make a comparison and to render his expert opinion as to substantial similarity.

In fact, it was eventually deduced by Prof. Stewart, consulting with Mark Rubel, a Nashville recording engineer, what Mr. Duckworth and his recording engineers did. They extracted the actual musical track from a recording of "Don't You Want To Stay," then digitally reproduced it and sped it up ever so slightly, so it resulted in the exact same music as originally recorded, but now sounding a bit different, in that it was now at a new speed. An expert would say it was composed in the key of E minor, one half step up the musical scale from E ♭ minor. Those dirty bastards.

Armed with this information, demand was made upon Mr. Duckworth and his cohorts that they immediately cease and desist from their unlawful activities and cough up their ill-gotten gains.

At first, they simply denied all wrongdoing, forcing the filing of a copyright infringement lawsuit in the U.S. District Court for Central California in Los Angeles. At this point, you again may want to pause and enjoy what I think is some entertaining reading by googling *Mattie Music Group et al v. Kendrick Lamar et al* (2:16-cv-02561).

Eventually, the case was ordered to a pre-trial settlement conference before a federal magistrate judge, Bob Besser and I appeared with Bill Withers and his wife Marcia. Mr. Duckworth and the other named defendants in the case and their attorneys also appeared, and what occurred I put under the heading of classic.

At one point, Mr. Duckworth was asked by the judge if he had anything to say.

The young rapper rose from his seat, stepped up to the podium, and addressed the judge. What followed was a "tear-jerking" apology – an "I'm so sorry" – an "I have respect for Mr. Withers" - an "I didn't know what I was doing" - a "Please forgive me."

Then the judge asked Bill if he had anything that he wanted to say. Bill stepped up to the podium and said, "Good afternoon, Your Honor. My name is William Harrison Withers, Jr., also known as Bill Withers. I have enjoyed the world of music for many years and I have been blessed in that other people have enjoyed the music I have created over those years. I have great respect for others who have created good music as well. I also know that times change and younger people and different generations develop what they call "their music," but what this young man and others like him have done to others' music, I find disgusting and unacceptable. I call what has happened here, in this case, 'pissing on my poetry.' Thank you for your attention."

Bill nodded his head in respect, turned, and walked back to his seat next to Marcia. The courtroom was still for an extremely pregnant pause, and then the judge announced the ensuing procedure. There would be a split caucus. She would meet with the defendants and their counsel first, privately, and then she would meet with the plaintiffs and their counsel, separately, and the intended result would be a meeting of the minds for a settlement and an avoidance of a trial.

We adjourned to a designated empty courtroom and awaited the judge. While biding our time, and he would probably deny this, Bill went up to the bench where the judge sits when court is in session, probably curious as to what is up there. I saw him reach down and apparently push a button up near the judge's bench. He returned to where the rest of us were sitting; I don't think anyone else saw what he had done. Soon, two court marshals came into the courtroom. They were confused because there was no judge on the bench.

Puzzled, the marshals inquired as to what was going on and had anyone been up on the bench.

I responded that we were in a settlement conference with a judge. They shook their heads and left. Bill winked at me.

About then, the judge came into the courtroom and said she had met with the defendants and their counsel and had a settlement proposal. We all nodded and waited for her to continue.

She then said directly to Bill, "Mr. Withers, I have to say, I am an avid fan of you and your music, but that will have no effect on what we do here today. Is that understood?"

Bill nodded and I responded, "Of course, Your Honor."

The rest is history. The judge was impartial, without a doubt. The case settled, as it should have. All parties were satisfied.

The end of a "Lovely Day" – pun intended.

What have you done to my poetry?
Bill Withers

RIPPED RIP RIPS

In early March 1985, John Candy invited me to Tampa/St. Pete, Florida. He was starring in a movie being shot there directed by Carl Reiner for Paramount Pictures entitled *Summer Rental*. He sent me a copy of the screenplay to read on the plane.

John was playing Jack Chester, a burned-out air traffic controller in Atlanta who was told to take some much-needed time off. Jack packed up his family, wife Sandy, played by Karen Austin, and three children, and headed to Citrus Cove, Florida, for a beach vacation. Of course, it would turn out to be something other than your normal family vacation.

When I arrived in Florida, I was met by a driver and taken to a house on the beach rented for John by Paramount.

John told me not to get too comfortable because we would be going down to the pier to look over the *Barnacle*, a dilapidated hulk of a boat to be used in the movie. When we arrived at the pier, Carl Reiner was there, looking nautical in his white shorts and striped boat neck shirt. He and John bumped chests like old college buddies and John introduced me.

Carl said affably, "Well, I hope we won't be needing a lawyer."

He and John laughed. Little did they know.

The *Barnacle* was a 27-foot sailboat with a weather-beaten, stained wooden frame and an American flag hanging off the stern behind a raised cabin above a wooden stern ladder. She was tied up alongside the walkway to a seafood restaurant of the same name. The movie proprietor of the Barnacle restaurant and owner of the *Barnacle* was a crusty, salty old pseudo-pirate named Scully, played by Rip Torn.

I was looking forward to meeting Rip Torn, not sure what to expect. He had a bad boy reputation, playing sinister characters, like escaped prisoners and Judas Iscariot, and, from what I had read, was considered somewhat of a hot head. I would not be disappointed.

John, Carl, and I walked down the planked entrance to the restaurant where we were met by Rip in his pirate persona. Inscrutable eyes, a sly smile, a swagger in his step, a bellowing baritone.

"Ahoy, mateys. Welcome aboard ye old *Barnacle*."

He appeared in his full Scully regalia, sporting an unkempt, scraggly beard, a dirty red bandana tied around the top of his head covering his snarled hair, a knotted clump of it above the back of his neck.

He ushered us into the restaurant. The staff treated him as if it really were his restaurant. He called a waitress over to our table, grabbed her by the wrist and, looking at us, said in his deep baritone pirate-like voice, "So, what does ya think o' this here wench, me boys, aye?"

Before receiving a response, he let go of her wrist and ordered a round of ale. The drinks came in tankards, of course.

Carl held up his tankard and, staring at it, told us it reminded him of a set of inscribed pewter mugs he received from Sid Caesar while doing *Your Show of Shows*. He said that Imogene Coca, Howard Morris, and he each received a set. The inscription read: "To My Favorite Mugs." He said he had great memories of working on that show.

Rip flashed his yellowed teeth in a wide grin and said he

remembered watching Carl doing schtick with Sid Caesar and that he broke up every time he watched the show.

I remembered watching *Your Show of Shows* with my parents and my father laughing so hard sometimes that he would come to tears.

In contrast to Rip, Carl was cordial and genteel. He spoke in a quiet, mild manner, which drew one's attention to him. He shared his experiences with everyone around him without a hint of being boastful. He also reminisced about the cast of crazy characters on Steve Allen's *Tonight Show* – Don Knotts, Tom Poston, and Louis Nye.

John piped in that what he loved most about *SCTV* was working with his goofy pals – Joe Flaherty, Eugene Levy, Andrea Martin, Catherine O'Hara, Martin Short, Dave Thomas, and Rick Moranis.

Carl asked, "John, what's that crazy duo you do with Eugene Levy? The polka guys?"

"The Shmenges, eh?" John answered.

Carl chuckled.

"Ye got a good one there, matey," Rip chimed in.

John grinned and went on to explain the origin of The Shmenges. Carl was particularly interested. John said he and Eugene had created The Shmenges on a lark and it took off. But sadly, he said, The Shmenges were to be no more. In fact, their final performance would be on HBO the following evening, their swan song – *The Last Polka*.

"*The Last Polka*, like *The Last Waltz*," Carl laughed. "I love it."

A dark-haired waitress walked by our table. Rip reached out and patted her on the butt. He closed one eye and gave out an "Arrrgh, move along, ye strumpet" – always playing the part.

The waitress smiled, probably because she thought she had to, and scurried away.

Carl grimaced, ignored Rip and, changing the subject, said

he had a great idea. After tomorrow's shoot, everyone would be invited to his house, where he would make dinner and we would watch The Shmenges – *The Last Polka*.

I thought to myself: Carl Reiner just invited everyone, including me, to dinner that apparently he would be preparing. I pinched myself.

Ignoring Carl's invitation, Rip rose to his feet, pulled up his trewes by the crotch, and made his way toward the head.

When Rip returned, Carl said he would be inviting Karen and Richard to join in the festivities the next evening. (Richard Crenna was playing Al Pellet in the movie).

I awoke early the next morning and headed down to the kitchen. There was the aroma of a pot of coffee brewing, and bacon and eggs, prepared by the housekeeper, were awaiting us.

After breakfast, John drove us to the morning's shooting location at a country club. I killed some time checking out the golf course and eventually found my way into the main dining area where Carl was shooting some scenes with John, Richard, and Karen. Rip was there, again in his Scully outfit, carrying on with a young production assistant. She pushed him away with a scowl.

After the shooting wrapped, John, Carl, Rip, Richard, Karen, and I enjoyed a drink in the club bar. Carl repeated his invitation for dinner. After dessert, he said, we will watch *The Last Polka*. He took particular pleasure in explaining exactly what *The Last Polka* was to Karen and Richard, and John basked in the recognition Carl was pouring on him. Rip and Richard begged off with other commitments, but Karen was all for it.

John and I arrived at Carl's and rang the doorbell. Carl was busy in the kitchen and we heard him shout "It's open, come on in."

Carl had given his housekeeper the night off and, as we stepped into the kitchen, we saw Carl methodically shredding carrots on a butcher's block. There was half a glass of red wine on the counter behind him and a pot of some delicious-smelling concoction simmering on the stove.

"Help yourselves to a cold beer, or there is an open bottle of red wine if you'd rather," he said in his friendly tone.

John looked at me, headed for the fridge, and took out two Stellas.

Taking a beer from John, I asked Carl, "So what's with the shredded carrots?"

"They're for the spaghetti sauce," Carl replied. "My mom always put shredded carrots in her spaghetti sauce."

The doorbell rang and John said he'd get it.

Karen entered, looking stunning in casual black slacks and a light blue pullover sweater, her shoulder-length auburn hair framing her bright blue eyes.

You would never have guessed she had been working all day, shooting scenes since early morning at the country club. She said hello to everyone and John pointed first to his beer and then the red wine and said, "Betch you'd like somethin' to drink, eh, lady?"

With a smile and in a smooth voice, Karen opted for the wine.

Carl stopped momentarily to fetch a wine glass for her. Then, returning to the butcher's block, he scooped up the mound of shredded carrots and gently folded them into the pot of bubbling tomato red jus. He picked up his glass of wine and motioned for us to adjourn to the living room.

After a half hour of conversation, Carl returned to the kitchen, filled a pot full of water, threw in a generous scoop of Kosher salt, placed the pot on the stove, next to the cauldron of simmering spaghetti sauce, and turned on the burner beneath it.

I decided to switch to red wine, topped off Carl's glass, and went into the living room to do the same for Karen.

Carl had deposited a large helping of pasta into the boiling water and started slicing a loaf of French bread on the butcher's block. The sweet smell of garlic scented the air.

The dinner was exquisite. We ate and talked and laughed. We all helped Carl clear the table and made our way into the television room just in time for The Shmenges and *The Last Polka*.

Karen sat next to John and would poke him and smile every time she saw him do something crazy on the show.

Carl was impressed. He laughed a low sincere chuckle at first that soon burst into a belly laugh.

John's pudgy round face was beaming. He was eating it up; he was in his glory.

In the car on the way back home, John kept saying, "Clair, he liked it. Carl Reiner liked it, he liked The Shmenges. Carl Reiner."

John had told me many times that he wanted to work with all the funny people, the funny people who made him laugh.

As I said good night and headed off to my room, John was still murmuring "Carl Reiner, Carl Reiner laughed at The Shmenges."

The Toronto Blue Jays, one of John's favorite sports teams, along with the Maple Leafs, held their summer training camp in Tampa/St. Pete. The weekend was approaching and, with no shooting scheduled for Saturday, John invited Carl and Rip to join us on a trip out to the Blue Jays camp to watch them play a preseason game against the New York Mets.

That Saturday, John drove the SUV over to Carl's place where Carl and Rip were waiting. I got out and jumped into the back seat behind John, Rip got in the back next to me, and Carl rode shotgun.

Rip was not Scully-dressed but rather looked like he was back home in Texas – Wrangler jeans, a washed-out chambray shirt, and Tecovas lizard boots. He looked at me and asked if I was ready to kick some ass. I smiled, not catching his drift, as he was reaching into a small duffel bag he had brought with him. He withdrew a 375 ml bottle of Jack Daniels and offered it to me. I passed, and he offered it to Carl and John, who also declined. He set it down unopened on the seat between us and, reaching again into the duffel, produced a small bag of doughnuts. Once again, John and Carl and I declined his offer.

Rip took out a chocolate-covered doughnut, took a healthy bite, screwed the top off the JD bottle, and washed down his breakfast snack with a slug of Old No. 7.

He smiled, licked his lips, and said. "Nothing like ye good ole Cap'n's breakfast, Daniels and doughnuts." He took another slug.

We got to the ballpark. Rip was getting rather loud. He half stumbled out of the car and made a beeline for the men's room.

Again, Carl tried to ignore him. I sensed he was a bit on edge.

The crowd was fairly small. We sat down in the front row of the bleachers behind a screen along the first base line. Carl chose to sit as far away from Rip as possible.

The Mets came up in the top of the second inning, and John got up and went over to the concession stand. He came back with four beers and a Blue Jays cap and jersey for each of us. He insisted that we don the apparel. It drew a lot of attention and laughs. John stood, raised his fist, took a big swig of beer, and shouted "Go Blue Jays." Everyone cheered. John again was in his glory.

After everyone's attention returned to the game, Rip suddenly stood up and hollered a delayed "Ya–Hoo." He looked around; people were staring at him. He shot his fisted left hand up into the air with his arm bent at the elbow and his right hand gripping his left bicep. He stood there motionless for a few moments and then sat down. Carl looked away.

The Jays won 4 to 2, so John was pleased. By the time we reached the restaurant Carl had selected for dinner, Rip had polished off most of Old No. 7.

John pulled the SUV into the parking lot of the restaurant and parked next to a gleaming cherry red Corvette to the right and a black Ford pickup to the left.

John and Carl headed toward the restaurant. Rip was half asleep. I nudged him and said we were at a restaurant and were going in to get something to eat. He stirred and tried to open his side door. We were parked very close to the Corvette. His door opened only part way, so he banged it against the Corvette. Once, twice, then again.

"Goddamned son-of-a-bitch."

I pulled him toward me, reached over and closed his door, and helped him get out on my side.

The four of us sat in a booth, and ordered drinks and dinner.

There was a bright full moon rising up in the east out the window to our left.

I noticed two guys across the way to our right, sitting in a booth, in jeans and boots, western shirts, and cowboy hats. As Carl told a story about his being hired to write for Sid Caesar, the cowboys paid their bill, got up, and left.

John asked Carl about working with Imogene Coca, which he compared to his work with Andrea Martin. Rip was dozing.

The cowboys returned and walked up to our booth.

One of them asked, "Did you guys come here in a black Mercedes SUV?"

John answered, "Yes, is there a problem?"

"Nothing more than the fact that some asshole pounded a nice hole into the side of my Vette."

"Hold on just a minute," Carl said.

"What are you talking about?" John queried.

Rip jerked awake but said nothing. I was sure he knew what was going down. He stared out the window, the moon shining on his florid face.

John said, "We are just trying to have a nice friendly dinner here, if you don't mind."

"Yeah, well pardon me all to hell, but somebody fucked up my car." The guy was getting hot.

Carl and John looked confused. Rip sat motionless. I stood up.

"I am sorry, gentlemen," I said. "Perhaps I can help you."

I turned to John and Carl and said I would take care of it. They looked at me like "take care of what?"

I motioned toward the door, scooped up one of the guys by the arm and walked him and his companion out of hearing range.

"What seems to be the problem?" I asked, knowing full well.

A Corvette's body is made out of fiberglass. The gash in the side of the Vette was big and ugly. There were small fragments of red fiberglass on the edge of the SUV's rear passenger door, Rip's door. As I feared, Rip, while ripped, had ripped a hole in the side of this guy's otherwise beautiful cherry red Vette.

I told the guys who I was, that I was an attorney, that clearly the damage had been done by one of my friends, and that the matter would be taken care of. They were not buying it.

One of them, the bigger of the two, asked, "Isn't that big guy with you in the movies?"

I said yes and that all of us were down here in Florida doing a movie for Paramount Pictures. In fact, I said, I was sure that Paramount Pictures would take full responsibility for the damage. I asked them to bear with me and that I would call my contacts at Paramount in the morning.

The big guy said, bullshit, and started back toward the restaurant. I grabbed his arm. I told him I didn't think it would be a good idea to go back into the restaurant and create a scene. I turned to the driver and pleaded with him. He agreed and told his buddy to back off.

"Chill out, man. We'll deal with this dude."

I gave the driver my business card and wrote down the address and phone number of John's beach house on the back. I told him that I would arrange for everything to be paid for; the damage would be repaired to his satisfaction at no cost to him.

I must have said that I apologized for my friend and the whole matter ten or twelve times. The driver got a pad and pen out of his Vette and wrote down the license plate number and a description of the SUV. He asked me for the names of the guys I was with. I told him their names were irrelevant. I could see dollar signs in his eyes.

"You know," he said. "This is gonna cost thousands of dollars."

I said, "Look, again, I am truly sorry about this. It will be taken care of, in full."

I took his name and phone number and told him I would call him in the morning to follow up.

All I wanted to do was to get these guys on their way. I had no real idea whether Paramount would pick up the tab. I had an inkling that Paramount would want to protect its project. I had seen it in the movie business before; the lioness protects her cubs. The key was avoiding, at all costs, the chance of bad publicity. And the last thing I needed was to get any of what happened to spill over onto John or Carl.

But I also had to contend with what John and Carl would think of me if they found out I told them nothing and instead contacted Paramount directly, without talking to them, and then the whole thing backfired. And what if Paramount reacted in a way that got Rip in a pile of shit?

What a fucking mess.

I decided to go with my gut. I would not say a word to John or Carl or Rip. I would persuade Paramount it was in the best interest of the studio and *Summer Rental* to step up and absorb the car damages as a cost of doing business.

The full moon was now directly overhead, shining brightly down on the left side of a bashed-in 1985 cherry red Corvette.

The driver was finally satisfied and decided to leave, but just as he was getting into the Vette, the other guy snorted, "If this shit ain't gotten straight in the morning, you can bet your sweet ass we will be paying y'all a visit."

I watched them drive off and then went back into the

restaurant and back to the booth. John had paid the bill. Carl was shaking Rip to wake him up.

"What happened?" John asked.

Neither John nor Carl had any idea of what Rip had done, as they were well on their way into the restaurant when Rip stumbled his way out of the SUV.

"It's a long story," I said. "I'll tell you about it in the morning."

Fortunately, when we got out to the parking lot, the Vette and the cowboys were gone.

Carl said, "Hey, John. Did you notice that super-looking red Corvette we parked next to? You should have had Paramount rent one of those for you."

John smiled. I didn't. Rip collapsed in the back seat of the SUV.

In the morning, I told John I was going to stay in the house and take care of some business. He told me to call when I finished and someone would pick me up and bring me to the set.

At 9 am L.A. time, I called my contact in legal affairs at Paramount. He was not happy to hear what happened and was reluctant for Paramount to get involved. I emphasized the potentially bad publicity problem and the need to keep John and Carl out of the picture. I said I thought that if he wasn't able to smooth things over, these guys would make a big stink; they might show up at a shooting location, and they no doubt would go to the press.

I pleaded for half an hour. He called his boss. His boss called me. He started out with "no way," but when the possibility of negative publicity sank in, he came around.

I called the driver and told him he would be receiving a call from someone at Paramount Pictures to deal with his car damage.

I waited for the next shoe to drop.

When I got to the set, John and Carl cornered me. At first, I thought for sure someone at Paramount had contacted one or both of them with the whole story. I held my breath.

John asked, "So what the hell happened last night?"

I let out a nonchalant sigh.

"Ah, it was all just one big misunderstanding, nothing to worry about."

Apparently, the appropriate arrangements were made by Paramount because I never heard another thing about it, thank God.

As for John and Carl and Rip—little did they know.

Get below and put a fish in your captain's ditty bag
Rip Torn

A HOLE IN MY HEART

Ireceived a call one Monday morning in late March 2020, and when I saw the caller ID light up with the name "Todd Withers," I knew.

I was fortunate to have spent some quality time with his father, Bill Withers, just a few weeks earlier. He reminisced about many things in his life, and I recall him saying, "Wherever you go, you take yourself."

As I pondered that, I remembered thinking about what Bill had told me was the secret to songwriting: Keep it simple and profound.

Looking at him, in his man cave that afternoon, I was reminded of his story of his having lighter black skin than most.

I said, "So Bill, tell me again about the time, in the diner, with the two Black ladies."

He laughed and began.

It started in a small country church. It was in 2007, and I had gone back to West Virginia to be inducted into the West Virginia Music Hall of Fame. I found myself reliving a lot of childhood stuff back there and wandered into this church located somewhere in the middle of my yesterday. I sat down in a pew by myself completely unnoticed. It felt grand.

The service was exactly the same as it had been decades before when I went to services with my Grandma; mostly Black folks with a sprinkling of White faces here and there and a down-home preacher with a soul-searching prayer delivery.

After the "find your way" sermon, as the preacher was leaving the pulpit, the choir broke into a stirring rendition of "Lean On Me."

I could still hear those wonderful voices singing my song as I walked out of the church and down the street to the local diner. I was seated at a small table by myself enjoying a mug of freshly brewed coffee with a touch of chicory. Two Black ladies I recognized as members of the church choir were seated together at a nearby table within earshot. I overheard them chatting about the sermon and couldn't help myself from getting up and going over to them.

"Excuse me, ladies, I don't mean to interrupt, but I just wanted to say I think you both have wonderful singing voices."

"Well, thank you, sir," the lady to the left replied.

"You know that was one of the finest presentations of "Lean On Me" I have ever heard."

"That is by far our favorite," the lady to the right said. "We could sing that song every Sunday."

"That makes me feel particularly heart-warmed, ladies, because you see, I wrote that song."

"You wrote 'Lean On Me'?" they questioned in unison.

"Yes, I'm Bill Withers."

The lady to the left blurted out, "You ain't no Bill Withers. Bill Withers is Black."

I laughed so hard, harder than I ever laughed before. Not being able to top that, I simply gave the ladies a "good day" nod and wished them a pleasant afternoon.

When he had finished reciting, we smiled and stared at each other for a long time.

I said, "I love that story."

He said, "It's best because it's true."

I said, "Yea." Then,

"Okay, so now let's live again the surprise birthday party in the airport hangar."

He smiled and again began.

I got this call from this lawyer who said some lady wanted me to sing some of my songs at a surprise 50th birthday party for her husband. She swore her husband was my biggest fan.

Now I told this lawyer that he knew damn well I didn't perform in public anymore and hadn't done so in many years and wasn't going to do so now. Not for a birthday party or a costume party, and certainly not for a political party. And furthermore, it wasn't the first time somebody swore they were my biggest fan. I figured that was that; that was the end of it.

But this pesky lawyer called me back and said the lady wouldn't take no for an answer and, as I was about to lose my temper, the lawyer mentioned some details about, among other things, the payment being offered for my performing services. I paused. My head was calculating what I would pay my guys if I could get them together.

Then I said to myself, wait a minute. You don't do this. What's the matter with you? I told the lawyer to tell the woman I appreciated her interest and generous offer, but I would have to take a pass.

The lawyer called again and, before I could say anything, he apologized and asked me not to kill the messenger. I listened as he explained that he had suggested to the woman's representative that the offer was too low, just to see what would happen. I was flabbergasted when he told me they doubled their former offer.

I was now again calculating and could not escape the reality that, for a forty-five-minute performance at a private, not public, event, I was being offered an amount per minute that no one in their right mind should refuse.

He stopped and gave me that familiar Bill Withers grin I

knew and loved. Then he said, "We had a good time, didn't we? And the old pipes weren't too bad."

I wanted to stay for hours more but sensed it was time for me to be on my way.

Then Bill said he wanted to show me his gym. As we walked across the living room, he pointed to several guitars in stands over to the left of a baby grand piano. He said the one on the right was a gift from Jose Feliciano and the one in the middle was given to him by Ray Parker, Jr.

I said, "You know I sued Ray Parker, Jr., right?"

As we continued down a stairway to the gym at a lower level, he asked me to tell him about the Ray Parker thing, but I never got the chance. He left a hole in my heart, and I'll bet he's listening to angels singing "Lean On Me" somewhere.

You ain't no Bill Withers
Bill Withers

DID HE EVER SHOW YOU
THE TRICK?

After finishing a round of golf, the boys and I went to the Grill room to have a few beers and settle up the bets, as usual. It was a small crowd and the chatter in the room was constant but not too loud. Having finished my beer and paying off my bets, I got up to leave. As I turned toward the door, I was summoned by a friend, I'll call him Rick Paisano, from the far side of the room, "Hey, Clair. Where you goin'?"

"I'm headed home, why?"

"Come on over here. What say we play a little Gin Rummy, you and me, mano a mano?"

I sauntered over to where Rick was sitting, not really interested in playing any cards. I'd rather go home and take a nap. But Rick already had a deck of cards and a scorepad in front of him, so I thought, what the hell, and sat down.

"Okay," I said. "What's the game?"

"Let's do five, ten. I'm feelin' lucky."

This means whoever wins the hand wins either five dollars or, if he "gins" or "cuts," he wins ten dollars.

We cut for the deal and he wins and is keeping score.

Rick is about my age, with a full head of thick, flowing white hair. He has a ruddy complexion and a habit of making a clicking noise in his mouth, like a nervous tick. I don't like the look on his face right now and wonder what he is up to. He just smiles, shuffles the cards, takes a sip of his beer, and starts dealing, eleven cards to me and ten to himself. He knocks his knuckles on the table and says "Good luck," just like the dealers in Vegas.

Now, I consider myself a fairly good Gin player, but I was not faring well in this game. I won five, he won ten. I won ten, he won thirty. One of the other guys I sometimes play Gin with would say he was beating me like a red-haired stepchild. And I can't get over the sarcastic smile on his face.

"Hey, Rick," I say, pointing at the scorepad. "Where am I?"

"You're down eighty-five bucks," he says through a toothy grin and a wink.

I want to choke him.

"I'll tell you what," I say in disgust. "Eighty-five bucks, double or nothing, says I can tell you what the next card is coming off the top of the deck."

"What do you take me for," he says. "You looked."

"No, I didn't, but go ahead and shuffle the cards, and pull one card out, face down, and, double or nothing, I will tell you what it is."

He shuffled the deck, spread the cards out face down on the table in front of him, and, with one finger, slid out a card.

"Here you go, Houdini. What is it?"

I said, "It's the four of diamonds."

He turned the card over and it was the four of diamonds. I could not believe it, but I smiled as if I knew that it would be that card. In truth, I was as amazed as he was, maybe more so.

He sneered at me and then took his pencil and crossed out the eighty-five dollars in his favor on the scorepad. We were back to even.

He got up and went over to where three guys were seated at

a nearby table. He tried to tell them what had just happened, but they had no interest and came back to our table.

"Bunch of stiffs," he said and sat down.

The guys at the nearby table heard him and gave me one of those "What's up with that guy" looks; one of them twirled his finger around his left temple as if to say "he's wacko."

Rick shuffled the cards again and dealt out our hands and we continued playing. Sara, the bartender, came over to ask if we needed anything.

I smiled at her and said, "Yes, I think I need a miracle, but bring me a Miller Lite instead, please. Rick, can I get you another beer?"

He ignored me, totally absorbed in his cards. I went right back to losing, even worse this time. After he beat me several more times in a row, I said, "Okay, Rick. Where am I now?"

"Now, let's see, you're down a hundred and ten."

"OK, one more time," I said. "Shuffle the cards, spread 'em out, pull one out, a hundred and ten, double or nothing, and I'll tell you what the card is."

"You are fucking crazy," he said, but he shuffled the cards, spread them out, pulled one out, with one finger, and said, "Go for it, idiot."

"It's the King of Spades," I said.

He turned it over and it *was* the King of Spades. I stared at it in disbelief.

Rick crossed out his one hundred-ten dollar winnings on the scorepad, put the cards back into their box, stood up, and said, "I am never playing cards with you again."

Before I could do or say anything, he walked out the door. I didn't know whether to laugh or gasp or cry or faint. Sara came over and said, "Where did your friend go?"

I said, "I'm not sure he is my friend any longer."

"What?" she said.

"Never mind. Just bring me my tab, please."

Two weeks passed. Finishing a round of golf with the boys again, I was sitting with them at a table, outside of the Grill room this time, having a few beers and settling up the bets as usual. Appearing out of nowhere, Rick came walking down the sidewalk toward us. He stopped, smiled at me, and then announced to everyone at the table while pointing at me, "You know what this son of a bitch did?"

Several guys looked up.

"He took a hundred and ninety-five dollars off of me with some kind of hocus pocus."

Someone said, "Yada yada, Rick."

Rick responded, "No, really. Wait 'til you see this." And he went into the Grill room and came back with a deck of cards.

He sat down at the table with me on his left and, this is important, a guy I will call Cary, on his right. Cary was very well known as an excellent card player, a successful gambler who frequented Vegas, and nobody's fool.

Rick shuffled the cards and announced, "I am going to deal one card face down to each one of you, and I am placing twenty-five dollars in the center of the table, and if anyone can guess the card in front of them, they win the twenty-five dollars, and I swear this bastard to my left will win."

Everyone was now paying attention.

I said, "Wait a minute, Rick. You're going to play also, right?"

"Right."

"Well, you can't win your own twenty-five dollars, so, if you win, I will cover your twenty-five, OK?"

"OK."

He dealt out one card face down to everyone. Rick went first and called out his guess. He was wrong. Cary went next and called out his guess and was wrong, as was everyone else before it finally got to me.

I said, "It's the ten of hearts."

I turned over my card and, believe it or not, it was the ten of hearts.

Rick said, "See, I told you. This guy is a fucking wizard or something." Then turning to me, he said, "I owe you twenty-five dollars."

Cary laughingly said, "I have seen this scam before, fellas, and I ain't fallin' for it. Rick, you are now going to bet me one hundred dollars that Clair can guess a card that you will place in front of him, face down, and if I say yes, you will slip him a pre-arranged card, and he will guess it correctly. I call bullshit."

Rick replied, "No, no. Here. You take the cards and shuffle them and you pull out the card and I will place five hundred dollars in the middle of the table and if you guess it right or I do or Clair does, the guy who guesses the card correctly wins the five hundred."

Again I said, "Wait a minute, Rick. You can't win your own five hundred, so, if you win, I will cover your five hundred."

"OK."

Calling us both nuts, Cary shuffled the deck and as he was shuffling, I swear to God, as sure as you are reading this, I saw in my head the seven of clubs. No matter what, I am going with the seven of clubs. But wait, I am going to go last. What if Rick or Cary guesses the seven of clubs? Not to worry. The odds are they will not. Let's go.

Cary finished shuffling and spread the cards out, face down, in front of him. Like Rick, he used one finger to pull out one card.

Rick said, "It is the five of hearts."

Cary said, "I think it's the Queen of Spades."

I said, "You are both wrong. It's the seven of clubs."

Cary turned over the card, and I swear again, it was the seven of clubs.

The three of us were equally astounded and said nothing for a long while.

Then Rick said, "I told you. This guy is a goddamned wizard."

Cary said, "I don't believe it." Then he turned over the rest of the deck, I think to be sure it did not contain more than one seven of clubs. Then he said to me, "OK, how did you do that?"

I told him I had no idea, but I did see the seven of clubs in my head while he was shuffling.

Of course, Rick had not actually put five hundred dollars in the center of the table. I offered to buy a round of drinks, but they both passed, so I closed out my tab and went home.

It didn't matter who I told what happened, nobody believed it. But then several weeks passed. I was sitting at my desk opening my mail and, low and behold, I received a check from Rick. It was made out to me for five hundred dollars and, in the lower left-hand corner, next to "Memo," he had written "Carnac - Seven of Clubs."

I laughed and made a decision. I went to the art supply store and bought a frame, just the right size, framed Rick's check, and hung it on my office wall.

Now, I said to myself, they will *have* to believe the story.

Again time passed and one Saturday, at the golf course, Rick came up to me and said, "Hey, did you get my check?"

I told him yes, I received it, and he asked why I hadn't cashed it. I told him I framed it.

"And it's hanging on my office wall."

"You're crazy," he said. "You won the five hundred fair and square. Cash it, you dope."

"Ain't gonna happen," I said. "The story and the proof of the story are worth more to me than five hundred bucks."

He called me an idiot, flipped me the bird, and left.

The following week, Rick showed up at the golf course again, walked over to my table in the dining room, and counted out five hundred dollars in five one hundred dollar bills, right in front of me. A mutual friend, Bob, was sitting at the table with me and asked, "What's that?"

Rick recounted the entire story and Bob just shook his head.

Rick turned to me and said he wanted me to go to my office, take my framed check off the wall, take the check out of the frame and write on the back "Void For Cash."

I said, "Wait a minute, Rick. Do you really think I would accept your five hundred in cash and then also cash your check?"

"Your kids," Rick said. "Your kids." And we all laughed.

The next week, Bob showed up at the club and handed Rick and me each a T-shirt. I unfolded mine, as Rick was unfolding his. On the small left breast pocket of each was imprinted the playing card image of the seven of clubs and, turning it around, the entire back was also imprinted with a very large playing card image of the seven of clubs. There was laughter all around. Rick and I put our shirts on and thanked Bob profusely.

One day, weeks later, my good friend and landlord, Michael Silver, came into my office to chat about something and noticed Rick's framed check on my wall. He asked, "Hey, what is this?"

I told Michael the whole story and, like everyone else, he was stunned. He said, "This could only happen to you. You are the luckiest bastard I know."

I smiled.

Michael said he stopped in to talk about an upcoming golf tournament at his club, a member-guest tournament, the North Ranch Rodeo. Mike usually played with Jack Smiley, but Jack couldn't make it, and Mike thought maybe he and I should hook up as partners and give it a go. I told him I would love to.

We did play in the tournament and we won it.

It was a month later and time for the member-guest tournament at my club. I of course invited Mike to play as my guest partner.

Prior to the start of the first round on the first day, Mike and I were out on the practice green, among a bunch of other members and guests, and Mike asked, "Hey. Is that guy Rick Paisano here? The five-hundred dollar seven of clubs guy?"

"Yeah. He's over there putting at the far end on the practice green," I said, pointing. "He's the guy with the white hair."

Michael casually made his way over to where Rick was practicing his putting and began practicing putting at the same hole. At an appropriate moment, Rick, being a personable guy, extended a hand toward Michael and said, "Hi. I'm Rick Paisano. I'm a member here. You must be a guest."

Michael shook Rick's extended hand and said, "Nice to make your acquaintance. I'm Michael Silver and yes, I am a guest. I play out of North Ranch."

"North Ranch. I've played there. Nice course. Welcome. So who is the member you are playing with in our tournament?"

"I'm playing with Clair Burrill. Do you know him?"

"Yes, I do. Clair and I are good friends."

Michael paused, as if in deep thought, and then said, "Did Clair ever show you the trick with the seven of clubs?"

Rick's jaw dropped and he stood very still, flat-footed, unmoving.

Michael tipped his hat and said, quite casually, "Nice to have met you, Rick. Play well today." And he walked away, leaving Rick standing there dead in his tracks.

Michael came back over to me and related what he had done.

"Excellent," I said.

I still have the framed check and the T-shirt. Michael and I did not fare very well in my member-guest tournament, certainly nothing like what we had done in his tournament.

Did he ever show you the trick?
Mike Silver

QUOTH THE RAVEN "NEVERMORE"

This chapter is dedicated to Bill, Pat, and Paul.

My brother Bill, five years older than me, was the quintessential musician. He practiced music, played music, wrote music, arranged music, and taught music. He lived music. He played nearly every musical instrument, but his most accomplished instrument, and the one he loved most, was the tenor saxophone.

My sister Nancy played the piano, my brother Jack played the trumpet for a while, and my mother sang in church. She had a beautiful voice.

So I grew up with music all around me, and when I was about nine years old, I was coaxed into taking piano lessons.

Alice Halstead was the church organist at St. Paul's Episcopal Church in Plymouth. I was an acolyte and while serving at mass, I could see her up close in the sanctuary. She was a frail, white-haired, wee slip of an older lady, barely visible sitting on her bench behind the massive keyboard of the church pipe organ with its fifty-six pipes looming behind her.

A spinster, Miss Halstead supplemented her church salary by offering piano lessons in her apartment on the third floor of the Cheese Counter building in the center of town. I rode there on my bike once a week after school, and for a dollar for a one-hour lesson, started by learning to play scales, over and over, dying for the time when I could play a whole song.

Her apartment had steam heat radiators and during the winter, frail as she was, she had the heat cranked up. The steam permeated the main sitting room where her piano was located and fogged up the windows to the point that you could not see out. She had the patience of a saint but was strict in her demands to practice, practice, practice. Bless her soul, she laid the foundation of my love for being able to express myself through music.

After years of bike rides and hours of lessons and steam, I finally was able to play whole pieces on the piano. One day, Miss Halstead called my mother and told her that I should come to St. Paul's and that my lesson would be on the church pipe organ. What a thrill. I sat on the bench next to her, with two keyboards and a wall of stops in front of me and a third keyboard below me, to be played with my feet.

She showed me two special pedals, the expression pedal, and the volume pedal, also operated by my feet. I loved the volume pedal and was reprimanded by her time and again for using it too often. For a year, I continued to take my lessons on the pipe organ.

My pipe organ playing reached its peak when I was asked to play a piece for my sister Nancy's wedding. Miss Halstead chose Chopin's "Barcarolle in F sharp major." I practiced and practiced and practiced and, on that special day, I pulled it off.

But one cannot play the pipe organ in the high school band, so when the time came, I switched to trombone. My piano and organ playing helped tremendously in taking up this new instrument because of my ability to read music.

At this same time, my best friend, Pat, came over from the Catholic grade school to the public high school and played drums in the high school band. One of the other drummers, a year older than Pat, was a guy named Paul, and Pat and Paul became friends.

The year was 1958. A few years earlier, in 1954, Bill Haley and the Comets had introduced our world to Rock 'n' Roll with their smash hit "Rock Around the Clock." Chuck Berry, Buddy Holly, and others soon followed, and teenagers across the country had their own music.

Sock hops in the gym with DJs spinning records were the craze. Years later, Don McLean would recall those days to us in his magnum opus, "American Pie."

> *"Well, I know that you're in love with him*
> *'Cause I saw you dancin' in the gym*
> *You both kicked off your shoes*
> *Man, I dig those rhythm and blues"*

The advent of the local rock band soon followed. Guitar sales, particularly electric guitar sales, soared. Pat called me to tell me one day that a local rock band had been formed in nearby Sheboygan. They called themselves "Denny and the Crown Jewels" and they would be playing for a dance at the Sheboygan Armory the following Saturday night. We had to go.

Not yet 16 and hence not entitled to drive a car, Pat implored his mother to drive us to the Armory, and, reluctantly, she agreed.

We stood in wonder, gazing up at these guys not much older than us, mesmerized. And we were standing in the midst of a bevy of cute young blue eyed girls obviously captivated by the band. They looked like they would do anything these guys would say. What do you think, Dr. Hook?

I looked at Pat, he looked at me, and we both said, "We gotta form a band."

That was the beginning. I talked to my parents and told them I wanted to buy a guitar. They were not keen on the idea. We bought you a trombone. Stick with that.

I saved my paper route money and my allowance. I talked privately with Bill and the next time he made a trip to Sheboygan to see Winnie Goodell, who had a music shop behind his house where Bill bought reeds for his sax and other music supplies, I begged him to take me along. He agreed.

Winnie gave me a catalog of musical instruments including inexpensive six-string acoustic guitars. I had my eye on a Stella for $29. When I had saved up enough, I approached my mom to tell her of my burning desire, and perhaps because I was her baby boy, she gave in.

On Bill's next trip to Winnie's shop, I went along again and ordered the Stella. When I picked it up and paid him for it weeks later, he threw in a book of basic guitar chords for beginners.

The action on the Stella, which I learned later is the distance between the strings and the fretboard, was high, making it not only difficult to play but also resulted in slightly distorted sound. Nevertheless, aching fingers and all, I fought on, trying to make music.

Remember Vera Carlyle, the Guidance Counselor at Plymouth High School? She lived down the block from our house and, in addition to providing a home for about ten cats, she took in boarders. One was a fellow named Duke Duval, a young man dressed in all black in his late twenties with slicked-back black hair and a noticeably large comb protruding from his back pocket, whom I came to know as he walked to and from Vera's house and his workplace each weekday.

Fortunately for me, I was sitting on our front porch one day trying to learn how to change from an E chord to an A chord on my Stella. Duke in his wanderings, no doubt hearing my feeble efforts, stopped in front of our house, listened, and then approached me.

"Hey, whatcha doin'?" he called out.

"I'm trying to learn how to play this thing."

"Can I see it?"

I handed it to him. He strummed a few chords and said the action was terrible. That's when I found out what action was.

He asked me if I had a minute, if I would like to come down to Vera's house and see a real guitar.

I asked my mom if I could go down to Vera's house, that there was a guy there who wanted to show me his guitar. Since it was Vera's house, she said okay.

I sat in a lawn chair in Vera's front yard while Duke went inside and came out a few minutes later with a black Gibson Johnny Cash model acoustic guitar. He played "Don't Take Your Guns to Town" as I sat and stared.

When he finished I said "wow" and continued to stare.

"You want to give it a try?" he asked and pushed the Gibson toward me. I was embarrassed and felt I shouldn't even touch his guitar, but he insisted.

"Do you know E and A and D?" he asked. "That's all you need to know to play that song."

He allowed me to play his guitar, and with his patient help, I got to the point where I could manage to change from one chord to the other. Not as effortlessly and melodiously as Duke, but a seed was planted. Now all I had to do was save up enough money to buy a better guitar.

I reported this breakthrough to Pat, and he and I began in earnest to make it happen – to form a band.

Eventually, I bought a Danelectro double pickup electric guitar out of the Montgomery Ward catalog, and Pat bought a Slingerland drum set. I couldn't afford an amplifier and an electric guitar doesn't make any sound without one, but I learned I could plug my guitar cord into the auxiliary port of Bill's tape recorder when he wasn't around. I drove my mom nuts twanging away upstairs in my bedroom.

Pat and I went to every dance where Denny and the Crown Jewels were playing. Pat watched the drummer, Denny Sachse, who played his drum set standing up. I watched Denny Berg, the lead guitar player, especially his left hand, as he wove his way through chord after chord and song after song. And when I couldn't figure out for myself what the proper chord changes were, good old Bill would say things like, you want to go from C to A minor, and then F and G. So I would look up in a chord book where to put my fingers for an A minor chord. Bill was priceless.

Pat and I were getting better, banging away together on 16-bar blues in the key of E in what had been his grandma's apartment upstairs in his folks' big white house. So now, we agreed, we needed a bass player. How about Paul? Pat suggested. He's a drummer, I replied. So, he's got rhythm, Pat insisted. Pat approached Paul and Paul was all for it. Plus, it turned out, he had money, at least enough to buy an electric bass guitar, the same make and model as Jerry Shields of Denny and the Crown Jewels played, and an amplifier. And his amp had multiple input ports so he and I could play out of the same amp. We were on our way.

To show you how much we did not know about this whole band thing, when Paul got his bass and it was time to tune it, we did not know what octave it should be tuned to relative to my guitar. So Paul kept tightening the tuning knob of the E string until he couldn't turn it anymore by hand. Pat got a pair of pliers from his dad's tool kit, and Paul kept turning the tuning knob with the pliers until the string eventually popped. He (we) were trying to tune it an octave higher than it should have been. We laughed, and Paul put on a new string; he tuned it an octave lower than before; it worked, and we were set to go.

We practiced in Grandma's room over and over. Then came the time that we needed to find a singer. Denny and the Crown Jewels, in addition to their lead guitar player, bass guitar, and drums, had a lead singer, who did not play an instrument, Gene Knause.

The lead singer would be the frontman, so he had to look good in addition to being able to sing. Pat, Paul, and I pulled out the most recent copy of our high school yearbook and started looking for a guy who could pull off being the frontman for our band and hoping like hell that maybe, just maybe, he could carry a tune. We decided on Bob Hall, a really good-looking guy in Paul's class, a chick magnet, we thought.

Paul approached Bob Hall with the proposition. There was one catch, Paul explained. If he (Bob) really was serious about wanting to join the band, he would have to purchase a microphone with a stand and an amplifier. He went for it. He wanted to be in the band.

While Paul, Pat, and I waited for Bob to get his equipment, we continued practicing. There was a very popular song by Gene Vincent and His Blue Caps entitled "Say Mama." Everyone loved to dance to it. It was basic 16-bar blues with a rock beat and clever lyrics. We learned the instrumental parts fairly quickly.

That same day, during a break in our practice session in Grandma's room, Pat asked what we should call ourselves. We agreed that each of us would come up with a suggested name. The following day, Paul and Pat had not come up with anything. When I suggested we call ourselves the Ravens, it stuck. Pat did not want the name of the band on his bass drum, so Paul and I, who by this time had each purchased an amp with a white mesh front, bought black plastic letters that spelled out "RAVENS" and attached them to the mesh front of each of our amps. It looked cool.

Then came our first rehearsal with Bob Hall. It was a disaster. After many attempts, it was clear that no matter how good he looked up front, he couldn't carry a tune. Paul and I set our instruments down, and Paul took Bob aside. Pat and I stepped outside.

"What are we going to tell him?" Pat asked me.

"I think Paul is breaking the news to him right now."

Pat and I went back inside. Bob looked deflated and Paul looked sympathetic.

"I guess I can't be a Raven," Bob said to us as we came back into the practice room.

"Hey, man," Pat said. "You gave it a try."

Then Bob said he wouldn't be needing his sound equipment, and I offered that we, Paul, Pat, and I, would buy it from him. At first, Pat said he wouldn't contribute because he wasn't going to use it. Paul jumped in and said it would be needed by the whole band. I agreed and Pat finally came around, so the three of us offered to buy it. Bob agreed and as he left us, he smiled and thanked us for giving him a chance. Again, it was sad, but the right decision.

With Bob gone, we turned our amps back on, Pat got situated standing behind his drum set, and I stepped up to Bob's, now our, microphone. I played the opening riff on my guitar, and sang the opening lines to "Say Mama" and that's when I became the lead singer of the Ravens.

Months later, we had a list of about twenty songs we could play well, and we figured we were ready to take a shot at performing in public. I approached the principal of Plymouth High School, John Richards, and suggested to him that our band, the Ravens, was available to play for a dance in the school gym. Dances, sock hops, were held in the gym after home football games in the fall. Mr. Richards balked at first, but I convinced him to give us a chance. The deal was sealed when I told him we would do it for free.

We set up in a corner of the gym where electrical power was available for our amps and, when the magic moment arrived, we opened with "Say Mama." The kids went wild. They danced like crazy and screamed for more. They had their own band.

Other bands were cropping up around us. The Furys had a lead guitar, bass guitar, drums, and a singer. The Renegades had all of that plus a rhythm guitar and a sax. Our trio couldn't compete.

I went to Bill. Please join the Ravens.

Bill was playing sax regularly in a dance band that played for weddings and anniversaries and similar occasions, but not sock hops or rock dances. He told me he wasn't into rock.

This was going to change. But first, a bit of Wisconsin history.

As early as 1940, some bars and taverns in Wisconsin began serving beer only and opened their doors to anyone 18 years old and older. The concept caught on to a point where cities and counties throughout the state began regulating the practice. The result was that the state became dotted with various cities and counties that allowed such establishments and others that did not.

For example, our county, Sheboygan County, allowed it, while most of the cities in the county did not, including Plymouth. Outside the Plymouth city limits, the 1880 Club served beer only to anyone from 18 to 80 years old. These establishments popped up throughout the state in areas that legally permitted them and they became known as Minor Bars and Teen Bars.

Curiously, Milwaukee County, the largest county in the state and the one that produced the most beer, did not permit them, nor did the City of Milwaukee.

Going back earlier in time, to 1934, a gent named Leo Weiler, lived in rural Ozaukee County, the county adjacent to Milwaukee County to the north. Leo built the original Weiler's Log Cabin Ballroom out of tamarack trees salvaged from a nearby swamp. Soon the large facility became a world-class dance hall featuring big-name bands of the 40s and 50s.

In 1958, Sonny Smith purchased the Ballroom from Weiler and expanded it. Sonny ran it successfully for a few years and then, seizing a golden opportunity, converted it into a Minor Bar serving beer only.

It turned out to be a bonanza for Sonny, with hundreds of teenagers ages 18 to 20 traveling from Milwaukee and other cities and neighboring counties where they could not drink beer to Weiler's, where they could, every Friday and Saturday night.

Paul heard about Weiler's from some of his friends who frequented the dances there. They said the place rocked with great bands, including The Legends from Milwaukee.

We decided we had to take a trip down to Weiler's, but there was a problem. None of us was 18. So we went on a Sunday afternoon.

Although there was a large parking area surrounding the dance hall, there were only a few cars parked outside near the entrance. We parked and apprehensively opened the door. We were met immediately by a man sitting on a stool just inside the door. He was an off-duty Ozaukee County sheriff's deputy and as large as a house. He demanded to see our ID.

I stepped forward and explained that we were not 18 but did not come to drink, but rather wanted to talk to the owner, that we had a band and wanted to see if we might be able to perform for a dance concert.

A stern-looking man in his fifties with hair in a buzz cut and a muscular build overheard me and motioned to the bouncer to let us in.

The conversation was short and to the point, as I am sure he did not want these underage minors to remain for long. He asked the name of our band and what we charged for a four-hour performance.

We had heard through the grapevine that The Legends were paid $80 and, knowing we could not compete with them, said our price was $60. Sonny's eyes indicated his interest. He said we would have to audition on a Sunday afternoon and suggested we come back in two weeks.

Outside, we stood in the cold next to Paul's car. We stared at each other in disbelief. We could not believe what had happened.

Then reality sunk in. Could we pull this off?

Paul said to me, "You have to talk Bill into playing with us. He will make the difference."

Pat agreed. I said I would see what I could do.

When I found the right moment, I cornered Bill.

"Look," I said. "You can play this stuff with your eyes closed. Come over to Pat's, bring your sax, and let's give it a try. Please."

He hesitated.

"We can make $15 a piece," I said.

Now you have to realize two things. First, the minimum wage at the time was $1.00 per hour and, second, the musician's union scale for a four-hour gig, which Bill received with his dance band, was $9.

He relented and his addition was awesome, phenomenal. He would listen to a record or a song on the radio and could play the sax part perfectly the first time through. Bill Doggett's "Honky Tonk," Duane Eddy's "Rebel Rouser," "Tequila" by The Champs, and Bill's favorite, Jimmy Forrest's "Night Train."

Audition Sunday arrived. We opened with Buddy Holly's "Rave On," which had become our theme song, and as it faded out, we moved immediately into "Night Train." We knocked 'em dead, as they say. Sonny, a few guys who wandered in from the bar, and Sonny's raven-haired daughter, Monica, listened, and they all actually applauded.

Monica came up to the stage and requested another Buddy Holly song, so we launched right into "Peggy Sue." Monica stood right in front of me as we played and I sang, and I knew by her reaction that we were going to be hired. She had a beautiful smile, she moved to the music and tossed her hair; I guessed she was probably 19 or 20, definitely out of my league and out of reach.

When we finished, she turned to Sonny and nodded her head. Sonny came over, put his arm around her shoulder, and said we had the job.

We played at Weiler's many Fridays and Saturdays and many other venues, but like all good things, the Ravens came to an end. Paul was the first to leave, going off to school in Maryland. Bill was next, pursuing a music teaching job in western Wisconsin. I threw in with a bunch of other guys and continued playing in several different bands before heading off to Harvard in the fall of 1962.

Pat, standing at his drum set in the back, committed suicide at age 42; Paul, playing his bass guitar to the left, succumbed to cancer at 69; as did my brother Bill, playing his tenor sax, at 71.

Quoth the Raven, the last remaining Raven, yours truly on the right with the Strat: "Nevermore"

ACKNOWLEDGMENTS

In addition to my immediate family members to whom my work is dedicated, and the dedication of Chapter 48 to my fellow Ravens, Bill, Pat, and Paul, I want to thank those without whom this book would not have come to fruition.

I was fortunate to spend time with and to represent many famous and talented people with whom I crossed paths. I am also particularly appreciative of the support I received from the wings. Thank you John Mitchell, Suzanne Merrill, Marcia Withers, Roberta Meshel, John Massa, Myron Hura, Michael Silver, John Durrill, and so many others.

Then there is Alexander Stewart, an exceptional musicologist, and Maurina Sherman, a former Con Law student of mine, who introduced me to Ivor Davis, a brilliant reporter and author of several books, including *The Beatles and Me on Tour*. Ivor encouraged me and pointed me in the right direction to Irma Wolfson, editor extraordinaire, and Jose Ramirez at Pedernales Publishing, a most patient and understanding man, who led me to the superb publicist, Kathleen Kaiser.

I would be remiss not to include my thanks to my former partners and best friends, Bob Besser and Gerry Margolis, may he rest in peace.

ABOUT THE AUTHOR

CLAIR BURRILL is a Harvard University and University of Wisconsin Law School graduate and has been representing clients in the entertainment industry for over forty years. His experiences as a musician and singer in several rock bands, and his love of music contributed largely to his understanding of his entertainment clients' ups and downs, and needs and desires, and his service as an officer in the U.S. Navy added discipline as a necessary adjunct to his successful law practice.

PHOTO CREDITS

SONG LYRIC CREDITS

The author is grateful for permission to quote lyrics
from the following songs.

A-11 - words and music by Hank Cochran, copyright © 1963 Sony
Music Publishing (US) LLC, all rights administered by Sony Music
Publishing (US) LLC, 424 Church Street, Suite 1200, Nashville,
TN 37219, international copyright secured, all rights reserved,
reprinted by permission of Hal Leonard LLC - p. 128

A Good Hearted Woman - words and music by Willie Nelson and
Waylon Jennings, copyright © 1971 EMI Full Nelson Music, Inc.
and Vagabond Dreamer Music, copyright renewed, all rights on
behalf of EMI Full Nelson Music, Inc. Administered by Sony
Music Publishing (US) LLC, 424 Church Street, Suite 1200,
Nashville, TN 37219, all rights on behalf of Vagabond Dreamer
Music administered by Downtown DMP Songs, international
copyright secured, all rights reserved, reprinted by permission of
Hal Leonard LLC - p. 53

All I Have To Do Is Dream - words and music by Boudleaux Bryant,
copyright © 1958 by House of Bryant Publications, Gatlinburg,
TN, copyright renewed, all foreign rights controlled by Sony
Music Publishing (US) LLC, all rights for Sony Music Publishing
(US) LLC administered by Sony Music Publishing (US) LLC,